POST-APARTHEID EDUCATION

Towards Non-Racial, Unitary and Democratic Socialization In the New South Africa

Mandla P. Mncwabe

UNIVERSITY
PRESS OF
AMERICA

Lanham • New York • London

Copyright © 1993 by
University Press of America®, Inc.
4720 Boston Way
Lanham, Maryland 20706

3 Henrietta Street
London WC2E 8LU England

Library of Congress Cataloging-in-Publication Data

Mncwabe, M. P.
Post-Apartheid education : towards non-racial, unitary and democratic
socialization in the new South Africa / Mandla P. Mncwabe.
p.   cm.
Includes bibliographical references and index.
1. Education—Social aspects—South Africa.   2. Education—South
Africa—Aims and objectives.   3. Education and state—South Africa.
4. Blacks—Education—South Africa.   I. Title.
LC191.8.S565M59   1993
370.19'0968—dc20   93–37902 CIP

ISBN 0–8191–8969–3 (cloth : alk. paper)

DEDICATION

To the memory of my late brother
and sister Bhekuyise and Zibuyile.

A QUOTATION

"The school crisis demands urgent and critical appraisal of the whole enterprise of education in South Africa. Such an investigation requires, first, that education and education policy-making be examined in their own right, within the specific terrains of public and academic debate or administrative policy initiatives, in order to uncover the assumptions which have informed 'commonsense' or 'expert' knowledge on these subjects over time."

Peter Kallaway (1986:2)
Apartheid and Education

LIST OF TABLES

ILLUSTRATIONS

TABLE OF CONTENTS

CHAPTER ONE

EDUCATION FOR BLACK PEOPLE IN SOUTH AFRICA:
THE GOVERNMENT'S UNFINISHED BUSINESS

CHAPTER TWO

THE CONVOLUTED STRUCTURE OF EDUCATION IN SOUTH AFRICA

CHAPTER THREE

HIGH BLACK TEACHER-PUPIL RATIO AND WHITE TEACHER RETRENCHMENTS

CHAPTER FOUR

MANDELA MEETS DE KLERK ON BLACK EDUCATION CRISIS

CHAPTER FIVE

GOVERNMENT SCHOOL ANNOUNCEMENT AND COMMUNITY RESPONSES

CHAPTER SIX

THE DOORS OF WHITE SCHOOLS CREAK OPEN

CHAPTER SEVEN

EDUCATION AND RESPECT FOR DIVERSITY OF CULTURES

CHAPTER EIGHT

THE EDUCATION RENEWAL STRATEGY - A FURTHER PLOY TO KEEP WHITE SCHOOLS WHITE

CHAPTER NINE

THE NATIONAL, NON-RACIAL AND DEMOCRATIC EDUCATION SYSTEM - THE ONLY SOLUTION

The convoluted structure of education in SA

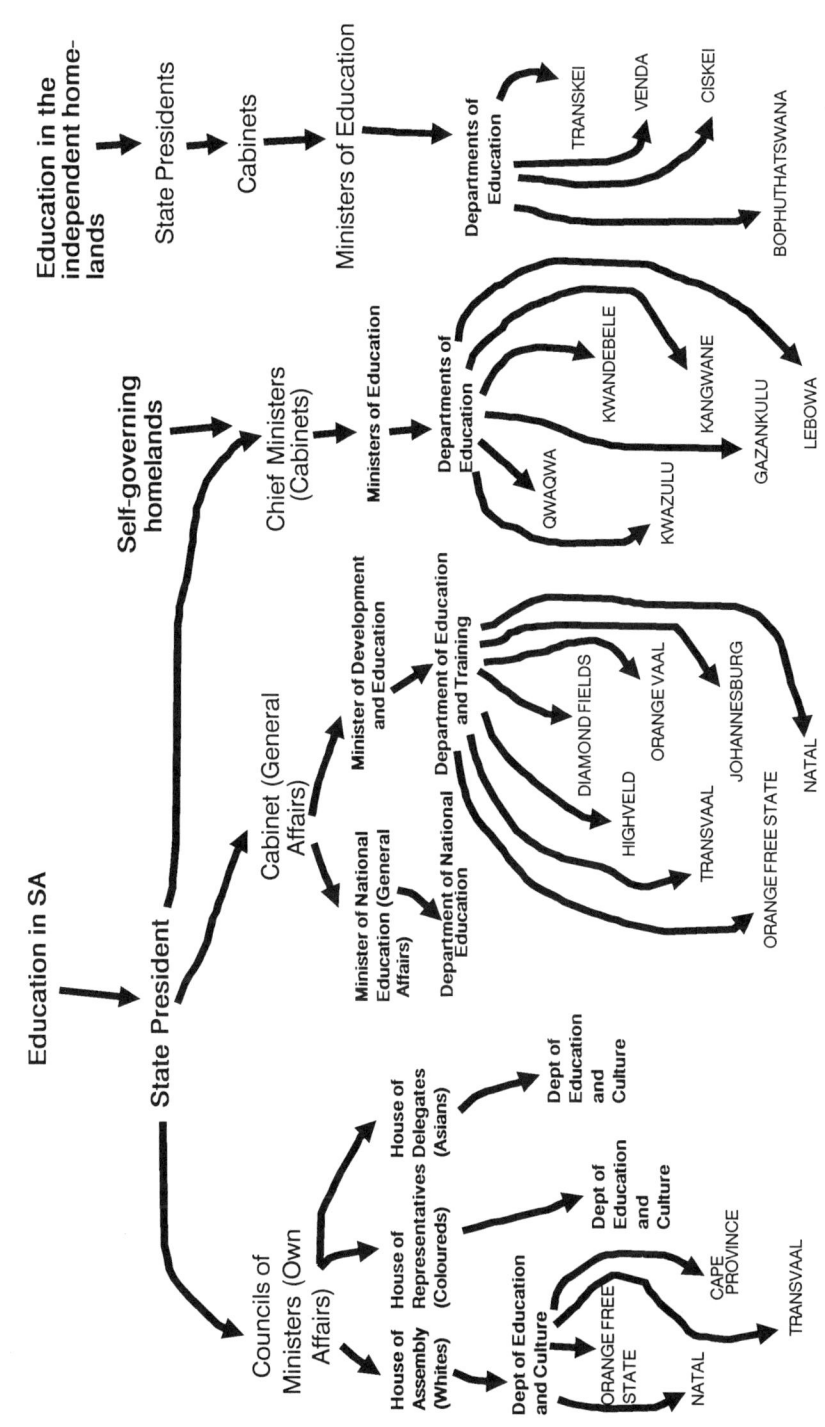

Education in SA → State President

Councils of Ministers (Own Affairs)

- House of Assembly (Whites) → Dept of Education and Culture → ORANGE FREE STATE, NATAL, CAPE PROVINCE, TRANSVAAL
- House of Representatives (Coloureds) → Dept of Education and Culture
- House of Delegates (Asians) → Dept of Education and Culture

Cabinet (General Affairs)

- Minister of National Education (General Affairs) → Department of National Education
- Minister of Development and Education → Department of Education and Training → DIAMOND FIELDS, ORANGE VAAL, HIGHVELD, JOHANNESBURG, TRANSVAAL, ORANGE FREE STATE, NATAL

Self-governing homelands

Chief Ministers (Cabinets) → Ministers of Education → Departments of Education → QWAQWA, KWANDEBELE, KWAZULU, KANGWANE, GAZANKULU, LEBOWA

Education in the independent homelands

State Presidents → Cabinets → Ministers of Education → Departments of Education → TRANSKEI, VENDA, CISKEI, BOPHUTHATSWANA

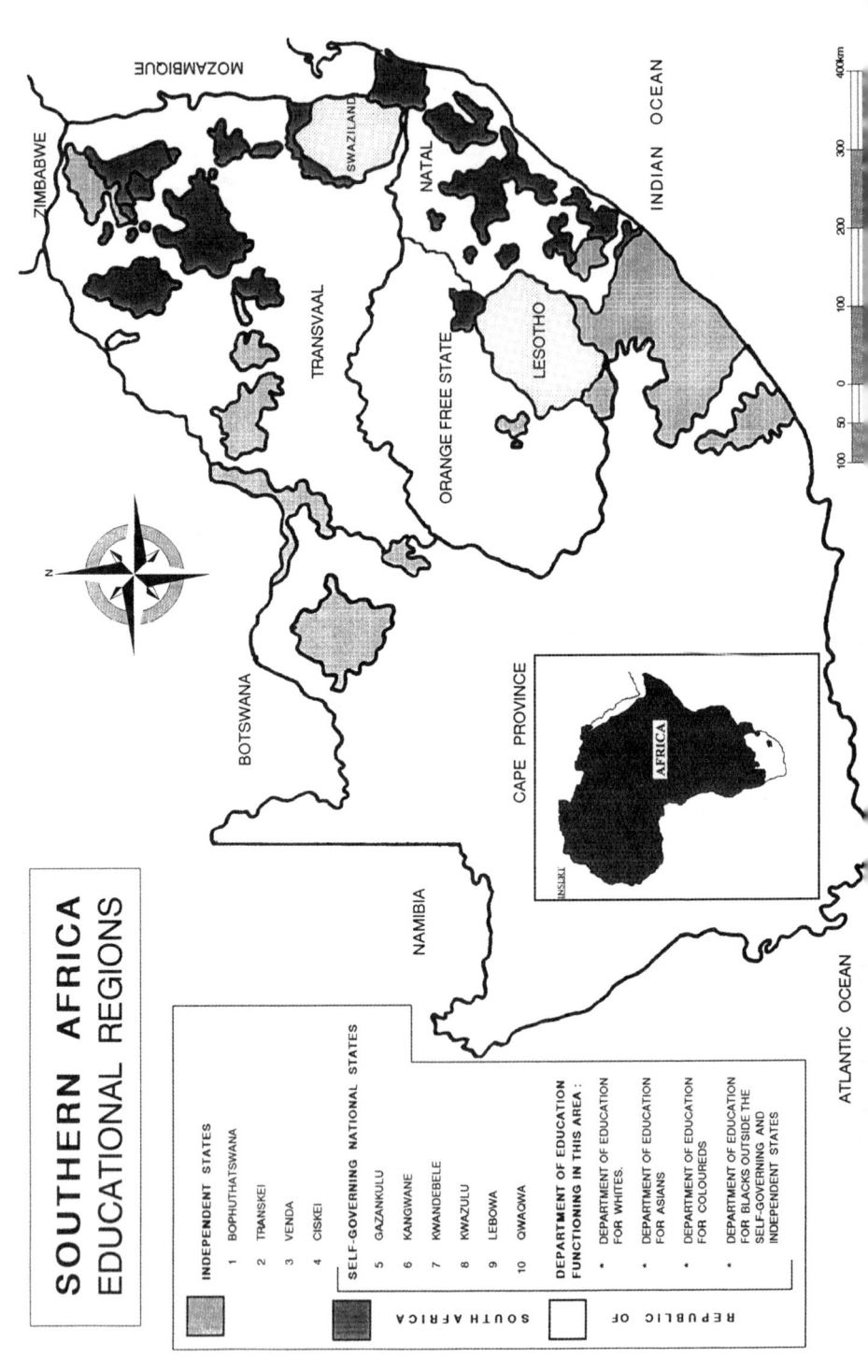

SOUTHERN AFRICA
EDUCATIONAL REGIONS

INDEPENDENT STATES

1 BOPHUTHATSWANA
2 TRANSKEI
3 VENDA
4 CISKEI

SELF-GOVERNING NATIONAL STATES

5 GAZANKULU
6 KANGWANE
7 KWANDEBELE
8 KWAZULU
9 LEBOWA
10 QWAQWA

REPUBLIC OF SOUTH AFRICA

DEPARTMENT OF EDUCATION FUNCTIONING IN THIS AREA :

* DEPARTMENT OF EDUCATION FOR WHITES.
* DEPARTMENT OF EDUCATION FOR ASIANS
* DEPARTMENT OF EDUCATION FOR COLOUREDS
* DEPARTMENT OF EDUCATION FOR BLACKS OUTSIDE THE SELF-GOVERNING AND INDEPENDENT STATES

ZIMBABWE

MOZAMBIQUE

SWAZILAND

NATAL

INDIAN OCEAN

TRANSVAAL

ORANGE FREE STATE

LESOTHO

BOTSWANA

NAMIBIA

CAPE PROVINCE

AFRICA

INSERT

ATLANTIC OCEAN

N

100 50 0 100 200 300 400km

INTRODUCTION

Faure, E. et al (1972:183) observes that:

> So great is the demand for education, training and industry today, and
> so great will it be in the years to come, that present institutionalized
> systems are and will be incapable of absorbing it. If they are to do so,
> they must abandon their rigid interior divisions.

This observation could not be more true of South Africa. In matters
educational South African administrators and planners tend to take a
conservative approach, to tread well-worn paths, seeking security rather than
risking imaginative innovation. In a way this is understandable. Their
students are 'in the pipeline' for six, twelve or more years, during which
period continuity is essential. The safe path, causing least disturbance, is
'business as usual' or 'more of the same'. But, as Coombs (1968:185) points
out:

> The old arrangements that had served them well before - the system of
> administration, the syllabus and curriculum and teaching methods, the
> self-contained classroom, the means of teacher training and recruitment
> ... have proved no match for the new situation. What seemed like
> 'business-as-usual' actually became 'business-worse-than-usual', as
> attested by the echoing protests against deterioration.

In the words of Professor Fafunwa (1967:32):

> You cannot use yesterday's tool for today's job and expect to be in
> business tomorrow.

Certainly new things in South Africa's education have been added and old
things improved, such as more relevant curricula, etc. but for the most part,
these have been superimposed like geological strata on bedrock methods and
logistics that have prevailed for generations. (Coombs, 1968:113).

By and large there has been no fundamental synthesis of new and exciting educational innovations and revolutions as have occurred in almost all spheres of life in the past fifty years. The self- contained and over-crowded classroom, with its rigid walls, - the monk's cell of the educational process - is still designed to accommodate one teacher, at a desk before a blackboard, facing a specified large number of pupils arranged in regimented rows and columns. At the sound of a bell, the whole process must get under way.

What is needed is a re-fashioning of the education system, a new synthesis, combining the best of the old and the modern, to form new, integrated 'systems' of education more geared to the twentieth and twenty-first centuries. The age-old equations:

education = "own affairs" schools
1 teacher = 45 students = 1 classroom

must be rethought and re-written, even if we are not too sure of what the new equations should be.

As Fafunwa says in the Preface to his New Perspectives in Education, **rather than dragging an educational system kicking and screaming into the twenty-first century, bold new adventures must be embarked upon.**

If Africa is to meet the challenges of the late twentieth century and prepare for the twenty-first, it will have to take giant steps, and cover in twenty years the process that took Europe centuries to achieve. The answer does not lie in increased budgets and numbers of personnel alone, but in adopting a radical or unconventional approach to the question of finding solutions for Africa's problems. (1967)

Raja Roy Singh, Director of the Unesco Regional Office for Education in Asia, in Bangkok, also points out that the only hope of meeting future demands for education is by adopting new approaches.

To say that you must stop them (young people) from seeking education till you are in a position to afford their education is a difficult, even if it were at all desirable, as asking the world to stop because you want to get off it. The demand for education is hitting the ceiling of available resources. We in the developing countries require more and more, and better education, but we cannot get either more or better, by doing the same things in education as we have done before, even though on a larger and expanding scale. That way is a blind alley. (1972:87)

Many developing countries opted for linear expansion of their educational systems to solve their educational problems in a reasonable time. But this has not proved sufficient. They have had to seek other alternatives, rejecting timid half-measures, **like opening few white schools to few black pupils**, which are costly, because of their very inefficiency and embarking boldly on innovations which hold promise for the future. The only escape from the economic squeeze causing shortages of resources in money, personnel, facilities, etc. is for the South African educational system to find ways to get more and better education from the resources they already have, i.e. to improve their efficiency and productivity. But, as Coombs warns, to do this on the grand scale that is needed will require much more than mere tinkering with familiar arrangements. It will require far-reaching innovations and drastic changes in the customary ways of doing things. It will require an educational revolution, comparable to the revolutions that made modern industry and agriculture more efficient and productive."

Since South Africa's conventional educational structures are not proving adequate to the task alternative structures must be designed. This re-designing of educational processes, the planning for educational change, is what Beeby calls 'today's main frontier of education planning'. He elaborates:

In this respect educational planning can learn some important lessons from modern design engineering as applied to other fields. The process begins with a clear definition of 'functional specifications' - i.e. the tasks to be performed within prescribed economic and other limitations. The object then is to examine various alternative 'systems' for accomplishing the desired result, to select the optimum one and develop it to fruition ...

New educational designs are usually patch-work versions of old ones and therefore rarely if ever go into orbit ...

This means that educational planning must move increasingly into creation and testing-out of new educational designs involving fundamentally new 'systems' of teaching and learning designed to achieve well-defined performance specifications with greatest effectiveness at least cost ...

If education is to help change the world and to help brighten the lives of more and more people, it must begin by changing and brightening itself. (1969:32)

Is is interesting to note that boldest reforms in educational innovation have been attempted in the less developed countries where formal school education has not been so well established universally and where, accordingly, it has been little encumbered by traditions and practices, good or bad. Third World leaders can write on relatively cleaner educational slates and, dropping any inhibitions, can strike out in new educational directions. In fact, as Edward de Bono, Director of the Cognitive Research Trust and the Centre for the Study of Thinking, Cambridge, states in an article in The Times Higher Education Supplement of 8th May 1981,

Education is an area where the Third World countries can leap-frog over the developed world simply because they are not sterilized by institutional senescence. All that is required is a decision and commitment of effort in a direction. (1981:4)

The essential difference between innovation and change lies in the fact that innovation is planned, the idea being that through planning one can increase the chances of bringing about any desired change. **So for educational change in South Africa to be effective it must be deliberately planned and rationally organised. If the innovation is some ad hoc process; if it is a pragmatic, haphazard affair, conjured up by not so well-intentioned administrators as Clase has done, not preceded by careful research, not based on adequate expertise; if it is a case of hit or miss, it will often be the latter.** And if South Africa is poor in human and material resources she cannot afford to waste scarce resources on misses. For resources to be wisely spent on hits then the innovations and changes must be deliberately planned and rationally organised according to certain principles. One cannot plan without some kind of theoretical framework. Practice must be principled by ideas. These principles of innovation theory must be used as pegs upon which to hang the stories of achievement.

Can Mr Clase claim the same about his theory and idea of opening White schools to Black pupils?

The opening of White state schools is seen by many, **myself included**, as a damp squib which makes not significant impact on the enormity of the education crisis, and does not begin to address the fundamental demand for a single, unitary, non-racial and democratic education system. It may also be seen as a momentous event where for the first time in the history of the nation racial segregation in state schools is beginning to crumble and the erosion of apartheid education is becoming a reality.

The opening of these schools is clearly not quantitatively significant in terms of the numbers of children who have been admitted a mere 5 360 Black pupils have been admitted to White schools in 1991 (the Weekly Mail, February 15-21, 1991) which is probably in the region of 0,8 percent of the White and 0,08 percent of the African school going population. **The departure to greener pastures of such a small number can offer no relief to a critically overburdened education system.**

The political significance of the police (the Clase models) which made this minimal opening possible has been contested:

- Firstly, because the models are fundamentally undemocratic in that they exclude most parents from decisions about where their children may go to school and they allow a small minority to make decisions for the majority - a further disenfranchising of the disenfranchised.

- Secondly, the significance of the Clase models may be dismissed because the policy is still fundamentally wedded to an apartheid - style commitment to race and to Christian National Education (CNE). This is perhaps the clearest indication that De Klerk has in mind of what he might mean by 'distinctive community-based education'.

So that amid the optimism of renewed world links following the government's commitment to remove the last vestiges of apartheid, there still remains the anomaly of racially-based education and the proliferation of 19 departments. If South Africa is to take the proverbial high road to economic success and social stability

everyone needs the self-empowerment that can only be obtained through a good education. It is the minefield of inequalities that has resulted, particularly since Soweto 1976, in thousands of ill-educated and unemployable young people, whose resentment must threaten every effort to build a new and peaceful South Africa.

The solution lies in the creation of a single ministry of education. Within these provinces and regions should be given autonomy to tailor education to their unique needs. Education currently takes up 19 percent of the national budget and though this is going to increase gradually every education rand must be carefully spent in the best possible way. The bitter legacies of apartheid will be truly removed when every child enters school on an equal footing in a national, democratic and non-racial education system. This is what this book is all about.

EDUCATION FOR BLACK PEOPLE IN SOUTH AFRICA: THE UNFINISHED BUSINESS

1.1 INTRODUCTION

In these years of political crisis, South African people are called upon the undertake arduous, hazardous and crucial tasks of social reconstruction: they are compelled by circumstances to make some of the grand choices of history, to determine in which direction they are to move, to make decisions which will deeply affect the life of South Africa for generations and indeed for centuries - decisions concerning the incidence of economic and political power, the distribution of wealth and income, the relations of classes, races and nationalities and the ends for which women, men and children are to strive for. In making these choices, South African persons and institutions engaged in the performance of educational functions will inevitably play an important role. To the extent that they operate in the real world, they will make their influence felt. They are called upon, not only to bring the heritage of knowledge, thought, and attitude abreast of general social advance, but also to make broad choices concerning alliances to be consummated, values to be reserved, interests to be defended, and social goals to be striven for. Before these persons, and perhaps countless others who have thus far remained inarticulate, can hope to become a positive and creative force in the South African society and education, they must come into closer communication, clarify their thoughts and purposes, draw like-minded South Africans into their ranks and merge isolated and discordant voices into a mighty instrument of group consensus, harmonies expression and collective action. Progressive teachers, professors, social critics, and reformers should develop both a critique of the existing social order and educational system and a positive programme for democratic change. They should constitute a continuing legacy, not only for democratic educational theorists, but also for South African radicalism as a whole. They should set a wheel in motion for the acquisition of the moral understandings and political skills necessary to pursue a vision of the common good through membership in diverse South African communities.

Education in South Africa is under the siege of conservatism. However new schools of thought about education liberal thought and radical (neo-Marxism) thought emerges to counter the conservative force in education. Education is the primary means for public and self-formation; ethics is an account of the virtues required for a free common life; and politics is the craft which all citizens must master to become fully human. These are some of the themes eminent in socialism liberation in South Africa. In view of this, education and politics have become merged. If democracy is not something that happens for us, but rather to us, then the political is the pedagogical and the point of both educational and political practices is to create the self-cultivating publics and self-governing persons whose possibilities create further possibilities for democratic practice.

Now, the development of the school crisis, between 1976 and 1980, appears to have had the effect of committing many social scientists to a more serious approach to the study and analysis of education in South Africa. This is expressed through the attempt to review the traditional schools of thought, and re-direct the theory and history of South African education. To some extent, it represents a broader widening of the debate, expressed, for example, by the publication of the De Lange Report in July 1981 as well as the release in July 1985 of a Human Sciences Research Council Report which identified APARTHEID as the cause of conflict in South Africa.

The outstanding feature of this development is the emergence of a new generation of educationist and historians of education with a view point startlingly opposed to the liberal and conservative tradition. Neo-Marxist educationist argue that any objective analysis of an education system must be accomplished with the use of the tools of political economy. They stress that the dominant traditional approach which presents education or schooling as an independent field of enquiry, divorced from the wider political, social and economic context within which educational policies are formulated, is no longer acceptable. Further, the attempt merely to describe the development of educational policy, without at the same time trying to problemitise either the process itself of schooling or the historical context of which it forms a part is also criticized. In short, the view of South African educational developments broadly accepted by the liberal academics for some time has come to be seen as inadequate.

Not only do Neo-Marxist educationist argue for the use of the tools of political economy, in addition, they maintain that these social scientists of the early 1970's who pioneered this approach in the broader fields of history and sociology have either neglected education or have examined it solely in relation to economy. The intention of this chapter is to make a comparative review of education in South Africa with a view to search for legitimacy.

1.2 BRIEF HISTORICAL REVIEW

BLACK EDUCATION in the Republic of South Africa has been neglected for many years. In consequence, there is now an entire generation of young black people that has been subjected to an education system gravely inferior to that provided for whites. This fact carries two fundamental implications for the social and economic well-being of the country. The first is the problem of those black people (at a conservative estimate, more than a million) who, in the words of Mr. R.V. Sulton, a member of the Commission of Inquiry into Labour Legislation under the chairmanship of Professor N.E. Wiehahn, "have not received a sufficient basic education for induction directly into industrial training programmes". The second is the overall inadequacy of young blacks who have completed part of all of their secondary level schooling within an education system so low in quality as to make it difficult for them to meet the demands of modern society.

Clearly, the long-term responsibility for renovating and re-structuring a system that has been disadvantaged for so long lies with the government, upon which also falls the necessity of taking immediate and radical action in some specific areas.

A recurring weakness has been the absence of specific targets for educational development. They were laid down only once: in the report of the Commission of Native Education of 1949-1951 (the Eiselen Commission) established under the chairmanship of Dr. W.W.M. Eiselen, one of the main academic exponents of the apartheid ideology and secretary of the Department of Native Affairs under the them minister, Dr. Hendrik Verwoerd. In its 'tentative scheme of educational development' the Commission suggested that the main aim should be to provide by 1959 enough places in the first four classes of primary schools to accommodate the anticipated numbers of children ages 8-11. Other objectives would be to furnish additional places in the higher primary schools to accommodate the increased number of children that might be expected to attend school for a longer period; to train the necessary extra teachers; and to teach in academic high schools all those who could be absorbed by "the development plan or the present Bantu (black) society". There were to be twice as many school places available in 1959 as in 1949.

In terms of the Bantu Education Act of 1953, control of black education was removed from the provincial authorities in Natal, Transvaal, Orange Free State and Cape Province, and from mission churches, and was placed with the central government's newly-created Department of Bantu Education. By 1959 the Eiselen Commission's targets for primary and secondary pupil enrolments had been met but there were only 5 656 student teachers rather than the 15 000 envisaged, and 1 379 pupils instead of the predicted 6 000 were receiving technical training. Indeed, it was not until 1975 that the projected 1959 level of teacher training was achieved, and the objective for numbers undergoing technical training was not reached until 1980. It should also be borne in mind that the targets for secondary education and technical training were set within the framework of what Eiselen called "the Bantu society" and the separate development of the "Bantu areas" (later to be designated the 'homelands', now 'national states'), and not of the social and economic needs of South Africa as a whole.

The enrolment of the planned number of children in primary and secondary schools brought in its train a far-reaching consequence: priority was given to quantity rather than to quality.

The main objective of the Eiselen plan was to provide educational facilities for all children in the age group 8- 11 by 1959. In a sense this was to be the introductory phase of a programme of compulsory schooling based on a very sound educational principle that anything less than four years of basic education was unlikely to be of any lasting benefit to the learner, and moreover a waste of public funds. However, the Commission under-estimated the growth rate of the black population and particularly the number of children of school-going age, and therefore set targets that were too limited.

The present crisis position has been reached also as a result of continual neglect of black education, in terms of financial resources, over the past of more than 30 years.

All this amounts to an indictment of decision makers, including many outside the political sector. During the last 40 years they have failed to attach due importance to black education; they did not have the foresight to recognise its position as the first line of national defence, nor perceive the social and economic consequences of starving it of resources. It is no accident that the two major upheavals of the last few years in South Africa - the student-orientated unrest of 1976 in Soweto, the black 'city' outside Johannesburg, and the more recent boycott of schools in many parts of the country by coloured (mixed race) and black pupils - should have centred on educational issues to express social and political disaffection. Among other things the Soweto pupils were saying that they had been let down by their education system and that they wanted an education as good as anyone else's, with the opportunity to use it, once acquired. Like their coloured counterparts, they placed these statements within a specific political perspective. As the Reverend Allan Boesak, the then student chaplain at the University of the Western Cape (an institution for the coloured community) and a leading spokesman for the predominantly Afrikaans Nederduitse Gereformeerde mission church, said: "The logic is simple, forthright and devastating: conditions are the way they are because we have inferior education. We have inferior education because we are regarded as second- and third-class citizens in the country of our birth" (Star, 14 November 1989). It is difficult to see how the black community could have reached any other conclusion in the light of data on teacher-pupil ratios, size of classes, high wastage, and unit costs of the educational system through which its children must pass.

Since 1976 the Department of Education and Training has indeed taken up many of these matters a great deal more seriously than before, and much of what is being done deserves support. However, financial and political constraints remain. In spite of considerably increased budgets, resources are still limited, the wide gulf between the black and white education systems persists, and the salaries of black teachers still compare unfavourably with those of white colleagues of like qualifications and experience, South Africa spends only about 19 per cent of its gross national product on education, and in allocating that level of resources lags behind many other less developed countries.

Above all, the improvements being instituted by the Department of Education and Training are not having the impact or acceptance that is necessary. The morale of teachers is at a low ebb, and black education is caught up in a crisis of trust and credibility caused by a rejection of the 'separateness' of the system and of the ideology which gave it birth. The solutions to this problem are political. The heart of the disease in South Africa's education system is its separateness and the ideology which is the rationale for that separateness.

This is not just a matter of administrative machinery. It strikes at the heart of the ideology on which the present system of black education is based. The arguments for 'separateness' revolve around everything from the nature of man, cultural differences, political solutions in a plural society and issues of relevance in education. These are all areas worthy of debate. But throughout, the decisions arising from the debate have been taken by the white establishment, deciding what is 'good for' the black man. Whatever divisions there are in the black community there can be no doubt as to its broad unanimity that the separateness of the system should be brought to an end.

Two opportunities for dealing with this fundamental issue have been lost. The first was in drafting the 1979 Education and Training Act, which replaced the Bantu Education Act of 1953 as the instrument for control and administration of the separate system of black education under the Department of Education and Training. While the Act facilitated many practical and material improvements, it did not come to grips at all with the isolation of black education, and merely perpetuates the 'tradition' of whites taking decisions for the black man. The second opportunity occurred when the Prime Minister, Mr. P.W. Botha, decided to reduce the number of state departments to achieve greater co- ordination and efficiency in the civil service. Initially, instead of incorporating the Department of Education and Training into the Department of National Education (which is concerned with education for whites), it was intended to combine it with the Department of Co-operation and Development, which is concerned with the legal and administrative control of almost every aspect of black life. The clear political statement accompanying this intention aroused strong opposition, not least from within the Department of Education and Training itself. As the Department of Bantu Education, the latter for 25 years had been closely associated with the Department of Bantu Administration, the forerunner of the Department of Co- operation and Development and the connection had severely damaged its relations with the black community. The decision was finally taken to maintain the status quo and leave the Department of Education and Training as a distinct, separate organisation responsible for black education. The essentially political, ideological nature of the decision, however, remains. The emphasis was placed on 'black' and a continuation of separateness, rather than on 'education' and co-ordination of the national effort in the development of human resources. This may well prove to have been a most disastrous choice. Recent boycotts, unrest and violence in coloured and black schools certainly seem to suggest so.

In May 1980, Prime Minister Botha suggested that he might be prepared to make the issue of separateness one of the terms of reference of a general commission of inquiry into the state of education in South Africa. On June 13, 1980 he announced that the Human Sciences Research Council (HSRC, a statutory body) had been instructed to begin a co-ordinated and scientific investigation at every level from pre-primary to tertiary education, and within 12 months to recommend to the Cabinet guidelines for a practicable education policy that would realise the "optimum potential of all [South Africa's] inhabitants", promote economic growth and improve the quality of life for everyone. As well as organisational structure and controls and financial arrangements, the investigation was to consider an infrastructure that would fulfil manpower needs and the "self-realisation" of all the country's inhabitants, and the provision of a programme "whereby equality in education for all population groups can be attained".

The inquiry, directed by a committee of 25 drawn from all sectors of the community, did not have the standing of the statutory commission that many educationist and community leaders had hoped to see. But that point aside, any new dispensation arising from it would win wide acceptance only if it is based on two principles. There had to be firstly, effective co-ordination, co-operation and overall planning at the highest national level to ensure that the educational needs of all South Africa's people are realised and that there is a just distribution of resources to offer equal opportunity for all in the educational process. Secondly, greater flexibility and freedom at the decentralised level was necessary, so that the needs of different areas and cultural groups (identified and defined by the group and not for it), and of different constitutional entities, such as the 'homelands', could be responded to in an effective and acceptable manner.

Such an approach implied the disappearance of the existing separate education departments for African, coloured and Indian pupils, and the re-organisation of the present Department of National Education. It would be naive to believe that this alone would necessarily bring about fundamental change or heal dissatisfaction; mere administrative re-structuring will remain a sterile process unless it is accompanied by a genuine willingness, and a declared intention, to share common resources and facilities, and a thorough assessment of where South Africa stands in the education. The HSRC investigation had to address some fundamental questions. What is education about? What is wanted from it? What should it achieve for the individual, for South African society? It had a need to investigate, discuss and negotiate a common future for education, and a public debate on the issue is probably the most immediate and positive step that could be taken to restore confidence and provide a climate in which reconciliation and reconstruction can take place.

1.3 REPORT OF THE EDUCATION COMMISSION OF THE SOUTH AFRICAN INSTITUTE OF RACE RELATIONS - 1979

In the aftermath of the Soweto unrest of 1976 in which general dissatisfaction with "black education" figured so prominently, the South African Institute of Race Relations appointed a commission to examine education in South Africa and to set out alternative policy guidelines for the country. Chaired by Professor G.R. Bozzoli, former principal of the University of Witwatersrand, the commission issued a report endorsed by the institute's executive committee in January 1979.

1.3.1 Principles

The Commission believed that a desirable educational system for South Africa had to be based on the following principles:

- There had been an emphasis upon equality of opportunity (for different geographical areas, sexes, social and ethnic groups), with supplementary allocation of resources for disadvantaged groups.

- No form of separation of the various race and language groups into separate education institutions had be laid down in laws and regulations, and every effort had be made to integrate educational institutions at all levels.

- The curriculum had stress not only the learning of basic linguistic, mathematical, and scientific concepts and skills, but also the stimulation of a critical scrutiny of society and encouragement in all pupils of an understanding and appreciation of the religions, music, art, literature, and history of other groups within South African society as well as their own.

- A comprehensive programme of adult education in cultural, political, and vocational fields with particular attention being given to the establishment of functional literacy and numeracy programmes for all those adults who do not have these skills, had be embarked upon.

- Education for the entire country had to fall under a single ministry, and the system of educational decision- making and management has to be designed to ensure effective participation of all interested parties at local and regional as well as national levels.

- Independent (i.e. non-state) educational institutions, often centres of excellence and innovation, had to be recognised, subject to state scrutiny in broad terms, to ensure basic compatibility with the spirit of society and the maintenance of acceptable educational standards.

The Commission considered principles to be essential, and the following proposals for a new South African education system were based on them. It must be borne in mind that although it was not possible to predict future political developments in South Africa accurately, it seemed likely that some form of constitutional structure would evolve, possibly for a transitional period preceding the establishment of a unitary political system.

1.3.2   Proposals for a new South African education system

1.3.2.1   Desegregation

In principle there should, in educational dispensation, be a little separation of ethnic and language groups as possible.

1.3.2.2   <u>Control and management</u>

There should be a high degree of decentralisation (on a geographical and not on an ethnic basis) to provide for maximum involvement of the local community in education.

1.3.2.3   <u>Allocation of resources</u>

Overall spending on education in South Africa is inadequate and the Commission recommended that public expenditure should rise from the then 4.33 percent to a least 8 percent of the country's GNP (noting that even this would be insufficient to equalise per capita expenditure on black and white pupils).

Allocation of resources should be such as to bring about a situation where education of an equally high standard would be offered to all groups at all schools and universities. This will demand major redistribution of resources.

1.3.2.4   <u>Specific educational levels</u>

1.3.2.4.1   <u>Schools</u>

Curriculum should reflect the multi-cultural nature of South African society. The drawing up of curricula and syllabuses should fall to a body of educationist including representatives of the teaching force and interested parties from outside the educational system.

Controversial social and environmental problems should be included in the curricula, (as well as courses) dealing with the handling of inter- and intra-group relationships.

Provision must be made for affirmative action in the form of special courses for the disadvantaged.

Textbooks. Many current textbooks contain material offensive to certain South African population groups. Therefore existing textbooks must be reviewed and where necessary amended or replaced. Multi-Cultural bodies should be responsible for the revision and selection of textbooks, which should be impartial and acceptable to all population groups.

Medium of Instruction. Recognising that at least for the foreseeable future it will be necessary for African pupils to switch from mother-tongue instruction to instruction in either English or Afrikaans, the Commission considers that there should be mother-tongue instruction in the early years of schooling, together with sufficient exposure from the beginning to the language of the parents' choice, which will later become the child's medium of instruction.

The nature of the transition from the mother tongue to another language as medium of instruction should not be rigidly prescribed. It should be possible for the child to become sufficiently proficient in the second tongue for the gradual change-over to have started by the third year of schooling, but this may be varied in accordance with the demands of the particular situation.

We also accept that the official language not chosen as medium of instruction should be offered as a school subject at both primary and secondary level.

1.3.2.4.2   Universities

All universities should fall under the same government department, and should be free to admit students and appoint staff, but shall not be free to exclude students on the grounds of race, language, or religion.

1.3.2.4.3   Intermediate qualifications

The importance of intermediate qualifications, particularly in the technological field, must be stressed. People who compose "middle level manpower" - including the technician in industry, the medical aide, the dental aide and responsible health personnel, the draughtsman, the survey technician, and other para-professional persons - are in very great demand. Yet while they are highly skilled, educated, and trained, they do not require the breadth of expansive university education essential for fully professional people.

1.3.2.4.4   Adult education

The inability of the various education systems in South Africa, and particularly those for blacks, to cope with all the needs of the country and its people makes adult education a high priority, which might even warrant the diversion of resources from the school system.

1.4   THE DE LANGE COMMITTEE REPORT ON EDUCATION - 1981

In June 1980 the South African government commissioned the independent but state-funded Human Sciences Research Council (HSRC) to carry out a comprehensive review of all levels of South African education. The HSRC chose Professor J.P. de Lange, the Rector of Rand Afrikaans University, to serve as chair of a distinguished steering committee of twenty- seven members, including several leaders in black education (e.g. A.C. Nkabinde, Principal, The University of Zululand; F.A. Sonn, Director, Peninsula Technikon; and R.E. van der Ross, Principal, University of the Western Cape). De Lange organized a massive research effort and a year after its creation the steering committee submitted a unanimous report to the government. The fifth and final chapter of the report proposed "A Programme to Attain Education of Equal Quality For All Institutions".

The abridged text follows.

The meaning of education of equal quality and the manner in which it should be achieved have received much attention during the past decades. Only limited success has been attained in introducing such education in different parts of the world.

The limited success can mainly be ascribed to bias, incorrect premises, and overestimating the importance of, for example, symbolic measures.

An attempt has been made to learn from experience in this regard. What follows is an exposition of

* Premises
* A short evaluation of the present educational system with equal quality as a criterion
* Problems in formulating operational criteria relevant to education of equal quality
* Proposed policy guidelines
* Implications of these guidelines
* Priority recommendations

1.4.1 Premises

The pursuit of equality basically involves the desire to adhere to a particular social-ethical concept regarding the structure of society, namely that the right of every individual to receive equal treatment in the allocation of collective benefits in the social structure should be recognized and guaranteed. This goal is not based on an assumption of sameness or uniformity between people. It does however postulate a common humanity and the right every person has to expect that organized society will acknowledge the intrinsic values of individuality and humanity and promote the realization of these values.

The demand for equality in education is of special relevance as a result of the restriction of available resources and when the real danger exists that as a consequence of the existing obstruction persons or groups may be denied their rightful share in the benefits that education offers. The term "rightful share" cannot be interpreted as an "equal share" in the arithmetical sense of the word, since no society can function on the basis of unqualified equality ... "Rightful share" should therefore be understood as being related to the concept "distributive justice". The demand for equal share in education is only viable as a principle of distributive justice - "equality-in-the-light-of-justice".

"Rightful distribution" in the first place demands that the rules of distribution be formulated and applied in an unprejudiced manner and, secondly, that the demand for fairness should be met.

Since distribution rules in themselves can be unjust, even if they are applied in an unprejudiced manner, the demand for justice with regard to distribution rules implies that in the rules there should be no discrimination between people unless relevant differences can be indicated, necessitating differentiation. The principle of "equality-in- the-light-of- justice" therefore does make provision for differentiation in the distribution rules and for this reason "rightful share" does not merely mean "the same share for everybody". Equal education therefore does not imply identical education for everybody.

The main problem in determining what a fair share is, lies in the differences between people that could be raised as conditions for distributive differentiation and consequently for categorizing. Justice demands that such differences should be relevant differences, i.e. they should relate to the benefit that will be considered for distribution ... The operational criteria for the application of the principle of equality (in the sense of "for each and everybody his rightful share") should therefore be related to the character and meaning of education.

A further problem is to determine what should be regarded as the "character and meaning of education". This question is basically concerned with the mutual relation between the education curriculum and those matters that are regarded as important by society. Which aims should be served by institutionalized education?

The answer probably lies in the balance between the following community values:

-       Formative religious education, i.e. to give the person taught an opportunity to experience formative religious education in accordance with his own convictions.

-       The maintenance and elaboration of cultural values, i.e. to equip the educational client (sometimes the learner, sometimes the parent, sometimes the community) with an appreciation of cultural heritage as well as with the critical and creative abilities essential for cultural renewal, taking into full consideration the requirements of the different cultural groups; and to give them a share in the control of the contents of the curriculum for the members of the cultural group concerned.

-     <u>Raising the material standards of living</u>, i.e. to equip the educational client wit the necessary skills to be economically productive in accordance with his individual potential, as part of the trained and active labour force; also to enable him to meet his individual needs as well as the collective needs of society.

-     <u>The development of innovative and adaptive abilities with regard to the demands of cultural change</u>, i.e. to equip the recipient of education with knowledge and understanding of the requirements of continual cultural change, for example how to adjust to new situations, to cultivate a productivity-orientated ethic of work, and to master new technological knowledge skills.

-     <u>The improvement of interpersonal relationships</u>, i.e. to equip the educational client with knowledge , interaction skills, and a sense of social responsibility which can promote mutual respect, trust, and co-operation between individuals and groups.

-     <u>The cultivation of positive civil attitudes</u>, i.e. to equip educational clients with knowledge regarding the history, geography, fauna and flora, system of government, etc. of the country, as well as with the problems and challenges facing society.

-     <u>The promotion of the overall quality of life</u>, i.e. to give the educational client the opportunity to develop as a complete, responsible individual: for example the cultivation of language, arithmetic, and manual skills; the cultivation of the ability to learn and evaluate independently; the cultivation of a personal system of values; the identification and development of the largest possible variety of individual talents; the improvement of physical and mental health; the cultivation of specialized professional skills as well as social and leadership skills.

1.4.2 Evaluation of the present educational dispensation

In the existing provision of education, differentiation occurs in different ways and on different grounds between educational clients. The same advantages are not available to everyone.

1.4.3 Problems connected with the concept of "equal quality in education"

The approach to the concept "equal quality in education" can be narrowed down to two points of view: that of educational achievements and that of educational opportunities.

Because of the extremely complex problems standing in the way of a positive definition of a "programme for equal quality in education for all population groups", an answer could perhaps be found by adopting the following as a point of departure: the reduction and elimination of demonstrable inequality in the provision of education available to members of the different population groups. Such inequalities can be clearly defined and documented as concrete, empirically determinable facts on the basis of several specific indicators:

- Accessibility, including freedom of choice in the sense of the absence of educationally irrelevant limitations.

- Curriculum content and standards, for examples subject choice, syllabuses, textbooks, evaluation criteria, examination standards, certification, and general administration.

- General compulsory education, for example a specific number of years agreed upon.

- Teachers, for example level of training, teacher-pupil ratio, etc.

- Physical educational facilities, for example the number and quality of buildings, equipment, sports facilities, etc.

- Financial resources, for example per capita expenditure.

1.4.4 Proposed policy guidelines

The progressive provision of adequate means to enable every inhabitant to obtain the essential minimum of knowledge skills, and values will be recognized and maintained as the highest priority in the programme for the provision of education.

No person will on educationally irrelevant grounds be debarred from available educational opportunities from which he might benefit.

1.4.5 Implications

The above guidelines are collectively aimed at establishing a new educational dispensation to promote the progressive implementation of the principle of education of equal quality for the different population groups. This does not mean that on a given date the education system will be reformed to such an extent the "equal quality education" will immediately be provided in an absolute sense. It is unrealistic to expect that such an objective can suddenly be achieved. The achievement of this general objective can nevertheless be systematically striven for through the achievement of definite aims and the determination of clear priorities in terms of specific action programmes.

The first guideline implies that provision should be made for the introduction of general compulsory education and compulsory schooling linked with "free" education for a certain number of years.

The second guideline implies the need for clarity on the methods and pace of eliminating restrictions on access to and the provision of educational facilities based purely on racial or colour discrimination.

The third guideline implies the needs for clarity concerning the model that will be used to determine the quality of the benefits to be provided for a particular category of educational clients.

The most important implication of the fourth guideline is that educationally irrelevant inequalities that are evident in the provision of education should be identified as clearly as possible and eliminated through educational reforms.

1.4.6   Recommendations on priorities

A system for the provision of education that is aimed at the pursuit and achievement of equal standards in education cannot be accomplished immediately. However, this should not be used as an excuse for sluggish and feeble attempts. It is regarded as a bounden duty to commence with a practical programme as soon as possible and to move purposefully towards the ultimate objective. The series of recommendations contained in this report were made with a view to establishing a basis for such a programme. The recommendations relate to the whole system for the provision of education and it is regarded as desirable to indicate which recommendations should be implemented as soon as possible.

1.4.6.1   Education management: Interim council for education

The restructuring of the system for the provision of education should occur with the highest degree of consultation and it is therefore recommended that an Interim Council for Education be appointed by the Cabinet or by a Minister appointed by the Cabinet, within the next few months.

1.4.6.2   Educational structure

It is recommended that the following matters be given priority:

-    The progressive introduction of nine years' compulsory education.

-    The introduction of a pre-basic bridging period aimed at school readiness.

-    The expansion of preparatory vocational education.

-    The establishment of the necessary infrastructure for the provision of non-formal education.

-    The granting of the right to Councils of autonomous educational institutions in higher education to decide who should be admitted as students.

1.4.6.3   Supporting services

Supporting services are of primary importance in the improvement of the provision of education and it is therefore recommended that the planning and establishment of a co-operative education service should be given priority. These are: curriculum services; educational-technological services; guidance services; health and social services; evaluative and diagnostic services for learning with handicaps; and co-operative educational services.

1.4.6.4   Recruitment and training of teachers

The key factor in the provision of education is the teacher. It is recommended that

-          a registration authority where all teaching staff may register should be instituted;

-          the registration authority should as its first priority after the necessary consultations decide on the categories in which teaching staff may register;

-          a model recruitment and selection programme should be developed for use by educational authorities after adaptations;

-          the training of teachers for general formative and preparatory career education (technical education in particular) should enjoy top priority;

-          "Standard ten" as the minimum admission requirement for teacher training should be applied as soon as possible and the facilities for those wishing to obtain this qualification should be provided and the continuous need for in-service training satisfied.

1.4.6.5   Physical facilities

The backlog with regard to the provision of the necessary facilities of an acceptable standard in respect of existing facilities, present shortages, and additional needs as a result of increased numbers is matter of extreme urgency.

1.4.6.6   Financing of education

There is no doubt that the provision of education of equal quality will require more funds. Bearing in mind that means are not unlimited, it is recommended that financially realistic norms for the provision of an adequate standard of education should be drawn up and revised from time to time by the central educational authority and should be used for the central authority's financing of education for the total population.

1.4.6.7   Planning for the provision of education

A sophisticated and continuous survey of the need for and change in the demand for education as a result of, inter alia, trends in population growth and shifts and changing manpower needs should enjoy top priority as the basis for the flexible planning of the provision of education.

1.5   THE LOST DECADE

This is the year (1991) in which the problems in black education were supposed to have been solved. Like that other magical target - 1978 - when, according to former Minister M.C. Botha, the exodus of blacks from "white" urban areas to the homelands would have started, 1990 was D-year for education. Seldom in our history has a commission report been so eagerly awaited - and so universally acclaimed - as was the De Lange Report on Education, presented to the then Minister of National Education, Dr. Gerrit Viljoen in 1981. It was a thorough and scholarly piece of research. It cut to the bone of our education problems - racially splintered control and inequality in funding and opportunities. Its recommendations were incisive, cogent and practical. It provided a much need blueprint for the years ahead - with 1990 as the culmination. But, as happened so often with similar probes (Tomlinson, Riekert, et al) this report - named after the chairman of the research group, Professor Pieter de Lange, then Rector of the Rand Afrikaans University - lay gathering dust on bureaucratic shelves. Or, even worse, the government treated it as a smorgasbord rather than a fixed menu - picking out certain suggestions that it found feasible to implement, leaving out vital recommendations that were supposed to have formed the bedrock of a new education system. "It is sad but true - the situation has worsened between De Lange and now", says Dr. Ken Hartshorne, a former head of the Centre for Continuing Education at the University of the Witwatersrand and one of the country's most respected educationist. He served on the executive committee of the De Lange probe and led the working group which investigated education structures and control.

It is difficult not to be pessimistic about the future of "black" education in particular and education in general because the problems encountered now by the Department of Education and Training are bound to have a domino effect on teaching as a whole. The Government has totally lost control over black schools, it is a frightening situation. I have little hope that any answers can be found before finality on a new political dispensation has been reached. For now, one can only look back on a decade of lost opportunities - and speculate on what could have been, had the De Lange proposals been implemented. De Lange's insistence on ONE education department route - building up the Department of National Education, yes, to act as some sort of mother body, but to retain Education and Training for blacks, and strengthening the autonomy of the various Own Affairs education departments for whites, coloureds and indians. Now it finds itself in a classic Catch 22 - situation. The government instinctively knows that one department and one education system is the only route to go, but it can't move until clarity has been reached on what the political system will look like. The result has been an uneasy and unsatisfactory holding operation: in white education playing around with options for the gradual integration of white schools and state funding for private institutions; in black education, applying Band Aids and interim measures in a effort to restore some coherence to a system that has failed the community and its children.

De Lange's recommendations on wiping out the backlog in educational spending, standards and facilities through imaginative planning and the rearrangement of the State's budgetary priorities have vanished almost without trace. A government scheme to implement a five year plan to achieve educational parity had to be scrapped within years of its announcement. However, the stark figures provide the best indication of how black the picture has become. Total government expenditure on education has increased fivefold, from R2,1 billion in 1980 to more than R10 billion in the current financial year 1990 (although the effect of the shrinking value of the Rubicon rand should also be factored in), yet the problems of overcrowding, too few teachers serving too many pupils and inadequate facilities have not been solved. The pupil-teacher ratio in 1980 was 19:1 for whites and a staggering 45:1 for black children. De Lange recommended that this be narrowed to at least 30:1 by 1990. In 1990, the ratio stood at 41:1 for blacks while the white rate "improved" to 16:1. In areas like the Transkei the ratio at primary schools is 61:1. The number of black pupils at school (excluding the "independent" homelands has risen in the 80's from 3,5 million to five million - equalling the total white population. There are now more black children entering Grade one each year than there are in the entire white school system.

The spending gap per capita has narrowed dramatically. In 1980 R1 was spent on a black child for every R10 spent on his white counterpart. In the present budget the ratio has been halved to 1:5. In real terms, however, the contrast is still stark: R2 800 a year for every white child, R600 for every black child. The training of teachers has been one of the few success stories in black education over the past decade. Whereas in 1980 less than 20 percent of teachers in black schools had an education level higher than matric, this has risen to about 60 percent at the end of the decade. Teachers with degrees have risen from 2,4 percent to 4 percent. A large section of the De Lange report dealt with the importance of pre-primary and primary education. The report recommended that imaginative steps be taken to bridge the gap between the home and the first years of formal education. It quoted alarming figures from the 1970's to show that less than half of black children entering grade one finished standard two in the required four years compared with 90 percent for white pupils. This situation has not improved. The biggest dropout percentage among black children still occurs at the end of their FIRST year of formal schooling. The long-term effect this will have on the economy will be shattering.

Numerous smaller recommendations by the De Lange Commission have not been implemented either, black schools still suffer from a serious shortage of school books, laboratory facilities, libraries and sports grounds while across town, in white schools, headmasters run swimming pools, tennis courts and athletics tracks like private fiefdoms, refusing even the school's parents the use of them, let alone sharing them with children from other population groups. In the ten years since De Lange, the education crisis has grown instead of diminishing. It would be wrong to accuse the Government of ill-will (or even a lack of will) to tackle the problem. Within its own budgetary constraints it did a commendable job. However, the root of the problem remains political - a preoccupation with separateness taken to the extreme of duplicating, triplicating and quadruplicating each and every educational structure. Fortunately, this approach now seems to be on its last legs. Whatever government combination comes into being in the New South Africa we will have to tackle the education problem as a matter of the highest priority.

1.6 CONCLUSION

To say that there is an education crisis in South Africa is a gross understatement. The reality of black education is dismal. Major problems such as under-funding, classroom shortages, overcrowding, lack of qualified teachers, and abysmal living conditions have all contributed to a state of affairs which cannot be, indeed is not, tolerated.

Fifty percent of the country's population is under the age of sixteen. This statistic gives the dimension of the problem. For every Rand spent on a black child's education, over R5 is spent on a white child. White classrooms are half-filled, whole school buildings stand empty, while black scholars cram into leaking, cold, miserable structures by the hundred. And black students are aware of these facts.

Black teachers are underpaid, subject to maladministration, and their resentment has manifested itself through strikes and work stoppages. The festering sore of inequality in education erupted in June 1976 and, since then, there has scarcely been peace in the schools. Teachers are perceived to be government stooges, not worthy of respect, and authority has totally broken down. School boycotts are more the norm than the exception. There are estimates that on any one school day, approximately 200 000 children scattered throughout the country are boycotting classes. Today's scholars have seen whites almost solely in the role of oppressor, as police invaded school premises to "maintain law and order" and as they crushed student protest. Black children are angry and deeply scarred. That they ignore the calls of their leaders to return to school, to halt the boycotts, to develop their potential through education, is understandable. These children have lost patience. They want action, and they want it immediately.

There is little understanding of the negotiation process. When their leaders where returned to them and their political parties were unbanned, expectations ran high. On the night of Dr. Mandela's release, Soweto could not sleep - jubilation kept it awake. Once again, just as in the mid- 1980's there was a belief that liberation was around the corner. The months have passed, and they see no tangible progress. The 'talk about talks' have no real meaning to them, no effect on their material lives. As far as they are concerned, they are still engaged in a struggle, their fight of freedom.

I quake as I wonder - have we all lost control of our youth? The prospect is frightening. It is even more disturbing in the light of their expectations. It is apparently clear that the vast majority of this 50 % of the population have totally unrealistic expectations of their entitlements under our future government. It is a commonly held belief that they will then be guaranteed jobs, high wages, housing and superior education. The economic reality of the situation escapes them. No matter what economic structure emerges, the country is simply incapable of achieving these expectations. Bear in mind also that we have produced almost two generations of whom the largest proportion is functionally illiterate, and the problem becomes even more serious. How will we accommodate this mass of unskilled labour? Not even under the most optimistic scenario can we ever hope to create sufficient new jobs.

We have a problem. The government of the future has a problem. H.G. Wells said that human history "is more a race between education and catastrophe". We are experiencing the truth of these words. Education has got to be the priority of government, present and to come, of the private sector and of all South Africans. This is our Achilles' heel.

Many committed educationist, with the private sector have been acutely aware of this for years. Their response has been to attempt to address the socio-political causes of the crisis, at the same time providing resources for education empowerment programmes. These programmes have been focused on the training of teachers in order to achieve the greatest multiplier effect.

But formal education is not enough. We have to look further, at education which will temper the impossible expectations. Students must be helped to gain an understanding of basic economics, and this must be done as a matter of urgency. I am not suggesting here that we attempt to propound the virtues of a free market system over socialism, or a decentralised economy versus a centrally- planned economy. Whatever emerges in the new era, the logistics of funding of massive social projects will be problematic. What I do believe to be important is to draw a distinction between wealth creation and wealth distribution. Wealth distribution on the other hand, may require a different tactic. These are obviously important negotiating issues.

There is need, also, for education surrounding the negotiation process. It needs to be understood - and this applies to whites as well as to blacks - that previously espoused policy is not cast in stone. Dr. Mandela has been explicit on this point, President De Klerk has said so time and again. Yet there are still those who see every movement, every concession, as a sign of weakness.

The responsibility for education on these two key issues lies with all of us. It is as imperative for black leaders as it is for white.

Tomorrow's government cannot succeed if it is perceived as not 'delivering'. The result will be anarchy.

THE CONVOLUTED STRUCTURE
OF EDUCATION IN
SOUTH AFRICA

2.1 INTRODUCTION

Why is South Africa experiencing such a prolonged and so fierce a conflict over the issue of education? Is discontent being artificially stimulated or are there factors in the South African situation which make such conflicts inevitable?

Arguments about one or another aspect of educational policies are common internationally. If it is not the curriculum, then it might be the provision of facilities for minorities or unequal opportunities for participation, the allocation of resources, the medium of instruction or the status of religion in the schools. And there are of course other possibilities.

But why is the conflict so intense in South Africa? Could it be because she has a culturally mixed society of because of her economic system?

Among the areas of tension confronting educational policy- makers is inevitably the overall allocation of resources among such sectors as primary, secondary, vocational, adult and university education, circular priorities and teaching methods at these various levels, ways in which the system should be controlled and managed, the role of private institutions, the use of international aid, and, in most of our sub-continent, the handling of the ethnic dimension.

While the education system is concerned with individual people and their opportunities for fulfilment, it is also geared towards the welfare of groups, and herein lies a primary tension which is reflected in educational policy.

Many tensions are inherent in the thrust towards equality of educational opportunity. One of the two more common meanings of this phrase is the policy whereby all people have the same chance of entering educational institutions. In the second meaning, the policy entails the provision of compensatory resources and/or opportunity for members of disadvantaged groups, providing supplementary financing for what have been called educational priority areas in Britain.

On the issues of control and management, we can note that the major policy tension is concerned with the degree of centralisation in control. This does not merely relate to the extent in which power may be given to local communities to manage at least some aspects of their educational affairs. The role of independent schools complicates the issue further.

In the school curriculum, the most evident policy tensions are likely to be experienced in decisions about the teaching of contentious material in history and geography, and other social subjects. The arguments are well known and require no further discussion. In a culturally plural society, however, there is the separate matter of how to deal with cultural material such as songs, literature and art. A school system designed to foster national unity would certainly seek to encourage a appreciation of cultural material from other social groups in all young people. Finally, in this section of curriculum content, one must mention the general argument about the extent of specialised or vocational education appropriate at the secondary level.

So much for the what of the school curriculum. Now, briefly, the matter of how. Two issues suggest themselves, one being that of language medium. The argument for being free to choose another medium for instruction after a few years of schooling. Just when the change-over should be made, where it is to be made, should partly be a matter of empirical evidence, but financial constraints will necessarily limit options. Teaching styles present a second problem in this area. However beneficial the more progressive and unstructured styles may be (and under certain circumstances they can be very beneficial indeed), this method of teaching can have disastrous results if the teacher is insufficiently educated and confident, and the resources are lacking which ensure that a more imaginative and challenging type of classroom climate can produce effective learning. Particularly when the educational levels of the teaching personnel are more heterogeneous, tension may develop between the need for a freer type of teaching and the constraints of the classroom situation.

One thing may be remarked on at this point. Areas of serious conflict are not those concerned with issues such as teaching method or details of institutional management.

Everywhere education can constitute an actual or potential source of political conflict, because the education system performs a number of politically relevant functions. Firstly, education influences the way in which young people interpret their experiences, the way in which they perceive the world, the meanings which they attach to the things they observe. Other institutions in society also have an influence on this process of 'making meaning'. Examples of such institutions are the family, peer groups, religious institutions and the mass media. The school institution is a particularly powerful agent in such a development, and the influence exerted on the young is open to manipulation by forces with considerable resources at their disposal. Clearly, the way in which young people come to interpret their social context will have a bearing on their political postures.

Where a society is comprised of a number of different cultures, we may expect considerable debate and struggle over the social aspects of the curriculum, the degree of local control in education, autonomy for university institutions, the allocation of resources, inter-group equality of access to educational opportunities and the way in which the education system is used in nation-building.

2.2   THE BUREAUCRATIC MONSTER OF NINETEEN EDUCATION DEPARTMENTS

In 1989 educationist Dr. Ken Hartshorne wrote: "It will be more difficult for the government to change the principle of segregated education systems than to free Nelson Mandela, negotiate with the African National Congress or repeal the Group Areas Act, because (the principle) lies at the heart of the ideology of separate development." Two momentous year on, Hartshorne's prophecy - however completely ludicrous it might have sounded at the time - has proved to be true.

The pillars of apartheid are in the process of being completely dismantled, people of all races can already use the same swimming pools and toilets, within months they will be able to live and own land within spitting distance of each other, and newly born children will be christened "South Africans" rather than "black", "white", "Indian" or "coloured".

Yet there are still 19 department of education: five administering white education, one each for Indians and coloureds, 11 (eleven) for black education - in and out of "independent" homelands and "self-governing territories" - and one umbrella department controlling the purse strings and setting different "norms and standards" for the rest.

In only a tiny minority of government schools can children of all races receive the same quality of education and learn side by side in the same classrooms. Educational opportunities for white and black students are still hopelessly skewed and the prospects of fundamental change in the provision of these opportunities are limited by severe financial constraints. It has been calculated that between two and three times the amount currently spent on education (19 percent of total government expenditure) would have to be devoted to education, just to equalise yearly expenditure on children of all races.

The system has lost credibility. It has been called a bureaucratic monster and numerous academics, educationist and community members believe that not until a single education system has been created will any semblance of normality be restored to the beleaguered area of education. On the eve of the opening of parliament, rumours circulated to the effect that State President F.W. de Klerk would announce an end to "apartheid education", or at least announce the government's intention to make radical reforms to the system in this parliamentary session.

The rumour turned out to be far from the truth. While De Klerk admitted the present educational system "shall and must be changed", he did not specifically mention "one education system or department". The further he went was to say: "Distinctive or autogenous education, conducted with government assistance within a single system by those who desire it, has to remain an option". (The Star, April 8, 1991)

For those expecting a clear statement on the future of South African education, there was disappointment at instead being bedeviled with convoluted national party double-speak. In government briefing sessions both Minister of National Education Louis Pienaar and Minister of Education and Training Stoffel van der Merwe gave the strongest indication that the education system could only be radically changed when a new constitution is drawn up. In other words, education will be one of the last areas to be reformed. The philosophy of separate education is cemented in the Republic of South Africa Constitution Act of 1983, which defines the concept of "own affairs" and defines education at all levels as an"own affair". It is this Act the government is unable - or unwilling at the present juncture - to dismantle.

The reasons for this reluctance are clear and centre not only on the excuses readily given that it will be necessary to wait to see the shape of the future constitution and that the economy cannot afford to restructure the system so as to spend the same amount on each child regardless of race.

The other important reason - not as often heard - is that education is an emotive subject and the government knows it stands to lose the support of a major sector of its white constituency if the education standards for whites are lowered, as would be inevitable with a wholesale redistribution of funds.

While Minister of Constitution Development, Gerrit Viljoen accepted at a briefing session in February 1991 that one education system is virtually inevitable (although he offered few clues to its shape), the road that has to be taken to transform the present tangled bureaucracy is a matter of debate - within and without government circles. Pienaar and Van der Merwe favour a more "bottom-up" reform: addressing the imbalances in the system within the current framework, gradually working towards a situation where there is an equal provision of education for all pupils, irrespective of what department they fall under. They plan to start bringing the currently divergent "norms and standards" regarding syllabi, exams, teacher/pupil ratios and school calendars in line with each other. Equal funding is currently impossible - as was shown by the breakdown of then Minister of National Education F.W. de Klerk's 10-year plan in 1989 which aimed at providing parity in funding. The existing backlogs will take even longer to rectify.

Eventually, Pienaar believes: "We will have to apply whatever we have to a basic education, and if you want education after that, you will have to pay for it. There is a great likelihood that education at a secondary level will not be as free as we would like. We just will not have the money to pay for everything" (Weekly Mail, 15-21 February 1991).

At the same time, the government is chipping away at the laws from the top, for instance by making limited provision for children of all races to attend previously white government schools. But more community-based educationist believe this is not enough. They say that children will not return to schools administered under the politically- discredited Department of Education and Training (DET) and resume "normal" education until the DET is dismantled and a unitary department put in its place. According to Professor Charles "M.C." Maphahlele, Dean of Education at the University of the North (Turfloop), the government's first priority must be the "top-down" formation of a single education department, in essence, a cosmetic change. "Expenditure on black and white pupils will not necessarily be equal immediately. Even if all schools are opened, there is no way black kids can travel long distances to go the white schools and it will take time to upgrade schools in the townships". (The Weekly Mail (February 15-21, 1991).

Prof. Johan Muller from the Education Policy Unit at the University of Cape Town said bureaucracy is too entrenched to create a single department "with a stroke of a pen". The most important step the government must take now, he believes, is to stop thinking in racial terms and to create the concept of "the South African child".

"The government's dilemma is that they know they need one department, but there are such different norms for everything - both in terms of facilities and variable financing - and they know they will have to have one set of norms in order to have one department. "But, on the one hand, they haven't got the money to give everyone the same as the whites, and on the other, the whites won't accept less. They are thus going to have to edge towards a solution in a crabwise fashion, shrinking the current bureaucracy from either end. "We will not see the creation of a single education system in a minute. At the optimum, we can expect a speeding up of shrinkage from both ends", (Weekly Mail, 15-21 February 1991).

Top-down or bottom-up? I think the government is trying both.

2.3   SHORTAGES

In response to a question in Parliament in May 1989, Dr. Viljoen said that based on a calculation of 40 primary pupils per classroom and 35 secondary pupils per classroom, there was a shortage of 1 782 classrooms at primary and 2 730 classrooms at secondary schools under the control of the DET as at March 1988, (Hansard, 2 May 1989). The corresponding figures for 1987 were 1 084 primary and 2 194 secondary classrooms. In 1988 the DET built 447 fewer classrooms than it had done in 1987.

Dr. Stoffel van der Merwe, who succeeded Dr. Viljoen as Minister of Education and Development Aid towards the end of 1989, said in Parliament in February 1990 that there had been a shortage of 60 343 classroom places at primary schools and 99 506 classroom places at secondary schools as at March 1989. The statistics, he said, applied to permanent classrooms in state schools administered by the DET. Private and state-aided schools, permanent classrooms used in the platoon system, and rented and temporary accommodation, had not been taken into account (Hansard, 27 May 1990).

Research conducted by the Education Policy Unit at the University of Natal concluded that in Natal alone, more than 1 million children between the ages of six and twenty had not been able to attend school in 1989 (Weekly Mail, 15 December 1989). According to government figures provided in 1988, there were 1 million children between the ages of seven to sixteen not attending school in South Africa and the non-independent homelands as at March 1987 (Hansard, 22 March 1988). In 1989 and at the beginning of 1990 it was apparent that the DET was attempting to find ways of reducing the number of African pupils making use of restricted secondary school facilities. The controversial measures were considered unacceptable by educationist and communities. It was also repeatedly stated that headmasters were being told not to enrol more pupils than allocated.

In January 1989 hundreds of pupils were allegedly refused permission to attend schools in Cape Town (western Cape) because they had come from the homelands (Business Day, 19 January 1989). Towards the end of January, the East London Progressive Teachers' Union said that only one fifth of pupils who had passed standard 5 had been admitted to standard 6 in Mdantsane (Ciskei), in an attempt to limit numbers in secondary schools. The union alleged that enrolment had been restricted following a directive from the DET (City Press, 24 January 1989). Research by South African Institute of Race Relations showed that pressure on school facilities was also evident in the Port Elizabeth region in the eastern Cape, where schools failed to enrol all of the pupils who applied (Cosser, Social and Economic update 7).

In December 1989 the regional director of the DET's Cape region, Mr. W. Staude, said that the demand for school places in Port Elizabeth (eastern Cape) was outstripping the supply. He said that a natural increase in the population and rapid urbanisation would result in an 'excess of pupils for the foreseeable future'. Despite the fact that 11 new schools had been built between 1987 and 1989, the need to 'platoon' to get maximum use out of school buildings would increase, he added. He provided the following breakdown of African schools and pupils in the Port Elizabeth/Uitenhage area in 1989: there were 17

state secondary schools with a total enrolment of 19 841 pupils and
579 teachers, 100 state 'primary' schools (some of these schools taught
up to standard 7 level) with 73 661 pupils and 1 757 teachers, 60 state-
aided schools with 5 830 pupils and 163 teachers, and two private
primary schools with 684 with pupils and 24 teachers. Two new
secondary schools were under construction and would be completed
in 1991 (Eastern Province Herald, 11 December 1989).

Facilities were under particular pressure in Soweto (Johannesburg) in
January 1989. In March 1989 student spokesmen called for the
provision of more schools and staff to alleviate overcrowding. Critics
of the DET alleged that excluding pupils from schools allowed the
department to keep pupil/teacher ratios at a reasonable level (Business
Day, 16 March 1989). According to research conducted by the
Education Policy Unit at the University of the Witwatersrand (Wits),
some 13 000 African pupils had enrolled in private 'academies'
offering secondary education in the Pretoria/Witwatersrand/
Vereeneging area in 1989.

City Press reported in April 1989 that 'the abolition of influx control
measures caused a surge of thousands of black people in cities - but
schools had not been readily included in resultant township
development. Massive townships are being developed by the private
sector, but hundreds of school sites remain empty' (23 April 1989).
The Chief executive of F.H.A. Homes (a housing developer for the
Urban Foundation), Mr. B. Longley, said that no schools had been
build in the 20 African townships which had been developed by the
company during the past six years. The problem had not been caused
by lack of proper planning, but by the 'abnormally high growth rate
of pupils in certain areas', Dr. Viljoen said, in response to queries
(City Press, 23 April 1989).

Following what were considered to be 'disastrous' African
matriculation results at the end of 1989, the National Education Co-
ordinating Committee (NECC) launched a back-to-school campaign,
urging all pupils, including those who had failed any examination, to
return to class in defiance of a DET ruling which would have excluded
all failed matriculants from schools. The DET agreed to

accommodate all pupils and extend the registration date to 26 January 1990.

It was reported at the end of January 1990 that more than 1 500 standard 6 pupils could not be accommodated at DET schools in Grahamstown (eastern Cape). Following a meeting between a delegation of parents, pupils and teachers and the DET's director for the area, Mr. B. Podesta, a spokesman for the delegation, Mr. T. Tisani, said that according to Mr. Podesta the current waiting list was not valid, that pupils had to re-register and that a new list had to be submitted to the DET. Mr. Tisani also alleged that Mr. Podesta had not committed himself to any possible solution once the new list had been handed in. Mr. Podesta told the press that he was not in a position to comment on the issue (City Press, 28 January 1990).

The deputy Minister of Education and of Development Aid, Mr. Piet Marais, said in February 1990 that the extension of the registration date to 26 January had resulted in waiting lists containing 30 644 names. He said that only 3 000 pupils on the lists had not yet been accommodated. He added that the number of high school pupils had increased by 60 000 since 1989 and that more than R230 million would have to be spent to accommodate them. Mr. Marais also expressed the opinion that the back-to-school movement did not seem to have achieved the desired educational ends (Business Day, 20 February 1990). The general secretary of the NECC, Mr. Ihron Rensburg, said at the time of Mr. Marais's statement that while the DET had supported the back-to-school campaign, it had done nothing to provide resources for the increased numbers of pupils. It was clear that there was gross overcrowding and an acute shortage of learning materials and that the conditions for qualitative learning simply did not exist. (Business Day, 20 February 1990).

According to the Department of Education and Culture (coloured own affairs), there was a backlog of 9 561 classrooms as at the beginning of 1990. The cost of eliminating the backlog in primary school classrooms was estimated at R660 million while that of eliminating the backlog in secondary school classrooms was estimated at R257 million. The department also said that at a production rate of eight secondary and 22 primary schools per year and not taking into account the national growth of the coloured school population, it would take ten years to eliminate this backlog. According to the Department of Education and Culture (Indian own affairs), there was no backlog in classroom accommodation at Indian schools in 1988 or 1989.

Speaking during the debate on the budget for education and culture (white own affairs) in Parliament in May 1989, the Democratic Party's spokesman on education, Mr. Roger Burrows MP, said that the more than 278 000 empty places at white schools in 1988 represented R1.6 billion in unused assets (Hansard, 15 May 1989). The Minister of Education and Culture in the House of Assembly, Mr. Piet Clase stated in parliament in the same month that 196 white primary schools and seven white secondary schools had been closed over the last ten years. The 66 primary schools which had been closed in Natal, the Orange Free State and the Transvaal could have accommodated close on 13 000 pupils. Pupil enrolment capacity figures were not available for the 130 primary and the two secondary schools which had been closed in the Cape (Hansard, 16 May 1989). In reply to a question in Parliament some days later, Mr. Clase provided figures which showed that in the eastern Cape, one white high school had an enrolment which was 20 % of its capacity. Others were two thirds empty. With one exception, all schools in Aberdeen, Cookhouse, Cradock, Graaff-Reinet, Jansenville and Oudtshoorn (eastern Cape hinterland) were under-utilised (Hansard, 18 May 1989).

According to the Education Policy Unit at Wits, in a statement issued in August 1989, there were 42 white schools risking closure, immediately or in the next five years, in Johannesburg alone. This number represented almost one quarter of all white schools in the city. Schools with a drop in enrolment of more than 50 % over the past five years risked immediate closure. There were seven schools in this category, and another seven schools close to it (The Star, 17 August 1989). In March 1989 teachers at two different white schools in Johannesburg alleged that one school was 'fiddling the books' to boost pupil enrolment and that another was 'turning a blind eye to people who pass as white' in order to avoid closure (Weekly Mail, 31

March 1989).

Mr. Clase said in March 1990 that 24 white state primary schools, with a capacity of 4 104 pupils, had been closed in 1989. Of these, 12 were in the Cape, one in Natal, one in the Orange Free State and ten in the Transvaal (Hansard, 12 March 1990). In May 1990 Mr. Clase said that 78 schools owned or controlled by his department were either not used or were used for purposes other than education as at 23 March 1990. Mr. Clase also said in March 1990 that, of the 515 928 places available at white primary schools in the Cape, the Orange Free State and the Transvaal, 449 240 were filled as at the latest dates for which figures were available. Of the 390 585 places available at secondary schools in the three provinces, 33 260 were filled. Information on enrolment at schools in Natal was not available (Hansard, 25 March 1990). There were 21 163 vacant places in white school hostels as at the beginning of 1989. During the last ten years, 16 white school hostels which could have accommodated well over 1 000 had been closed down.

2.4   BLACKS' EDUCATIONAL NEEDS

At a macro level the South African Government is trying to commit itself to the upholding of fundamental human rights in a free, open and just society. This is the basic need for all Blacks in South Africa. All the other needs are the symptoms of this need. The problems underlying education in South Africa are not merely educational but are underpinned by political issues.

Why are the White and Indian children not boycotting their classes and burning down their schools? Why are the White teachers not putting their "chalk down" and taking to the streets? The writer is not condoning these actions. They are despicable, but the questions remain.

South Africa's education system does not allow any child free access to any public education institution. For various reasons including financial, socio-cultural background, etc. even private schools practice what is called selective discrimination in terms of elitist ideology which has the same effect as an apartheid ideology, only it is couched in a more civilised languages. That sounds an unkind remark to make about schools that are trying their best to uphold the highest educational standards, but that is another matter. South Africa does not have a single system of education which is legitimate and credible, characterised by a policy of cultural diversity. This system would take into cognizance the different languages, different cultures and historical heritages and differences of the third world and the first world. Unless this happens, education in South Africa does not serve the purpose of national unity.

At best it is a divisive force in terms of race and ethnicity and creates a suitable climate for conflict. At worst it alienates those Black children who attend the so called non-racial schools. Under the present set of circumstances both non-racial and racial schools are equally alienating in different directions.

The problem of accommodating an ever increasing pupil and student-numbers during the next two or three decades has been highlighted by various researchers who provided alarming statistics. Just to take one example from Prof Booysen's figures.

Table 2.1

PROJECTION OF NUMBERS OF MATRICULATED SCHOOL LEAVERS IN SOUTH AFRICA BY RACIAL GROUP (IN THOUSANDS)

YEAR	AFRICAN	COLOURED	INDIAN	WHITE
1989	25,1	4,2	5,0	31,0
1999	61,2	6,9	5,6	26,2
2009	98,2	11,2	6,9	28,6

Source: Booysen - The challenges of numbers, 1990

This indicates that even if all the White schools were opened and Blacks would have free access, this would not resolve the problem of large numbers. The need is for the provision of equal availability and equal quantity of facilities. More and more schools of poor quality will not help. The above is retarded by the present patterns of financing education which is not equitable. An insufficient progress is being made towards creating equal educational opportunities for all learners. The amazing feature in the financing of education for the non-voters is that it required a complete collapse of education in the Johannesburg region and an unprecedented demonstrations by teachers and some adults before the government could produce another R8 million for school books. Finally, the educational programmes are not relevant for both the learner and eventual employer.

The Minister of National Education appointed a Committee to devise a Strategy and Programme for Educational Renewal (SER) to look at:

- system affairs
- linkages between formal and non-formal education
- distance education
- university and technikon education
- instructional programmes at universities and technikons
- at colleges of education
- the school and technical college curriculum
- entrance requirements for universities
- usage of educational technology
- projected manpower needs
- remuneration of educators
- resources for teacher training colleges
- privatisation of education
- cost effective classroom and school buildings, etc.

The Minister mentioned that these investigations are aimed primarily at solving education management problems and not at researching fundamental educational issues. This investigation is mentioned in order to raise two following issues:

Whereas there is a need for a strategy and programme for Educational Renewal, this must be done within the context of the fundamental needs and aspirations of the majority of this society. The problems in Black education have been fuelled by events of unrest, stayaways, demonstrations and collapse of discipline amongst pupils and teachers. There is a perception in Black society that education is in a severe crisis and that the education authorities are slow and unable to address the pressing problems encountered in the education system. The pressing need therefore is to address the crisis in education by strategies to rehabilitate large numbers of children who have been brutalised by violence and completely disoriented by unrest.

Secondly, this investigation consists of twenty (20) working committees out of which only four (4) committees have Black representation. The 20 Committees have a total of 165 members drawn mainly from the various education departments and educational institutions including a few experts. Of these 165 persons, only ten (10) are Black. This is an amazing under representation at a time when the whole country is trying to find a way of enabling all sectors of this society to participate effectively in matters which affect them.

The writer has indicated that the educational needs of the Black people relate to the issues of

- freedom, justice and human rights
- free access, equal availability and equal quality
- culture diversity
- provision for ever increasing numbers
- adequate financing
- relevance
- participation

This suggests that all the present educational structures must be reformed and others disbanded in order to create a climate that will have legitimacy and credibility. When that happens education shall contribute its share towards building a new and a prosperous South Africa.

2.5   CURRENT EDUCATIONAL STRUCTURES

The present education model in South Africa is based on the principle of "own and general affairs". The publication of the Governments' White Paper on the Provision of Education in the Republic of South Africa, 1983 and the passing of the National Policy for General Education Affairs Act, 1984 (Act No. 76 of 1984) established a situation where the Department of National Education was made responsible for general policy in all the Education Departments in the areas of

- the financing of education
- educational programmes
- conditions of services of personnel, and
- registration of teachers.

The government argues that this arrangement established a single unitary education system because the formulas for financing all education are handled by this one department, the determination of educational programmes and the conditions of service of teachers are also handled by the same department for everybody.

However, in addition to the Department of National Education, there are three other Executive Departments of Education and culture in the Republic of South Africa which are racially based and operate in terms of the Tricameral Parliament one each for the House of Assembly, House of Representatives and House of Delegates. This constitutional arrangement is completely unacceptable to a large majority of the South African society because the Blacks were completely left out. To add insult to this injury there is a fourth Executive Department of Education and Training catering for Blacks in the Republic of South Africa. The setting up of this Department even violates the principle of "own affairs" because Blacks are not members of this R.S.A. parliament. Therefore, the education for

Blacks is treated as a "general" affair and is determined by the Tricameral parliament in which the Blacks are not represented. Can you imagine a better insult? The legitimacy and credibility of this department can never survive this insult.

The grand apartheid design then created ten other Departments of Education and culture which are ethnically based and located in the various independent and self- governing national states. This complicates an already untenable situation because these departments are completely powerless to determine their own fate both by design and incapacity to do so.

The cherry on the top for Whites is that although they all resort under the Department of Education and Culture, House of Assembly, they still have the four historical provincial education departments. This gives us an affective nineteen separate formal structures of education to cater for the 8 million children in this country. All the formal schools are registered and/or administered by one or the other of these executive departments.

At the non-formal level, various agencies administer some form of education ranging from literacy classes to industrial in-service courses. The new feature in Black education are the various structures which claim to provide alternative education in the wake of the collapse of formal schooling in some areas. The author's opinion about these structures is that at best they are a waste of time and money and effort which could have been well spent in a well organised school system. At worst they perpetuate the disruption of formal schools and some people who promote such structures will not sent their own children to these schools.

2.6   CURRENT OVERALL EDUCATION POLICY

Education in South Africa in 1991 continued to be administered by 19 different major education departments. At the present moment African education is administered by the following 11 departments:

*   the Department of Education and Training (DET), which administers the education of Africans in the white- designated areas, and the African matriculation examinations in these areas and in all homelands excluding the Transkei. The DET is directly responsible to the minister of education and development aid;

*   the education departments of the four 'independent' homelands:

    -   the Department of Education, Republic of Bophuthatswana;
    -   the Department of Education, Republic of Ciskei;
    -   the Department of Education, Republic of Transkei;
    -   the Department of Education, Republic of Venda; and

*   the education departments of the six non-independent homelands:

    -   the Department of Education in Gazankulu;
    -   the Department of Education in KaNgwane;
    -   the Department of Education and Culture in KwaNdebele;
    -   the Department of Education and Culture in KwaZulu;
    -   the Department of Education in Lebowa; and
    -   the Department of Education in QwaQwa.

Coloured education is administered by the Department of Education and Culture (coloured own affairs) of the House of Representatives.

Indian education is administered by the Department of Education and Culture (Indian own affairs) of the House of Delegates.

White education is administered by the Department of Education and Culture (white own affairs) of the House of Assembly, which controls four provincial departments (Cape, Natal, Orange Free State and Transvaal).

The Department of National Education is responsible for the following aspects of education for all race groups in South Africa (excluding the 'independent' homelands):

* the professional registration of teachers;
* the salaries and conditions of employment of staff;
* the norms and standards regarding syllabuses, examinations and certification of qualifications; and
* the norms and standards regarding the financing of the capital and running costs of education for all population groups.

The minister of national education is therefore able to determine general policy only in respect of certain matters provided for by the National Policy for General Affairs Act of 1984. While all teachers with equivalent qualifications and levels of experience receive the same salary irrespective of race, pupils of different race groups write different matriculation examinations and the norms for the financing of education vary according to race group. According to South Africa's constitution, education is defined as an 'own affairs'. However, the government is enforcing separation only in pre-primary, primary and secondary institutions (schools, teachers' training colleges and technical colleges) administered by the Department of Education and Culture (white own affairs) and by the DET. The situation with regard to white schools changed in 1991.

Tertiary institutions are free to decide which students to admit. Schools administered by the House of Delegates and the House of Representatives admit pupils of other races under certain conditions. The House of Representatives does not apply the same number or types of exclusionary criteria. Once preference has been given to pupils living in the residential areas served by the coloured administration's schools, principals are free to enrol pupils of other races. According to research by the South African Institute of Race Relations, it is becoming increasingly common for coloured schools to admit African pupils from neighbouring townships where space is available. The House of Delegates has been repeatedly criticised for allegedly limiting African enrolment. Research by the Institute showed that while non-Indian pupil enrolment had risen by over 4 000 between 1988 and 1989, less than 12 % of non-Indian pupils admitted in 1989 were Africans (SAIRR, 30 May 1989).

Private schools are allowed to admit pupils of all races and a substantial number of these receive a subsidy from the Department of Education and Culture (white own affairs), on condition that their enrolment consists of 50 % plus one white pupils. Whether this proviso is in fact adhered to by all schools receiving subsidies is not certain.

In June 1989 the then minister of education and development aid, Dr. Gerrit Viljoen, told an interviewer that 'strongly subsidised' private schools would probably become the preferred model for schooling in free settlement areas (Business Day, 13 June 1989). Later in the month, the then minister of information, Dr. Stoffel van der Merwe, told the federal congress of the National Party (NP) that the government wanted to extend the system of state-subsidised private schools to meet the need for mixed schooling in these areas (Beeld, 29 June 1989). Following these announcements, there was confusion concerning these non-racial private schools, since private schools also fall under the jurisdiction of racially separate state education departments.

According to research by the Institute, the government envisaged creating an additional education department to deal with schooling in free settlement areas. Whereas the size of the envisaged subsidy was still unclear, it would be substantially greater than the subsidies currently received by private schools. Some National Party MPs suggested that white schools which are underutilised and which are situated in free settlement areas, should be closed and reopened as non-racial private schools (SAIRR, 25 August 1989).

Speaking at a press briefing shortly after the state president's opening address to parliament in February 1990, the new minister of education and development aid, Dr. Stoffel van der Merwe, maintained that opening the entire education system to all races would lead to 'tremendous chaos' and would have a negative effect on political stability and on the economic system. Dr. Van der Merwe said that education needed to be organised 'on separate lines' because cultural needs differed. A single education department in South Africa would not improve the provision of education, he insisted (Business Day, 6 February 1990). In January 1990 Dr. Van der Merwe had said that the government was looking at the possibility of opening white schools to African pupils after normal school hours to alleviate the problem of overcrowding in African schools. He had added, however, that white schools were not within his jurisdiction and that opening them might not be economically viable, owing to the distances between these schools and African residential areas. He had not discussed areas which were informally desegregated, such as Berea, Johannesburg (The Star, 27 January 1990).

On 23 March 1990 the South African government, through its minister of education and culture (white own affairs), Mr. Piet Clase, announced two possible additional models for the provision of education by this department. According to government, these additional models would make it possible 'for parents to exercise their choice with regard to the determination of an admission policy for a specific school'. (See Chapter 5). According to the first model, state schools would be able to apply to become private schools and decide which pupils to admit, subject to the provisions of the constitution and the applicable education legislation. The government would finance such schools 'on a more substantial basis than that which currently applies to private schools' and would make existing school facilities available 'on reasonable conditions'.

The second model would 'give the school community the right to authorise the admission of pupils from other groups to a particular state school'. If this second model were approved, 'admission of this nature would have to take place without the nature and character of the school being disrupted'. Pupils from the community directly served by the school would be given preference regarding admission.

The government indicated that in the case of both models, the approval of a high percentage of the parents of all enrolled white pupils would be required. The figure he provided was '90 % for example' (Media Statement by Mr. P.J. Clase, 23 March 1990). It was doubtful whether such a high percentage of parents had ever voted in favour of opening a white school to all races (see Chapter 4 and 5). According to the announcement, provision would be made for pupils and staff who did not agree with the majority decision in favour of either model. The government also said that the department would continue to maintain 'the underlying principles of Christian, culture-orientated, mother-tongue education'. The two models, together with the necessary technical details, were being referred to the provincial educational councils, the Teachers' Federal Council and the Federation of Parents' Associations of South Africa, for comment and advice before 15 June 1990. Following this, consideration would be given to the approval of one or both possible models with a view to implementation on 1 January 1991.

A new national council for African education, the National Council of Education and Training, was inaugurated by Dr. Viljoen in May 1989. According to the minister, the 24- member council would henceforth be the highest consultative body advising the government regarding the education of Africans in South Africa. As an interim body, it would influence DET policy until African communities obtained full participation in political structures and were able to decide on education policy and practice. (Dr. Viljoen had committed himself to the African control of African education in accordance with the government's five-year reform plan of 1989). Whereas members of the old council had by and large been appointed by the minister in charge of African education, Dr. Viljoen said, it now consisted of [indirectly] elected parent and community representatives from the eight regions falling under the DET, as well as of 11 representatives appointed by African teachers' and inspectors' associations and by colleges of education, technikons and universities. Five education experts were to be appointed by the minister. At the beginning of 1989, school committees in DET schools had been replaced by school management councils. These councils were elected by parents and were designed to increase community participation in and control of African education. The chairmen of the school councils would belong to area committees, and chairmen of area committees would be seconded to a regional council, which would in turn elect a chairman from among its members. This chairman would be seconded to the council. According to Dr. Viljoen, the council would be entitled to be briefed on all aspects of educational planning, policy and funding and would advise the DET on any relevant matter. It would have direct access to the DET's director general and to the minister of education and development aid. However, it would not have the power to enforce its decisions or to veto DET decisions (Quarterly Countdown, 13).

Shortly before the council's first meeting in May 1989, 13 chairmen of area committees representing 330 schools in the DET's Johannesburg region (comprising Alexandra and Soweto) refused to elect a member to serve on the new body. During a meeting with Mr. De Beer, they said that the government had not canvassed parents' views on the structure of the council; that they objected to the five nominated expert members, who were drawn from current and former DET employees, mostly school inspectors; and that they feared operating within the structure in its present form because, although their role was merely advisory, they would be blamed by their communities for unpopular government policies on education. A parent who had attended the meeting said that 'we see no reason why these experts cannot be elected by parents ... We will not serve with them. We've chosen to operate from the region's management councils and area committees and all problems of the region will be dealt with at the level' (Sowetan, 15 May 1989). In October 1989 the area committees of chairmen and women of school management councils in the Orlando East and Orlando West areas of Soweto announced their decision to withdraw from the above structures altogether. The 17 schools they represented would cut links with the DET owing to the following: the unilateral decision by the DET to continue with the policy of screening pupils before admitting them; the continuing detention of pupils and parents involved in a search for an acceptable education policy; the re- introduction of 'veld schools', which were nothing more than 'brainwashing camps'; and the failure of management councils to take the initiative when there were crises in schools (New Nation, 27 October 1989).

One of the major issues to be raised by the alternative education movement (including the banned National Education Crisis Committee (NECC)) and by various educationist throughout 1989 concerned the devolution of the control of African education from the department to parents and communities. The DET was continually accused of failing to keep communication channels open and of addressing urgent issues too slowly or not at all. The DET denied the allegations.

Speaking on the occasion of the launch of the new National Council for Education and Training Dr. Viljoen argued that educational processes had been damaged and retarded by the politicisation of schools. He said, 'We all know that irreparable damage was caused by misguided people and pupils who boycotted and tried to reduce education to a state of ungovernability in the cause of the false and misleading slogan of "freedom before education". Fortunately black leaders, students and communities have come to realise that there can be no meaningful and lasting freedom, political emancipation, democracy or even good administration unless it is built upon a firm basis of sound education'. He added that the slogan should state: 'Education is a prerequisite for real freedom' (The Star, 17 May 1989).

2.7   CONCLUSION

True education cannot divide and separate. Education should unite all South African groups spiritually and socially by the propagation of reason. Black pupils' call for an end to separation in education in 1976 and 1980 was a major reason for commissioning the de Lange investigation. By rejecting the report's call for a unitary education system, the government has ignored the problem. The creation of a single ministry of education is still of the highest symbolic significance. This remains the only basis for legitimacy of the entire system in the eyes of the majority of its users. Press reports reveal that black leaders and student groups continue to regard their education as inferior. The government's present stand of 'separate and equal' poses the crucial question for black education, namely, if you are probing to achieve equality, can you have separateness? The answer from the viewpoint of the blacks is no. If the system has alienated blacks, the majority of its users, then the future prognosis for education in South Africa is bleak.

Because of the fragmentation of the educational system, there is a lack of a national perspective on the main problems. For instance, the problems of teacher supply, quantity and morale are not tackled as a national problem in terms of the need of the country as a whole. Education within the borders of South Africa is not looked at in its totality: divisions abound between education in homelands and 'white' areas, education in rural and urban areas, and education in the four provinces and the different population groups. Generally, the education system seems inflexible and resistant to change.

Blacks have been alienated from the education system by the historical neglect of their inferior, separate education and the government's refusal to establish a single education ministry and policy for education. They reject their unequal, separate education as a reflection of the apartheid system. Their alienation is expressed in student unrest at schools and universities and in the poor morale of most black teachers. The new education structure has left most of the blacks 'out in the cold' since they have only been given token representation on most educational bodies and more than half of all black pupils in the homelands have been excluded from its effect.

Education is an emotionally charged issue for blacks - for them it is 'the way out of the predicament they find themselves in'. With education so important to improving their life chances, a real threat exists that if the education system continues to alienate the majority of its users, the unrest which has become endemic in the black system may well become an epidemic again as in 1976. Even the present 'crisis management' of black student unrest points to the general lack of management skills in the formal education system.

The crucial factor in the provision of equality education has been identified as the teaching corps. The problems of its morale, supply and quality seems insoluble even in the long term. In the absence of a well planned, co-ordinated innovative national strategy for improving the quality and quantity of black teachers, in particular, current efforts in this field have little hope of reaching a critical mass. As long as the quality and supply of teachers remain poor, the vicious cycle of poor teaching, a high drop-out rate, few graduates and too few well-qualified teachers will continue. Because of lack of quality education, vast numbers of black pupils continue to drop out of school and fail the matriculation examination. There is every indication that the black matriculation pass rate may continue to fall in the short term, particular if a single examination system is introduced.

Blacks who have struggled in the system as far as matric have had their hopes raised on securing a certificate which will open avenues to tertiary institutions and the job market. In the near future these hopes of more than half the black matric pupils will be dashed. Due to the vast numbers involved, this situation continues to be a serious social, economic and political threat. Accreditation and evaluation seem to be the powder-keg issues of the future and their problems loom over the formal and non-formal sectors of education. In the formal system the examination system has been shown to be unreliable, invalid and open to abuse.

If education is viewed from the perspective of the private sector there are serious problems. The education system is not meeting the immediate or long-term interest of the private sector. The private sector is already making a significant contribution to education and clearly it cannot solve all South Africa's ills.

In a paper entitled Equal opportunity in education in South Africa delivered at the National Education Conference, Sonn retorts the following:

> The critical shortage of skilled manpower in South Africa has perhaps highlighted the South African dilemma more than anything else. Experts concerned primarily with economic growth emphasize the need for all of South Africa's people to be trained to take up the jobs waiting to be filled in commerce and industry. They insist that this must be done on the equal basis to each according to his ability and production (ibid, 10).

'Separate and equal' has been proven to be a contradiction in terms. Equal education opportunity, therefore, possibly only appears within a political system where all people participate fully in a just sharing of power. Hence the process of re-distributing educational resources and creating equal educational opportunity must take place either concurrently with political change in South Africa, or should lead the way to a just society.

The three black population groups in South Africa have consistently demanded one education department (for everybody) since they realise that there will never be equality of provision if their education departments are separate. This view is supported by the American Judge Warren in his words about the famous case of Brown vs Board of Education 347 US 483 (154).

> To separate (black children) from others of similar age and qualification solely because of their race generates a feeling of inferiority as to their status in the community that may affect their hearts and minds in a way unlikely ever to be undone.

The explicit meaning of this statement is that segregation of white children from black children in public education has a detrimental effect on the black children. The impact is even greater when it has the sanction of the law for the policy group. A sense of inferiority affects the motivation of a child to learn. Segregation with the sanction of law, therefore, has a tendency to 'retard' the educational and mental development of the black child and to deprive him of some of the benefits he would otherwise receive in a unitary education system.

In educational terms, there are legitimate and illegitimate reasons for educational differentiation. Entwistle (1978, 8) provides the following checklist.

> Equality of educational opportunity implies that no-one should be prevented through social or economic impediment from getting the best possible schooling from which he can benefit. Irrelevant matters to do with social class, economic status, nationality, sex, ethnic origin, religious affiliation, race or

> geographical location should have no bearing upon access to schooling ... demonstrable differences in intelligence, achievement, talent, interests or tastes, may justify differential educational provision. Everything hinges on this distinction between differences which are educationally significant and those which are educationally irrelevant.

An analysis of the above quotation points to the fact that educational diversity based on educationally irrelevant factors is discrimination; educational diversity based on educationally valid factors is differentiation. 'Equal' education may ignore the need for differentiation because of the slogan of 'equality' and so may discriminate by seeking to treat all in the same way. Conversely, the South African education system discriminates while it claims to be differentiating.

What has emerged from this Chapter, is that despite the debates, reports and talk about reform, as long as apartheid, ideological separation and racial discrimination are entrenched in the existing education system, there can be no genuine reform, since the system fails to satisfy the needs of the people it is supposed to serve. This opinion is also supported by many educationalists and academics of all racial groups. Until quality is given the same emphasis as quantity, the educational dispensation will be regarded merely as perpetuating the dominant ideology. The present crisis, unrest and school boycotts seem to indicate that such pessimism may well be justified and that the situation will persist until the perennial flash-points of apartheid have been abolished.

> Virtually all humanity, except a few die-hard South African racialists in Government, and to the right of Government, regard apartheid as being abhorrent, immoral and insupportable ... (Dalling The Star, 16 February 1985).

There is little doubt that there are certain fundamental features of educational dispensation in South Africa that contribute substantially to the present crisis. As already mentioned, education in this country is unavoidably and inextricably bound up with the politics of apartheid, the fundamental of which is self-development through the separation and segregation of the various races on ethnic, cultural and languages differences. The South African society embraces a wide variety of cultures, but is controlled by a white minority that prescribes education for all. Thus, an intrinsic pattern for conflict predominates, based on the belief that the black majority see their education designed to fill a particular place in South African hierarchical society. They not only have no say in the education provided, but also regard the education provided as discriminatory, irrelevant to their aspirations and attuned not to their own needs but to the needs of the dominant white minority.

> ... Blacks have always had an educational environment which was attuned not to their needs but to those of the whites (Mphahlele 1983, 73).

Most people believe that the answer to the problems in South Africa lies in the education that each South African receives, whether he is white or black. Only as a homogeneous group can problems be solved and a stable future be ensured. At present the education system does not even serve the minority group responsible for formulating the policy adequately. Most educationist of all racial groups are aware that bold steps are urgently needed in education, but that little hope exists for such changes as long as racial groups are required to live and be educated in isolation from one another by law.

The present education system is embedded in the ideology of apartheid and Christian National education, which facilitates social control of the majority through differential access to educational resources and opportunities, through a curriculum which propagates the values of the minority, and through denial of chance for the majority to participate in decision making about educational policy. However, it would take a long time before this country could extend the present expensive schooling pattern to all sections of the community, assuming that the education provided for the white population is accepted as ideal. Corke (1978, 101) argues against those who believe that a satisfactory education can be provided for all along the lines of the separate and independent systems for the four population groups.

> To achieve four independent systems, each similar in scope to that of the existing white model, would involve increasing total expenditure on education from the present R950 million per annum (R650 million on the white system) to around R4 700 million per annum.

The fiscal system in South Africa could not bear such expenditure. Therefore, the government now finds itself in a dilemma to which there seems to be no permanent solution. Nonetheless the segregated system is maintained, even though the conviction persists among blacks that despite vast material improvements, segregation implies differences in quality, content and expenditure. No matter what else is done, if the dominant white minority is truly committed to educating all the inhabitants of South Africa (regardless of colour or race), it must create an educational system free from discrimination that recognises the intrinsic worth of each individual. Apartheid could have no place in this, for it is seen by many educationalists as a recipe for social and economic disaster and the root cause of the present crisis in South African education.

HIGH BLACK TEACHER-PUPIL RATIO AND WHITE TEACHER RETRENCHMENTS

3.1 INTRODUCTION

A total of 344 teachers had been made redundant, retired early, or retrenched because of a surplus of staff, the Minister of Education and Culture, Piet Clase, said in the House of Assembly on the 27th of February 1991. In a written reply to a question from Ken Andrew (DP member of Parliament for Gardens), Mr. Clase said 28 teachers in the Transvaal, Natal and Free State who qualified at the end of 1990 were not able to obtain posts. No figures for the Cape were available. In 1990 a total of 9 368 white student teachers had bursaries from the State at a total cost of R31 575 million.

3.2 BLACK TEACHER NUMBERS AND QUALIFICATIONS

In 1988 there were 177 057 teachers in African Schools (including all ten homelands), 35 665 in coloured schools, 12 015 in Indian schools and some 56 000 in white schools.

According to research by the South African Institute of Race Relations there was a shortage of 5 531 primary and 1 350 secondary school teachers in schools under the Department of Education and Training (DET) in 1988. Although the total number of teachers had risen by 7 % between 1987 and 1988, the shortage of teachers had increased by 27 % in the same period. Calculations were made according to hypothetical pupil/teacher ratios of 35 to 1 in primary schools and 30 to 1 in secondary schools. If the more than 1 million African children not attending school in the white-designated areas and the non- independent homelands had to be accommodated using the pupils/teacher ratio of 30 to 1 recommended by the report on education of the Human Sciences Research Council (the De Lange committee report) in 1981, an estimated 74 000 additional teachers would have been required in 1988. Figures for the 'independent' homelands were not obtainable (Cosser 1989).

If a post-standard 10 teachers' certificate or diploma is regarded as the minimum qualification for a teacher, it is evident from the tables below that 46 % of teachers in African schools in the white-designated areas and non- independent homelands, 29 % of teachers in coloured schools and 0,3 % of teachers in Indian schools were not adequately qualified in 1988. The respective figures for 1987 were 54 %, 34 % and 2 %. The following tables give a detailed breakdown of African, coloured and Indian teachers' qualifications in 1988. Information on the qualifications of teachers' in the Ciskei was not obtainable. In the Transkei, almost 49 % of teachers were not matriculated in 1989. In white schools, most teachers were in possession of a professional qualification. Further information was not obtainable.

TABLE 3.1:   QUALIFICATIONS OF TEACHERS IN AFRICAN SCHOOLS (excluding TBVC) : 1988

Professionally qualified with	White-designated areas	%	Non-independent homelands	%	Total	%
Std 6	2 508	4,7	1 514	2,2	4 022	3,2
Std 8	14 980	27,9	12 763	18,2	27 743	22,4
National technical certificate	2	-	5	-	7	-
Std 10 with primary teachers' certificate	13 484	25,0	19 608	27,9	33 092	26,7
Std 10 with junior secondary teachers' certificate	2 460	4,6	3 161	4,5	5 621	4,5
Std 10 and 3 years' teacher training	10 604	19,7	13 076	18,6	23 680	19,1
Degree	2 240	4,2	2 978	4,2	5 218	4,2
Sub-total	46 279	86,1	53 105	75,6	99 383	80,1
No professional qualification, but with Std 8 or lower	4 084	7,6	3 763	5,4	7 847	6,3
National technical certificate	84	0,1	24	-	108	0,1
Senior certificate or matriculation	3 055	5,7	13 129	18,7	16 184	13,1
Degree	246	0,5	249	0,3	495	0,4
Sub-total	7 469	13,9	17 165	24,4	24 634	19,9
Total	53 747	100,0	70 270	100,0	124 017	100,0

a Transkei, Bophuthatswana, Venda and the Ciskei
Source: SAIRR Survey, 1989/90

The minister of education and development aid, Dr. Gerrit Viljoen, said in Parliament in February 1989 that 22 teachers had been retrenched or made redundant in African schools at the end of 1988. Of these, 11 had been retrenched to accommodate recently qualified teachers who were contractually bound by the department. Another 11 temporary teachers had been retrenched because they 'had chosen not to join' the Department of Education in QwaQwa following to incorporation of Botshabelo into the homeland. They had also not been prepared to accept posts in the Orange Free State. Nine of the 11 had been fully professionally qualified (Hansard, February 28, 1989).

In December 1989 it was reported that 124 under-qualified and unqualified ('temporary') teachers in Soweto (Johannesburg) were being retrenched by the DET. The retrenchment was widely criticised on the grounds that schools in the township were far too full and that pupil/teacher ratios were unsatisfactory. The director of the DET's Johannesburg region, Mr. Peet Struwig, stated that Soweto had a surplus of teachers, that qualified teachers needed to be placed and that the teachers who had been laid off could be employed in 'other' regions where there was a desperate shortage of teachers. Posts which became vacant in Soweto were simply not filled. He added that the DET had retrenched only 124 of 234 under-qualified and unqualified teachers (The Star, December 4, 1989). He also promised that the DET would help those teachers in the process of qualifying by granting them study leave.

According the minister of education and culture (white own affairs), Mr. Piet Clase, 5 247 persons (representing about 9 % of the total number of posts) had resigned from teaching posts in the four provincial departments of education in 1988. He gave a number of reasons for the resignations. The only province affected by the resignations was the Transvaal, but there were only 39 posts vacant out of a total of 28 090. (Hansard, February 14, 1989).

In February 1990 Mr. Clase told Parliament that 223 teachers at white own affairs schools had been retrenched or made redundant during 1989 (Financial Mail, March 2, 1990).

3.3   TEACHER TRAINING

According to the annual report of the DET, there were 15 teacher training colleges for Africans under its control in 1988 (one more than in 1987), with a teaching staff of 826. There were another 28 under the education departments of the six non-independent homelands (as opposed to 27 in 1987), with a teaching staff of 1 283. Enrolment at all these colleges totalled 27 638 (24 805 in 1987). In 1988 Bophuthatswana had five teacher training colleges with a teaching staff of 261, and a student enrolment of 3 399. Venda had 2 577 student teachers, enrolled in three teacher training colleges employing a teaching staff of 222. Information on the Ciskei and the Transkei was not obtainable.

The following teaching degrees and diplomas were awarded to (predominantly) African education students at African universities in 1986, 1987 and 1988 (DET RP 61, 1989).

TABLE 3.2: TEACHING DEGREES AND DIPLOMAS AWARDED AT AFRICAN UNIVERSITIES: 1986, 1987 AND 1988

University	1986 Degrees	Diplomas	1987 Degrees	Diplomas	1988 Degrees	Diplomas
Bophuthatswana	67	31	58	17	58	6
Forth Hare	49	35	81	59	55	74
The North	236	106	303	150	N/A	N/A
Transkei	12	90	11	76	7	138
Vista	5	1 679	42	2 566	54	734[a]
Zululand	141	173	203	267	N/A	N/A
Total	510	2 114	698	3 135	174	952

a   Vista University also awarded 1 924 teaching certificates in 1988 (Administrative Registrar, Vista University, 10/01/1990).

The following numbers of (predominantly) African students enrolled in the education faculties at African universities in 1987 and 1988 (DET, RP 61/1989):

TABLE 3.3: STUDENT TEACHERS AT AFRICAN
        UNIVERSITIES : 1987 AND 1988

University	1987 No of students	1988 No of students
Bophuthatswana	759	816
Forth Hare	429	687
The North	2 280	3 393
Transkei	773	1 152
Vista	15 875	18 836
Zululand	1 714	2 178
Total	21 830	27 062

In addition to the above, a number of African students enrolled
for degrees and diplomas in education at the University of
South Africa and at some of the predominantly coloured,
Indian and white universities.

There were 8 187 student teachers registered at 13 colleges of
education under the Department of Education and Culture
(coloured own affairs) in 1988 (RP 47/1989). At the end of
1988, 1 179 students qualified as teachers at these colleges. For
information regarding the number of coloured students who
obtained a qualification in the education faculties as
universities in 1987 and 1988, see the tables overleaf.

The Department of Education and Culture (Indian own affairs)
controlled two teacher training colleges in 1988 and 1989, with
an enrolment of 602 pre-service students in 1988 and of 455
such students in 1989. Altogether, 242 students qualified as

teachers at these colleges at the end of 1988.

For information regarding the number of Indian students who obtained a qualification in the education faculties at universities in 1987 and 1988, see the tables below. There were 8 487 white student teachers enrolled at 19 colleges of education in 1988 (NECC, January 1990). Information on the numbers of students who qualified as teachers at the end of 1988 was not obtainable. Mr. Clase said in March 1990 that statistics were not available on the number of students who had qualified teachers in the past ten years. For information regarding the numbers of white students who obtained a qualification in the education faculties at universities in 1987 and 1988, see the tables below.

The following two tables, based on information provided by the Committee of University Principals (CUP), show the number of African, coloured, Indian and white students who obtained some or other qualification in education (for example a degree, an undergraduate or a post-graduate diploma) in 1987 and 1988 (CUP, November 1, 1988).

TABLE 3.4: NUMBER OF EDUCATION STUDENTS
QUALIFYING AT UNIVERSITIES : 1987

	African	Coloured	Indian	White
Cape Town	30	106	10	291
Durban-Westville	2	4	331	3
Natal	16	26	50	309
The North	426[a]	-	-	-
Orange Free State	5	6	-	304
Port Elizabeth	-	3	1	167
Potchefstroom	-	1	-	468
Pretoria	1	-	-	608
Rand Afrikaans	1	11	-	355
Rhodes	16	14	5	84
Stellenbosch	-	9	-	421
Unisa	223	89	248	868
Vista	2 608[b]	-	-	5
Western Cape	2	441	5	2
Witwatersrand	124	9	47	382
Zululand	520[c]	-	1	1
Total	3 974	719	698	4 268

a   This total is 27 less than that provided by the university itself (see above)

b   This total is five more than that provided by the university itself (see above)

c   This total is 52 more than that provided by the university itself (see above)

One reason for differences in totals between the various tables above may be that figures supplied by the CUP are those which universities supply to the government according to the South African Post Secondary Education formula. This formula includes students from faculties other than education, who earn what are considered to be education qualifications even though they are not issued by education faculties. Universities frequently use criteria from those of the formula when they issue information on qualifications and other issues.

TABLE 3.5: NUMBER OF EDUCATION
            STUDENTS QUALIFYING AT
            UNIVERSITIES : 1988

	African	Coloured	Indian	White
Cape Town	34	104	14	244
Durban-Westville	15	4	308	-
Natal	86	20	82	280
The North	461	-	-	-
Orange Free State	7	5	-	263
Port Elizabeth	-	11	1	132
Potchefstroom	1	-	-	493
Pretoria	-	-	-	634
Rand Afrikaans	6	21	-	494
Rhodes	24	14	8	83
Stellenbosch	-	5	-	505
Unisa	303	89	285	770
Vista	2 754	1	-	-
Western Cape	13	13	760	1
Witwatersrand	116	10	36	407
Zululand	594	-	-	2
Total	4 414	297	1 493	4 308

In January 1989 the Transvaal Teachers' Association submitted a request to Mr. Clase to allow empty places at teacher training colleges in the Transvaal to be filled by students of all races (Business Day, January 13, 1990). Also in January, the KwaZulu Department of Education and Culture announced that 100 teachers from KwaZulu were being admitted to a (white) provincial teacher training college in Natal and that permission for their admission had been granted by Mr. Clase.

The teachers were all in possession of three-year teaching diplomas. The statement also said that classes would be fully integrated, as coloured and Indian students were already studying at the college. The education manager of the Urban Foundation in Natal, Mrs. M. Padayachee, who had been closely involved with the project, said that it was the first time African teachers had been able to obtain qualifications of matriculation plus four years' teacher training (Business Day, January 12, 1989). However, the development at the Natal College of Education did not indicate any changes in government policy, according to a statement by Mr. Clase's department, issued in response to the announcement: 'The training of 100 students from KwaZulu is done in accordance with the constitution which provides for the rendering of services by one department to another' (The Star, January 13, 1989). The education spokesman for the Progressive Federal Party, Mr. Roger Burrows MP, said that he welcomed the development but pointed out that the college was a correspondence college and had no campus or hostels. The college, which had until recently been a fully fledged institution training full-time students, had resorted to becoming a base for correspondence courses owing to a drastic drop in enrolment (Financial Mail, August 18, 1989).

In reply to a question in Parliament, Mr. Clase said in May 1989 that there were 3 567 vacant places in colleges of education falling under the control of his department. Of these, 1 354 were in the Cape, 1 004 in Natal, 238 in the Orange Free State and 971 in the Transvaal (Hansard, May 2, 1989). This amounted to 570 vacant places less than the number announced by Mr. Clase in March 1988. According to a briefing paper prepared for the National Education Co- ordinating Committee by the Education Policy Unit at the University of the Witwatersrand in January 1990, there had been 4 910 vacancies at the 19 white colleges of education in 1988.

According to figures which were provided by various white colleges of education in July and September 1989, the number of empty places may have been on the increase. For instance, the Johannesburg College of Education (Transvaal) said in September 1989 that, although it had an enrolment capacity of 2 500 students, it would register only 1 000 students in 1990 (The Star, September 27, 1989).

In July 1989 the Natal Education Council appointed a committee under the chairmanship of Mr. Justice W.H. Booysen to investigate the rationalisation of teacher education under the Natal Education Department. Many educationist expressed the fear that 'rationalisation' in fact spelled closure. The Edgewood College of Education, which had been designed to cater for 1 200 student teachers, was training half that number in 1989. However, the rector of the college, Professor Andre le Roux, said that it was virtually important that the Natal colleges not be closed down. He estimated that Edgewood would cost approximately R100 million to replace. He emphasised the need for the opening of all white colleges to African student teachers. Professor Le Roux quoted the minister of education and culture in KwaZulu, Dr. Oscar Dhlomo, who had said earlier in the year that KwaZulu would need to double its present teaching force of over 26 000 teachers almost immediately to remedy existing pupil/teacher ratios and to deal with the massive population explosion in the region (The Natal Witness, July 11, 1989). Professor Le Roux also advocated the diversification of the role of training colleges on lines which would help to address the country's massive educational needs, outside and beyond the school system (The Natal Witness, July 11, 1989).

3.4   18 000 WHITE TEACHERS FACE RETRENCHMENT

A total of 18 000 white teachers - 8 500 in the Cape - could face retrenchment, as the pupil ratio was raised from 1:18 to 1:30, Mr. Roger Burrows, the Democratic Party MP for Pinetown, warned on February 27, 1991. Mr. Burrows said in an interview that at present there were 55 000 white teachers. Changing the ratio would mean that 18 000 would lose their jobs. Mr. Burrows said the allocation of money was controlled by a formula - this was multiplied by what was known as the 'B factor'. That factor was now 1,51 for white education and about 0,66 for black education. The aim was to achieve an average of 1,0 and this would mean the loss of anything up to 20 000 jobs.

Mr. Burrows said that there were only two real possibilities if racial barriers fell - either to move the teachers to schools where they were needed or to bus pupils to where the teachers were located. Mr. Burrows said in areas of the Cape there was a very low density of white pupils and in the future these schools would be faced with closure or the option of being thrown open to all races, as had already happened in some areas. A further possibility was that a certain number of teachers would be allocated to a school and if more were wanted they would have to be financed by the local community. This would introduce market forces into the professions which could determine salaries and other conditions of service.

The director of the Natal Teachers' Society's call for a moratorium on cuts in teacher staff and closing of schools must be given serious attention by those in charge of education in Natal. There is an acceptance that the 'own affairs' system has got to be abolished with the greatest urgency, not just in education but in all areas where it applies. But we question most seriously the way in which the Natal Education Department proposes going about it and add our voice to the call for another look at the programme of transition.

Change there must be, but it must be gradual and it must be applied intelligently to take advantage of needs that will be created as the programme of upliftment progressed in black education. Simply to look at white education in isolation and to put 2 000 teaching posts - between 25 % and 30 % of the teaching body in Natal - on the line will achieve nothing more than to create a tremendous sense of insecurity within the profession and a rapid outflow of teachers seeking security elsewhere. The result will be a rapid decline in education standards, and that we cannot afford.

Millions have been spent on training these teachers. Quality education is desperately needed, and success or failure in providing it will determine whether South Africa is to become a relatively prosperous, productive country or another Third World basket case. There is a critical overall shortage of teachers. But in a panicky lurch from the grotesque "Own Affairs" dispensation to a more equitable teacher/pupil ratio, Pretoria can come up with nothing more imaginative than retrenchment of the best- trained teachers. The Natal Education Department should be combined with the KwaZulu Department of Education and Culture and the Indian and Coloured education authorities in Natal. That way teachers will keep their jobs, children will be educated and taxpayers will get a return on their investment.

3.5   THORNY SIDE OF "EQUAL EDUCATION FOR ALL"

There are two ways to describe the unequal teacher-pupil ratios that exist in South Africa. One says the black segments of the system have too few teachers. The other says schools controlled by the Assembly, the Delegates and the Representatives have too many. From the first perspective, justice required that black schools be provided with as many teachers as the other schools have. The alternative view requires a reduction in the number of teachers in the other segments of the system so that black schools can have more teachers. This seems to be the Government's strategy. It is being opposed by some of Natal's teachers. They reject the idea that, in a unified and non-racial education system, they will have to teach 35 to 40 pupils rather than 20 to 30.

Principals in the Assembly's schools have objected to the Natal Education Department's ruling that no extra teachers will be sent to open schools, even if there is an influx of black pupils. And about 9 500 teachers who belong to the Teachers' Association of South Africa (Tasa) held a sit-in because the Delegates wanted to decrease staff and increase teaching hours. The Natal Education Board (NEB) also believes black teacher-pupil ratios (TPRs) are too high rather than that the other ratios are too low. It has called for 32 000 additional teachers to staff black primary schools in KwaZulu/Natal. They are required to reduce the TPR in these schools from 1:51 to 1:30 (17 3000), as well as to provide schooling for about 441 000 children in rural areas who are not at school (14 700). The NEB also calculates that a TPR of 1:35 reduces the number of additional teachers required to slightly less than 24 000. If it had used a TPR of 1:40, the shortfall it is alarmed about would have been reduced even further to less than 18 000. The difference between these three figures is highly significant because it costs a lot of money to educate a teacher. It is the difference between an affordable R98 million to educate 18 000 teachers for a 1:40 ratio and an unaffordable R176 million to educate 32 000 teachers for a 1:30 ratio.

Because even R98 million is a lot of money, it is necessary to examine TPRs in the light of the World Bank's policies for adjusting, revitalising and expanding primary schooling in Africa. Its research tells us that "within broad limits (between 25 and 50 pupils) changes in class size influence pupil achievement modestly or not at all". This means that the TPRs in the Assembly (1:18), the Delegates (1:21) and the Representatives (1:23) are unnecessarily low. If teachers from these departments could be moved to black schools, the TPR for the whole country would be 1:32. And if they could be persuaded that a TPR of 1:40 is not too high, then there 'are enough teachers for the 1,5 million children who should be at school but are not being educated. There are significant inequalities in the TPRs that black schools have. If all the homelands are lumped together, one gets a TPR of 1:44. If they are separated, QwaQwa emerges with a more than adequate ratio of 1:32. At the other extreme, KwaZulu has a ratio of 1:50, which is where the World Bank draws the line.

Similarly, although the DET as a whole has a TPR of 1:37, the ratios for its regions range from Johannesburg's 1:31 to Orange-Vaal's 1:41.

These figures challenge the objections that many of Natal's teachers have to large classes. They also pose a string of thorny questions about teachers in a unified and non-racial education system.

* What is a adequate TPR for a Third World country like South Africa?

* How many schools refuse to have teachers who do not come from the local community, or who belong to a different tribal, racial or ethnic group?

* Who can discourage teachers from demanding small classes (less than 30 pupils) and resisting placement in rural schools?

* If teachers refuse to teach large classes (between 35 and 40 pupils), and cannot be moved from better to worse segments of the system, what alternatives are there to retrenchment, or to a reduction in student teachers?

* If teachers are going to have large classes, how should they be educated?

None of these questions is easy to answer and all of them points to another problem: when will, F.W. de Klerk and Nelson Mandela start telling us that a post-apartheid education system will be more equal, but at a lower level than teachers and parents who fall under the Assembly, the Delegates and the Representatives are accustomed to? Both of them, as well as everyone else who advocates "equal education for all" in a unified and non-racial system, should learn from Winston Churchill. When the UK had its back to the wall, he was brutally frank about what it would cost to defeat Hitler. He got more support than our leaders get because the hardships that he promised people were credible. In South Africa, teachers and parents must start knuckling down to two uncomfortable facts. Although the position of black rural teachers can be improved considerably, they cannot get as much relief as they would like. And urban black teachers, as well as those who are in the other segments of the system, will have to teach 35 to 40 pupils rather than 20 to 30. If urban teachers and parents refuse to accept that this is part of the price that has to be paid to create an equal and non-racial education system, then the inequalities that exist will continue in a post-apartheid South Africa.

3.6 RATIONALIZATION OF COLLEGES OF EDUCATION

Academics and education organisations called on the Government to make all white schools and colleges, which are due to be closed, available for the education of black students. This appeal followed the announcement in Parliament on Monday June 12, 1991 by Minister of Education and Culture Piet Clase that five white colleges of education would be closed as part of a major rationalisation of teacher training. The National Education Co-ordinating Committee (NECC) accused the Government of acting in bad faith by imposing "ready-made solutions" without consulting the people. NECC said what was particularly disquieting was the fact that the announcement came at a time when thousands of black students were being turned away from their colleges because of lack of space. "The point that needs to be emphasised is that while thousands of students are being denied access to teachers' training colleges, over the past years tens of the so-called white colleges have been running empty or half empty. This classic example is the shortage of space at the Soweto College of Education (SCE), while the Johannesburg College of Education, about 30 km away, is half empty." (Star, June 12, 1991). The rector of the Soweto College of Education, SCE, Michael Morapeli, revealed that between 5 000 and 8 000 applicants were turned away every year because the college could accommodate only 250 first-year student teachers. According to 1990 figures, there were 1 150 students at JCE and 350 vacant places. At Goudstad Teachers' Training College there were 807 student teachers with 693 vacancies. NECC dismissed Mr. Clase's announcement, that councils of these white colleges would be authorised to admit blacks as another attempt by the Government to leave the question of access and control of education institutions in the hands of white administrators. It also said Mr. Clase's announcement amounted to the implementation of the recently released Education Renewal Strategy proposals, even before the document had been discusses by interested parties.

Democratic Party spokesman on education Roger Burrows said closing colleges and dispersing lecturing staff implied a planning rigidity on Mr. Clase's part. If all teachers' training colleges fell under a central planning authority and generated teachers for all South African schools, the present "nonsensical closure" of major city colleges would not happen. Executive director of the Natal Teachers Society Dave Rayman said that there were more than 400 000 children of school-going age in Natal/KwaZulu who were not in school. Another 688 teaching posts in Natal would be scrapped in 1991. "The rationalisation of teachers' training colleges will lead to the destruction of the education structure in Natal". (Star, June 12, 1991). The general secretary of the Teachers Association of South Africa, Cliffy Kothia, said it was ironic that at a time when there was national consensus about the critical need to accelerate the pace and extent of providing for educational needs, the Government saw fit to do just the opposite. Professor Hennie Maree, president of the Teachers Federal Council, said the drop in enrolments at white schools made the closing of the colleges necessary. The new admissions policy would now make it possible for the college councils to decide whether to admit student of other races. "It is still the primary function of education colleges to train teachers for the Department of Education and Culture. The greater autonomy of college councils makes it possible to render a service according to identified needs but within the framework of existing legislation". (Star, June 12, 1991). The Conservative Party said the rationalisation of teachers' colleges was a further price whites had to pay for the equal treatment of all in an undivided South Africa. "The fact that so many colleges are being phased out is not a reflection of the moderate drop in student numbers at white schools, but is an indication that the Government has already accepted that the student-teacher relationship in white schools must be drastically weakened," said CP spokesman on national education and culture Andrew Gerber. (Star, June 12, 1991).

The unfortunate aspect of the whole issue is that while black schools desperately need qualified teachers, white teachers are being retrenched and white teachers' colleges are being closed. In the Cape there were eight white teachers' colleges. Now there are three. Five were closed. In the Transvaal literally hundreds of college lecturers are being retrenched. In Natal there were three white colleges of education, now there is the threat that there will be only one. There is the threat of the imminent destruction of the white teacher education system. In the primary schools in KwaZulu, the average teacher/pupil ratios are as high as 1:51. According to the Natal Chamber of Industries, if the teacher/pupil ratio in those primary classes is to be improved to 1:30 or 1:35, the additional teachers required would amount to 17 305 or 11 304 respectively. Furthermore, according to Hansard, Democratic Party MP Roger Burrows has declared that 36 percent of all black children in rural areas between the ages of six and 14 years do not attend school at all. It has been stated that 441 000 black children - almost half a million children - in rural KwaZulu do not attend school. (Some put the figure as high as 800 000). To cater for these children at least an additional 12 6000 teachers would be required to achieve a teacher/pupil ratio of 1:35 with 14 7000 teachers being required to maintain a teacher-pupil ratio of 1:30. In short, 32 000 teachers are required to provide primary education for children in KwaZulu.

To address the black teacher shortage in higher classes of secondary schools still more teachers are required. The position is exacerbated by significant numbers of unqualified and partly-qualified people in the ranks of practising teachers in the KwaZulu education department. Despite this desperate need for teachers, white colleges of education are being closed down. The euphemism used is "rationalised". In April 1991 P.J. Clase, the Minister of Education and Culture (House of Assembly), released figures which demonstrate that there are 4 393 vacant places in the 12 white colleges of education in South Africa. He cautioned that some of the colleges might have to close for reasons of "rationalisation". "Rationalisation" should mean the rational, reasonable use of colleges, but it has come to mean "closure".

The rational use of colleges of education surely means the optimal usage of the lecturing staff and the physical amenities to train teachers to supply the needs of schools such as those in KwaZulu. In the face of such dire need, it would surely be irrational to close colleges of education. On April 24, 1991, Mr. Clase released a Press statement which was widely welcomed. It devolved the admission of students to the college councils. This is an ideal for which colleges have striven for many years. Mr. Clase's statement means in effect that colleges that wish to do so may admit students on a non-racial basis, which would enable white colleges to fill their vacant places. College staff would be fully employed and college facilities fully utilised. Minister Clase's Press release said that "because of financial considerations a further measure of rationalisation of colleges of education will be effected". (Sunday Tribune, May 12, 1991).

Financial constraints arise because the rationalisation is being effected on an "own affairs" basis. Provincial colleges are financed by provincial education departments which are "own affairs" departments. Such departments are financed for white education only, and with the drastic decline in the white pupil population there is a concomitant decline in the financial education departments. For example, Edgewood College of Education is financed by the Natal Education Department. The formula which finances the Natal Education Department is largely determined by pupil numbers. There has been a dramatic decline in pupil numbers in Natal. There were 1 700 fewer pupils in white schools in Natal in 1991, than there were in 1991 and this trend has been apparent for some years now. Consequently the Natal Education Department limited finances and could not afford to subsidise additional students at Edgewood. Moreover, the Natal Education Department does not need additional teachers for its white schools. Vast numbers of white teachers are, in fact, being retrenched. The essence of the problem is that we are rationalising on an "own affairs", apartheid basis.

In the national interest, it is essential to keep all provincial colleges of education open. Provincial education departments such as the Natal Education Department will not have the money to keep such colleges as Edgewood College of Education open. It is imperative that the national treasury vote funds to prevent the destruction of these national resources. The new South Africa will have a single ministry. Colleges of education will be funded on a non-racial basis. In order to keep colleges alive and viable in the meantime, interim funding will have to be provided by the central government. The immediate reaction of government to this proposal is likely to be: money is in short supply, central funding is not available. This is a myopic view. It virtually means that we will destroy the whole infrastructure of teacher education now, only to have to start de novo to build it up again, at considerable cost, in years to come. To destroy centres of excellence such as colleges in the face of such need, is sheer madness. On one hand we have the KwaZulu government building a college on the South Coast for 450 students at a cost of R64 million - 450 additional students could be admitted to Natal white colleges with little extra cost. On the other hand, we are contemplating the closure of colleges which are staffed with highly qualified personnel and equipped with the most sophisticated libraries, laboratories, audio-visual facilities, sports facilities, etcetera.

Minister Clase's statement ends with these words: "After the minister has had final discussions with all the interested parties, he will make an announcement in this regard (i.e. with regard to rationalisation) - probably within the next few weeks." (Sunday Tribune, May 12, 1991). Minister Clase's statement was made on April 24. No "final discussions" with "the interested parties" in Natal have as yet been held. Interested parties such as the Natal Teachers' Society and the Council of the University of Natal are anxious to be consulted before finality is reached. It must be remembered that the University of Natal awards 53,9 percent of the diplomas and degrees offered at Edgewood College of Education. No doubt the organised teaching profession and universities in close co-operation with colleges in other provinces also believe that they are "interested parties" and must be included in "final discussions". The government is doing all it can to promote productivity. Without education and training there can be no productivity. Without productivity there can be no economic growth. In order to provide a productive work force, education is essential. We cannot afford to close colleges of education. In order to use them to best advantage for all the people of South Africa, it will be necessary to hold a national forum to negotiate the best use of colleges of education in the future.

It seems that education, perhaps the most vital tonic for a health economy, is caught in the cobweb spun by apartheid education under the tricameral system - "own affairs". As the country moves, inevitably, towards a single education department, and as the demand for education and training programmes grow, teachers are about to be retrenched in their thousands, schools are standing empty, and training colleges are under threat. The authorities have a word for these cut-backs: rationalisation. Many may ask, with some justification, what is rational about a policy that threatens the future of teachers and institutions when:

*   The number of black grade one pupils is growing by between three and four percent a year?

*   More and more teachers are needed to deal with the million-plus black pupils - more than the total number of white children at school - that begin grade one each year?

*   There is a greater demand today than at any time for education facilities?

*   There is a desperate need for a solid foundation in education (pre-primary) as the country moves towards a democratic future?

It is the state's function to deal with these needs. It should begin by reviewing the shortsighted rationalisation policy and find ways of utilising its "redundant" white resources - both material and human. A solution must be found in the interest of all.

3.7   CONCLUSION

According to the Research Institute for Education Planning (RIEP) at the University of the Orange Free State, there would be just over 14,5 million pupils of all races in South Africa (including all ten homelands) by the year 2000. The following table, based on figures provided by RIEP, provides a breakdown of projected pupil numbers in primary and secondary education in the year 2000.

TABLE 3.6:   PUPIL ENROLMENT PROJECTION : 2000

	African[a]	Coloured	Indian	White	Total
Primary education	8 613 800	722 800	160 500	594 100	10 091 200
Secondary education	3 722 200	269 500	88 900	338 100	4 418 700
Total	12 336 000	992 300	249 400	932 200	14 509 900

a Including all ten homelands

The number of teachers, black and white, trained annually will have to be increased significantly to keep abreast of the tremendous increases in the pupil population projection as shown by the above table. There is an alarming shortage of academically and professionally well qualified teachers, particularly in black schools.

Vos and Brits (1987:120) have indicated that in order to meet the increasing demand for education in the future, considering a teacher-pupil ratio of 1:30 as an ideal, the following numbers of teachers must be trained by 2020:

TABLE 3.7: NUMBERS OF TEACHERS TO BE TRAINED BY 2020

*	Blacks	:	245 405
*	Whites	:	24 981
*	Coloureds	:	22 708
*	Asians	:	6 964

	Total	:	300 058
			=====

If by the year 2020 our education system will need 300 058 teachers, irrespective of colour or nationality, can Mr. Clase afford to retrench 18 000 white teachers over the next three years? Can the projected number of pupils in the year 2000 (14 509 900) be properly taught without 18 000 teachers? Can we ever hope to reduce and keep the teacher-pupil ratio of 1:30? Mr. Clase will do well to consider seriously the HSRC (1981) warning:

Without a corpse of well-trained and talented teachers, any endeavour aimed at a system of education by means of which the potential of the country's inhabitants is to be realized, economic growth promoted, the quality of life of the inhabitants improved and education of quality provided of for everyone, cannot be successful.

MANDELA MEETS DE KLERK ON BLACK EDUCATION CRISIS

4.1 <u>INTRODUCTION</u>

Negotiations for a new South African constitution cannot survive in a vacuum. However vital, a new political dispensation is only part of the solution to the country's problems. Parallel to the modelling of a new constitution must be the creation of negotiating forums to deal with other issues crucial to the survival of a fledgling democracy: law and order, education, housing and health.

In Cape Town, the first step towards negotiating a new deal for education for all South Africans took place when President F.W. de Klerk lead a Government delegation in a meeting with extra-parliamentary leaders headed by Nelson Mandela of the African National Congress. The two sides were reportedly keen to use the occasion not just for an armchair debate on theoretical issues, but to grapple with the real administrative problems that have plagued the hopelessly warped education system for so long. Mr. Mandela's deep concern over the disastrous failure rate in black schools came through clearly when he openly distanced himself from the "liberation before education" slogan. Mr. De Klerk also expressed a determination to negotiate a new deal for education.

This common purpose must in future be translated, without delay, into a plan to unify the education system to effect rapid and systematic expansion and upgrading.

The Government has been pursuing an educational scorched earth policy. Over the past 12 years, 274 white schools were closed while thousands of white teachers were made redundant. In practical terms, if the whites don't need it, then nobody else is going to get it. The policies that have been pursued have sabotaged the educational and life prospects of millions of young South Africans.

4.2   ANC PLANS FOR EDUCATION WELL RECEIVED

Proposals on education by the ANC received a favourable reception from Minister of Education and of Development Aid Dr. Stoffel van der Merwe. He called for negotiations on a new system and the avoidance of disruptions in the meantime. Dr. Van der Merwe stressed that the Government was not reacting to ANC proposals in a confrontational way as these had also not been couched in such a style. Government policy was that all differentiation along racial lines in education must be removed.

Dr. Van der Merwe explained that he was reacting to the ANC memorandum as President De Klerk would have only limited time to refer to education in his speech at the opening of Parliament on the 1st of February. Referring to the ANC call for the laying of a foundation for one education department, he said this process had already started with the Department of National Education serving as the controlling body for all other education bodies. Salaries and working conditions in all these departments had been brought on par and there were no longer discrimination based on colour.

Another request, for a special education fund to deal with backlogs, had already been addressed and he hoped more could be done. In 1990 R750 million had been set aside for this purpose, black education had received R675 million, coloured education R60 million and Indian education R15 million. A sum of the R2 billion which had been set aside for the Independent Trust would also be used for this. From 1988-89 to 1990-91 Government spending on black education had increased by 34 percent. As far as participation by the community in the education system was concerned, he had since the middle of 1990 been trying to get black organisations to do so. Dr. Van der Merwe said he was confident that problems with the supply of text books could be ironed out. As far as school buildings were concerned, priority would be given to allocating buildings no longer being used by one race group to another.

4.3   GOVERNMENT READY TO NEGOTIATE NEW SCHOOL SYSTEM

The Government was prepared to negotiate a single ministry of education for a new South Africa, the Minister of Education and Development Aid, Dr. Stoffel van der Merwe, said in January 1991. However, he emphasised that practical and logistical considerations meant that any moves to create a unified system could not happen overnight. If, following negotiations, it was decided that a single ministry should be created, the next step would be to design such a system and work out ways of implementing this. The Government did not wish to commit itself to a particular model of education. Education was so important to all people that all interested parties should have a say in what a new system should look like. Dr. Van der Merwe said there was clearly a need to replace the current system, which contained large race-based funding discrepancies. "Government policy is that discrimination must be eliminated. We do not have an apartheid education policy, but an anti-apartheid one. There is still, however, an apartheid legacy which will take time and money to change." (Mercury, January 10, 1991). The Government was not dragging its feet, but the process required an enormous amount of work.

Responding to a document of education proposals handed to the Government by a 'broad group of educationally concerned persons' with ANC connections, he said he was happy with the non-confrontational tone of the documents. "I think it holds lots of promise that we can get something going to better the living conditions and future prospects of millions of South

Africans." (Mercury, January 10, 1991). Dr. Van der Merwe said the group's demand for a single ministry of education was not something the Government could implement immediately, even if it wished to do so. "You cannot just abolish a law as there must be something under which a system can operate. My plea is for the community to say what we must do in the meantime, as students are losing time which it is not possible for them to recoup later." (Mercury, January 10, 1991). Dr. Van der Merwe said that the Government agreed in principle with several of the demands outlined in the document, and many were already in operation. The foundation had already been laid for a single education system, with the Department of National Education acting as an umbrella body laying down general policy which was binding on all education departments; deciding on budgetary allocations and setting education standards for all pupils. Discrimination in the area of salaries, benefits and working conditions had also been eliminated, he maintained.

Referring to the request for the Government to create a special emergency education fund to eliminate historical backlogs, Dr. Van der Merwe said this was exactly what the Government had done in 1990. R750 million had been set aside for black education and additional education funding was also made available through the Independent Development Trust. The Department of Education and Training's bona fides were also demonstrated by the growth in its budget over the last two years (1989 and 1990). Dr. Van der Merwe said there was a chance that the Government's defunct plan to eliminate funding disparities could be revived.

4.4   IT IS GOING TO TAKE MORE THAN JUST MONEY TO BRIDGE THE GULF

The Department of Education and Training embarked on a massive campaign to alleviate backlogs in the capital expenditure on education. An amount of R337,5 million allocated to the Department from R1 billion State President's fund would be used to finance the erection of new schools and additional classrooms in the eight regions of the Department during 1991 and 1992. These building projects were in addition to the normal building programme of the Department. Of the 54 new schools to be erected as part of this project, fifteen were allocated to squatter areas. Nearly 400 additional classrooms would be built at school where present space is insufficient to accommodate the rapidly growing numbers of school children. The provision of school facilities on farms would receive special attention. Twenty million rand was allocated for this purpose.

More than 700 extra classrooms for black school children were being build during the 1990/91 financial year with funds from the R1,15 billion set aside in 1989/90. Budget for redressing socio-economic backlogs, Minister of Education and Development Aid, Dr. Stoffel van der Merwe disclosed in Parliament in February 1991. In the Johannesburg area the extra money was being used to build the new 25-classroom Ithute Primary School in Alexandra and a 15-classroom extension to the Thaba Jabula Secondary School in Klipspruit. Democratic Party Gardens MP Ken Andrew asked Dr. Van der Merwe whether the non-recurrent sum of R150 million and the education portion of the R1 billion had been spent. Dr. Van der Merwe said the R150 million had been divided between his Department of Education and Training (73,95 million) and the six self- governing territories (76,05 million).

Of the R1 billion, the department and the six self- governing territories had each received R337,5 million. The R73,95 million and R150,009 million of the R337,5 million given to his department was being spent during the 1990/91 financial year. The full R337,5 million was being used for the reduction of backlogs in school buildings. Of this amount, R150,009 million would be spent during 1990/91 and the balance of R187,491 million during 1991/92. He said the full amount of R73,95 million had been spent country-wide during the current financial year - R72,713 million on operational expenses and R1,237 million on schools. Of the R150,009 million, R122 million was being allocated to reducing backlogs in school buildings and R28 million for school books. Dr. Van der Merwe said the R150,009 million was being used to build 717 black classrooms around the country.

The state spends 30 percent more on education than on defence, excluding the police force. And education accounts for 19 percent of the budget - the largest single item. Expenditure on education in 1990/91 increased by 16,1 percent on last year to a total of R13 495 million. However, since inflation hovered around the 15 percent mark, the increase in real terms was nearer one percent. The Department of Education and Training (for black pupils) received R2 379 million, an increase of 21,9 percent on 1989/90. However, black pupil numbers were estimated to have increased by five percent, leaving the increase in expenditure on black education at less than one percent in per capita terms. The bulk of an additional R750 million set aside to address current backlogs in the system was spent on black education.

Over R1 600 million more was spent on the 973 444 pupils (preliminary figures for government schools) registered under the (white) Department of Education and Culture (House of Assembly), then on the 2 157 775 registered with the DET. The gap between per capita expenditure on black and white pupils continued to close. In 1990/91, 3,8 times more was spent on each white pupil than on each black pupil, whereas in 1989/90 the ratio was 4:1. In 1980/81, the disparity was 5,8:1. However, as Democratic Party spokesman Ken Andrew pointed out, in absolute terms, the gap between per capita expenditure could be said to be growing, since in 1989 (the last year for which accurate figures are available) per capita spending grew by R360 per white pupil, but by only R191 for Africans.

In 1986, F.W. de Klerk, then the minister of national education, introduced a 10-year plan, at the end of which it was hoped there would be equal education for all races. The plan was based upon a 4,1 percent annual real increase in expenditure on education. However, in July 1989, when the economy began to flounder and the overall growth of the education system continued to grow at 4,4 percent per annum, the plan was abandoned. Professor Johan Muller from the University of Cape Town called this "perhaps the single most depressing policy feature of 1989". (The Star, February 13, 1991). It is thought that for official parity in education to be achieved, an increase in expenditure of between two and three times would be required. This would take an estimated 50 percent of total state expenditure, clearly impossible in a changing South Africa, where other important social priorities have to be met.

4.5   EDUCATION SYSTEM MUST FIRST GAIN
          CREDIBILITY

For black education to become effective it needs to earn credibility within the community. "The system must be held accountable to the community for the adults it produces," says education consultant Gillian Maskell. (The Star, February 14, 1991). And African National Congress education department head John Samuel adds: "In the short term we need to redress the imbalances between black and white education. We need to reallocate financial resources equitably - and, more urgently, we need to use our resources more efficiently. Not only is the bureaucracy controlling the system inefficient - the system itself has a vast casualty rate, because the quality of black education is so poor." (The Star, February 14, 1991).

Poor education standards are due largely to the fact that many black teachers are inadequately qualified. According to the National Education Crisis Committee (NECC). In the longer term, educators must take into account the relationship between education and economic growth. Schools cannot be turned into factories - but the structure of the system needs to reflect the demands of a developing economy.

The formal school system needs more exit points. At present, only matric is awarded certification - yet not all pupils are suited to an academic education. Exit points earlier in the system would equip people with needed skills before diverting them into appropriate directions - whether apprenticeships, on-the-job training or continued academic education. "Education needs to be context-sensitive," adds education consultant Elizabeth Burroughs. "The same skills do not suit pupils in Soweto and those in the northern Transvaal". (The Star, February 14, 1991). While catering more specifically for the needs of non-academic pupils, the system needs to develop leadership potential where it exists. "We need to move away from authoritarian, militaristic education models towards a democratic approach." says Ms. Holland. (The Star, February 14, 1991).

Already an increasing number of black and white schools are allowing student representation on their governing bodies. Also of crucial importance is the need to restructure the curriculum, to enable the system to develop people who are equipped for later life. Purely academic subjects have an important place - but it must be in the context of an education that allows practical skills training. Specialisation is a fact of life in any technologically developing economy, and aptitude tests can indicate quite early on where a child should be placed for his education.

4.6   <u>BREAKTHROUGH IN EDUCATION TALKS</u>

Negotiations for a single education system achieved a "breakthrough" on February 25, when Mandela and De Klerk delegations met. At a press conference, Mr. Mandela described the meeting as a "breakthrough" for efforts to change the education system, while Democratic Party education spokesman Roger Burrows said it looked as though the working group would increasingly become an "effective interim administrative structure" for education. National Education Minister Louis Pienaar stressed, however, that the Government would have the final say in implementing any recommendations by the group.

Education and Training Minister Dr. Stoffel van der Merwe said at a Government press briefing that Mr. Mandela's delegation had put on the table its proposal for a single education system or department. There had been little time to discuss it but Mr. Mandela's delegation had agreed that there should be scope for "sub-systems" - a reference to "own" schools based on cultural but not racial criteria. Dr. Van der Merwe expressed reservations about creating a single executive education department which could become an "unadministrable bureaucratic monster". But whether there was one or several departments, in the end there could still be one system. Sources on both sides made it clear that the present unequal funding for education was going to be the big bugbear in negotiations.

The demand for a single budget was the first item on the agenda of Mr. Mandela's group. Dr. Van der Merwe said some members of the delegation liked to see an immediate equalisation of spending on all races, which the Government regarded as impossible. This was the sort of matter which the working group would deal with. He indicated that the working group's deliberations could still influence the allocations for the various education departments in the 1991 Budget to be delivered on March 20. Mr. Pienaar said the group would also discuss the reports of the Government's investigation into a major educational renewal strategy which was now being completed. The two Ministers pointed out that the February 26, 1991 discussions would have to be broadened because they did not represent all major groupings. The PAC and the Federal Council for Educationist were among those not represented. The working group would comprise Dr. Van der

Merwe and Mr. Pienaar, their two directors general and Dr. Van der Merwe's Deputy Minister Piet Marais.

Mr. Mandela's delegation was represented by John Samuel of the ANC's education department, Ihron Rensburg of the National Education Co-ordination Committee, Professor Shabani Mangamyi, rector of the University of the North, Neil McGurk of the Association of Independent Schools and Sedupe Ramokgopa of Azapo. Meanwhile, Minister of Education and Culture Piet Clase told Parliament that he was prepared to accept a single education ministry in a single education system. But if this became a "single, massive, executive education department which must provide forced integrated education to six million pupils, then I reject it as unrealistic". (The Star, February 26, 1991). Different communities had to be given the right to maintain "own" schools based on "own" values, with State support equal to that of other schools. Mr. Clase said the present four-model white education system could form the basis of a new education system under a new constitution. DP finance spokesman Ken Andrew accused Mr. Clase of following a "scorched earth' education policy.

4.7   SCHOOL CRISIS GROUP SET UP

The education crisis summit between the Government and a broad-based delegation of educationist agreed that there was a need to 'fundamentally change' South Africa's education system. The teams, led by President De Klerk and ANC deputy president Nelson Mandela, also agreed to set up a Joint Working Group to look into 'critical and immediate' issues, which left many black schools around the country in turmoil. However, no emergency plan was instituted to relieve the immediate problems of overcrowding, and the lack of facilities and materials plaguing many black schools. Neither did the Government agree to provide a special cash injection for black education - either immediately or in next month's budget - to help it out of doldrums.

But the Minister of Education and Development Aid, Dr. Stoffel van der Merwe, acknowledged that the meeting and the deliberations of the Joint Working Group 'can have an influence' on the allocation for education in 1991/92 Budget. In 1990 the Government made available and additional R750 million above the amount originally budgeted for a 'crash' building programme for more black schools. Although time did not allow the two sides to discuss many of the issues raised at the 'frank and open' discussions in depth or 'adequate detail', the Joint Working Group was appointed to look into both the short term issues and 'procedures to establish a fully representative forum to discuss a new education system for South Africa.

A joint statement issued by the two parties afterwards said they recognised that 'time is of the essence'. Mr. Mandela told a Press conference that the meeting had dealt with the problems "in a very constructive spirit in which sensitive problems had been handled honestly." (The Star, February 26, 1991). Explaining his earlier remarks to children - upon emerging from the meeting - that there was 'nothing to worry about', he said later that this was because 'issues are being addressed urgently'. Dr. Van der Merwe said that the Government was impressed by the fact that there was "a large area of agreement about the nature of the problem, the urgency of the problem and that is should be tackled speedily." (The Star, February 26, 1991). He believed the meeting had brought the two sides closer together but added that there remained areas - like budgetary allocations for black education - where the sides differed on how rapidly discrepancies could be eliminated.

Mr. Mandela emphasised that the group he led to the talks was 'not an ANC delegation' but included representatives from the South African Communist Party, Cosatu, Azapo, the South African Council of Churches, the University of Western Cape, the Peninsula Technikon, the South African Association of

Independent Schools and others concerned bodies. The Minister of National Education, Mr. Louis Pienaar, said the delegation led by Mr. Mandela was not fully representative of educational interests in South Africa and the Government could not 'limit itself' to dealing with the Joint Working Group in searching for solutions to the country's educational problems.

Eventually, a much wider forum would have to be formed so that the inputs of other groups could also be taken into account. The Joint Working Group had to make its first proposals in a following week and was expected to report back within the next four to six weeks. The two sides would then meet in full session again to consider the outcome of the 'spade work' done by the Joint Working Group, and decide on appropriate action. Government members on the working group are the Minister of National Education, Mr. Louis Pienaar, the Minister of Education and Training, Dr. Stoffel van der Merwe, his Deputy Minister, Mr. Piet Marais, the Director General of National Education, Dr. J.G. Garbers, and the Director General of Education and Training, Dr. J.B.Z. Louw. The other members are Mr. John Samuel, head of the ANC's education department, Mr. Ihran Rensburg, general secretary of the National Education Co-ordinating Committee, Professor Chabani Mangamyi, rector of the University of the North, Mr. Niel McGurk, of the South Africa Association of Independent Schools, and Mr. Sedupe Ramokgopa, from Azapo.

4.8   JOINT WORKING GROUP GETS MIXED RESPONSE

Government proposals for a joint interim education committee to manage the transformation to single education system and to deal with the crisis in black schooling was flatly rejected in progressive circles, before it was even formed at a government and ANC meeting. At the time of going to press, the ANC and National Education Co- ordinating Committee (NECC) were in a meeting to discuss proposals from government for an interim education monitoring committee. Early indications were that these organisations were unlikely to support the move. It was believed that National Party leader F.W. de Klerk had hoped to announce the formation of such a committee during the opening of parliament.

Sources closed to the NECC expressed concern that any interim education monitoring committee would be ineffective while the apartheid government was still in place. A joint interim monitoring committee would only be effective if there was an interim government in place, sources argue. There was also concern that such a committee would have to share the blame with the state for any future education crisis under an apartheid government.

Euphoria over the new education joint working group set up in a bid to break through the education impasse may be misplaced, educationist warned. The working group, made up of anti-apartheid educationist and government representatives, was established at the request of the delegation led by African National Congress deputy president Nelson Mandela in its three-hour meeting with President F.W. de Klerk during the last week of February 1991. The working group's brief is to address not only the "burning issues" - the lack of textbooks, classrooms and other facilities - but also "procedures to establish a fully representative forum" to discuss a new education system. In the view of the delegation, the government was then forced to concede some of its hegemony in an arena of crucial political importance. It committed itself to ongoing discussions which would focus on popular demands: a single education body, recognition of representative local structures such as parent-teacher-student associations, and funding.

The establishment of the working group also meant the government had been prevented from executing a political sleight-of-hand - that of postponing, until a new constitutional dispensation has been thrashed out, the focus of any real attention on the central issue, the inequities which pervade the system. But in the opinion of Professor Johan Muller of the University of Cape Town, the breakthrough could have come too fast, too soon - and could yet founder on a sandbank of political expediency. In his view, the government was casting about for a legitimate structure on which it can offload its responsibilities - a move which would effectively muffle any political repercussions. By agreeing to allow the responsibility for running schools to devolve to local community structures, the government could also ensnare anti-apartheid organisations in a trap that it could later argue was sprung at their own request. Confronted with sorting out the mess on a local level, without resources and in the absence of a national strategy to address inequities, communities could find themselves plunged into a nightmare. As Muller pointed out, while anti-apartheid educationist are engaged in researching educational policy options, their work is still its infancy. "Politicians going out to bat armed only with popular demands could get bowled." (Weekly Mail, March 1-8, 1991). His views were supported by Saleem Badat, an educationist at the University of the Western Cape, who warned that the formation of the working groups had fuelled expectations which would be difficult to meet. Central to Muller and Badat's reservations about the working group were fears that it could result in organisations like the National Education Co-ordinating Committee and, to a lesser extent, the ANC, being caught in a legitimacy crisis. Neither believed that the working group will be capable of adequately addressing the "burning issues" around which popular protest is likely to grow. While the government has no unified strategy charting a path to truly equal education, the anti- apartheid educationist have not yet travelled sufficiently far along the road of alternative options. "Calling for the doors of learning and culture to be opened is a good goal to aim for and should not be set aside, but in itself doesn't begin to specify the concrete means of achieving that goal". (Weekly Mail, March 1-8, 1991).

4.9   A GOLDEN OPPORTUNITY MISSED

The government missed a golden opportunity of making a bold statement about the future of education in the country when it met with the delegation led by ANC deputy president Nelson Mandela. While it was accepted that the establishment of the joint working group represented some movement, it is believed nonetheless that it still fell far short of the demands that are now current in education. The government should have come out boldly and taken the issue of education outside the ambit of the National Party, the white Parliament and, indeed, the negotiation process.

Effectively, it was still the government that would continue to determine the form and content of education policy for the majority of the people. Certainly this new arrangement meant that the Nationalists had finally acknowledged that they could no longer run education on their own. But it was no longer such acknowledgements that was wanted. For over a decade now it had been crystal clear that, although government continued to determine policy, it could no longer implement it because the products of Bantu Education had come back to haunt the system that produced them. It had been hoped that the government would have recognised that what was needed was bold action backed by resources accessible only to the government and supplemented by expertise from various communities. Education still remained the single most potent area of South African life - and by day there was movement closer to the zero hour that would devastate whatever had thus far been achieved.

This is to be expected from a generation that has known nothing but frustration in its entire educational life and has had one hurdle after the other placed in its path. In this edition we carry a typical example of the type of frustration that students and parents have been subjected to in their desperate struggle to get education. That this was happening at a time when the government was talking about a new deal for all South Africans made everybody wonder about its actual agenda. This was solace, nevertheless, in the fact that the people who serve on the working group were tested educationist whose commitment to a people's education was beyond question. They would not allow themselves to be used as a toy telephone.

4.10   <u>SCHOOLS OF SCANDAL F.W. DE KLERK MUST FIX</u>

Politicians may be making breakthroughs regarding education policies but the classroom crisis cannot wait for a new school system. As African National Congress and government leaders held education crisis talks in the elegant Tuynhuis, 90 Standard Six pupils sweltered in their makeshift Zo-Zo prefabricated classroom in Alexandra. "This is the reality of the crisis", said Mary Metcalfe, secretary of the Alexandra Education Co-ordinating Committee (AECC). "Stoffel van der Merwe (Minister of Education and Training) and the DET officials need to get past the bureaucracy and figures and come an see the picture behind the figures - maybe then they will make the enormous extra effort required to resolve the crisis." (Weekly Mail, March 1-8, 1991). Metcalfe, a teacher at Realogile High School in Alexandra, battled to be heard above the noise created when 30 desks, each with three, sometimes four - 14-year-old pupils crowded around them, are squashed into a room barely 12 m square. There was no space for the teacher to move between desks, no room on the desks for the pupils to place their books - assuming they had any.

Through the broken windows, the sounds of the densely populated township drifted in. There was no longer a playground - for where the small playing area used to be, there are now 10 overcrowded classrooms. Down the road, at the crumbling Skeen Primary School, 80 tiny Grade One pupils sat on red and blue plastic chairs or knelt on the floor, using the chairs as makeshift desks. The stench from the blue plastic toilets was overpowered. As the principal, T.M.S.

Matlhabegoane, explained, there was no water with which to clean the toilets, no water, in fact, at all. Pupils begged buckets of water from neighbouring houses when desperate. The school had been pressing the Department of Education and Training for toilets - and classrooms - for years, to no avail. "You can go on for a while without electricity and telephones, but not without toilets", said the principal. (Weekly Mail, March 1-8, 1991). A delegation from the AECC, the South African Democratic Teachers' Union (Sadtu), the Congress of South African Students (Cosas) parents and community leaders was organized to meet DET officials.

The wholesale welcome for the initiatives arising out of the meeting - perhaps most importantly the setting up of a joint government-ANC working group to look at the crisis - pales into insignificance in the face of the problems in many thousands of schools across the country. "The rhetoric seems encouraging to an uniformed observer, but they do not know the extent of the crisis - if they did they would not be so optimistic," said Metcalfe. (Weekly Mail, March 1-8, 1991). Most schools in Alexandra are beset with similar problems: overcrowded classrooms, lack of teachers, appalling sanitary conditions and, consequently, disastrous academic records. Eastbank High School has no premises, despite a pupil enrolment of 1 100 in this, their first year. They managed to get hold of the buildings vacated by another school, but have had to pay for renovations out of school funds, as the DET has not given them money. The principal reckoned the teacher- pupil ratio is close to 1:100. Each school has a tale to tell, of how they have been waiting for two, three, maybe more years for money promised by the DET. While the primary schools are pathetic, the conditions in the high schools are volatile. At one of them, tensions created by the shortage of furniture and overcrowding came to a head when two vandals who had been stealing chairs were identified and "chastised" by Cosas. The students took violent revenge on the vandals, an expression not so much of their anger at the two men, but more of their frustration at their impotence in the face of the lack of resources. Failure rates in Alexandra schools reflected the learning conditions. About 80 percent of 1990 matric students failed, well above the national average of 63 percent. High failure rates each year mean that in January school intake is swollen with pupils repeating a year, compounding overcrowding. This is the situation that ANC deputy president Mandela and President F.W. de Klerk face - and it is in no way confined to Alexandra.

4.11   CONCLUSION

The meeting between delegations led by President De Klerk and Mr. Nelson Mandela to discuss education addressed the issue that lies at the very heart of the turmoil in this country - a knowledge that the dice are loaded against blacks. It is no coincidence that the Soweto uprising of 1976 was sparked by a schools protest or that black education has been the focus of unrest ever since. Blacks, starting from a position of historic disadvantage, see themselves as condemned to perpetual inferiority by the system of separate education introduced by Verwoerd. The meeting appeared to have been businesslike. It could have ended in promises and platitudes but instead a joint working group was established to thoroughly go into all the issues before there was another meeting between the delegations. The nuts and bolts of education have fortunately been thoroughly explored already by the De Lange Commission, the Buthelezi Commission and the Natal/KwaZulu Indaba, so the working group's investigation need not be a lengthy process.

South Africa needs a system of education which is non-discriminatory on grounds of race or ethnicity, appropriate to future skilled manpower needs and affordable. It would probably be most effectively organised on a regional basis with a central authority setting core curricula and standards. It would have to offer every South African the opportunity to realise his or her potential. If President De Klerk and Mr. Mandela could agree on this and set a realistic timetable for implementation, much of the bitterness would be removed from the wider political bargaining.

South Africans have seen enough "breakthroughs" in recent times to be wary of undue euphoria; not to mention working committees that end up not working so well. Still, nobody should discount the initial progress on education problems said to have been achieved in talks at Tuynhuis between the Government, the ANC and others. Still less the working group that will take the discussions further. After the political solutions - indeed before them - education is an apartheid legacy demanding top priority. The inequalities between white and black schools are gross. Black matric results have never been worse. Many township schools are in a state of anarchy. The problems are daunting, the solutions not easily or quickly found. Essentially a more equitable application of resources and a single education system, as advocated for many years, are key parts of the solution. These things are more easily said than achieved: a lot of hard work lies ahead. Yet a start has to be made, and joint talks between State and community is a promising one.

GOVERNMENT SCHOOLS ANNOUNCEMENT AND COMMUNITY RESPONSES

5.1 INTRODUCTION

On 11 January 1990 the minister of education and development aid, Dr. Stoffel van der Merwe, speaking at a press conference in Johannesburg, declared that the schooling system would never be forcibly desegregated under the present government. He said that 'havoc' would ensue from the sudden desegregation of schools. According to Dr. Van der Merwe, a 'survey' had shown that integration would solve less than 20 % of the shortage of space in African Schools. In reply to a question as to whether schools would be desegregated if the Group Areas Act of 1966 were scrapped, Dr. Van der Merwe asserted that desegregation would be unnecessary as 'people would still want to go to their own schools'. He expressed the opinion that 'the world-wide tendency was not towards centralisation of education', citing the examples of Switzerland, with 26 education departments, and of the United States, with its more than 3 000 school boards (The Citizen, 12 January 1990). From the report of a Sowetan interview with Dr. Van der Merwe later in January 1990, it was confirmed that the 'survey' referred to by the minister was the 1988/89 Race Relations Survey. The executive director of the South African Institute of Race Relations (SAIRR), Mr. John Kane-Berman, clarified the position of the SAIRR in respect of the minister's statement. He said that while Dr. Van der Merwe had not misquoted the Institute, 'the fact that opening the white vacancies to blacks will not solve the whole problem is no reason not to do it and solve part of it at least. This would eliminate waste in a country which cannot afford waste' (Sowetan, 1 February 1990).

According to the Department of Education and Culture (coloured own affairs), 8 106 pupils not classified as coloured attended departmental schools in 1989 (Department of Education and Culture, Coloured own affairs). In 1988, 7 240 such pupils had been admitted.

Schools falling under the Department of Education and Culture (Indian own affairs) admitted 654 African, 3 818 coloured and nine white pupils in 1989 (Department of Education and Culture, Indian own affairs). In 1988, the Department had admitted 1 455 children not classified as Indian.

Speaking in Parliament in March 1989, the Progressive Federal Party's education spokesman, Mr. Roger Burrows MP, contended that the department of the minister of education and culture (white own affairs), Mr. Piet Clase, was out of step with the new mood of change in the country. He said that parents' bodies at over 20 white state schools had voted in favour of integration and that Mr. Clase has to consider opening state schools where the majority of parents were in favour of this. Mr. Burrows also argued that the new leader of the National Party, Mr. F.W. de Klerk, and the acting state president, Mr. Chris Heunis, had both indicated that the government would be taking a new look at the rights of people who wanted to associate with others outside the 'group context' and that Mr. Clase's department was the only one 'digging in its heels' against this (Hansard, 7 March 1989).

In April 1989, 21 schools, including some of the 'oldest and best-known white schools in the country', formed the Open Schools Association with the purpose of pursuing, through legal means, the right of schools to admit pupils on merit, without reference to race, colour or creed. The chairman of the association, Mr. Rodney Mazinter, said that the association felt it was self-evident that an ever-growing number of parents across language, racial and cultural line considered their children's future in South Africa to be inextricably bound up in the happiness and contentment of all the country's people. The association also said that it would pursue with equal determination the right of all schools to engage staff on merit alone (Sowetan, 24 May 1989).

In July 1989 a number of organisations, educationist, and pupils and their parents at the white Johannesburg High School for Girls, which was to be closed at the end of the year owing to a large drop in pupil numbers, called on the government to open the school to thousands of children of other race groups who lived in the area but had to travel up to 60 km a day to attend 'own affairs' schools. Mr. Clase replied that the school would be closed, in accordance with an earlier request by the school's management council. However, the chairman of the council, Mr. J. Foster, asserted that the request to close the school had come only after recommendations had been made to Mr. Clase to open the school to all races (Business Day, 27 June 1989). In a press release, the minister said that while he was aware of the controversy surrounding the future of the school, 'controversial discussion relating to the matter will serve no constructive purpose'. The school was closed at the end of 1989 and re-opened as a private multi-racial school early in 1990. In a media statement in September 1989, Mr. Clase had said that the grounds and buildings could be made available to a private school at a 'reasonable price' (Mr. Clase, Media Statement, 28 September 1989).

In August 1989 a number of individuals and anti-apartheid organisations launched the All Schools for All People campaign in Johannesburg. In the same month thousands of black pupils were prevented from marching to white schools in the Cape province to protest against segregated education (Business Day, 22 August 1989). On 23 March 1990 the government announced that its Department of National Education was considering two possible additional models for the provision of education. State schools might apply to become private schools, financed on a 'more substantial' basis than that which currently applied to private schools; or they might remain state schools but apply for the right to admit pupils of other race groups. In both cases, the approval of a very high percentage of parents - 'for example 90 %' - would be required. The two models were being referred to the minister's statutory advisory bodies and their comment would be submitted before 15 June 1990. Either or both of the models would probably be implemented on 1 January 1991.

The national director of the Independent Schools Council, Mr. M. Henning, said, shortly after the government's announcement, 'The government's proposals for community- controlled and privatised schools are not only a pragmatic step in finding a transitional solution for transitional times but a move in line with the spirit of the age.

They will, of course, be strongly contested ... Privatisation is an emotive and controversial subject ... An important point needs to be made - that the proposed "privatisation" of state schools, which is the second option in the government's model, is more in the nature of community control with state funding ... Ownership will remain with the state. For this reason these models should not be seen as that sort of privatisation which involves the selling off of state assets ... The next step will surely be the extension of community control either through other education departments or in a single ministry ... Community control is widely seen as the only solution to the crisis in African education' (Sunday Tribune, 1 April 1990).

According to a statement by Mr. Mazinter in March 1990, none of the schools which had voted in favour of becoming non- racial had recorded a vote of 90 % of parents in favour of the decision. However, in many cases the 'yes' vote had been 80 % or more, he said (The Citizen, 26 March 1990). It was reported in the 1988/89 SAIRR Survey (p248) that 70 % of teachers and of parents at Pretoria Boys High School had voted in favour of opening the school to all races. In May 1989 Pretoria Girls High School decided in principle that the school become multi-racial, following a poll in which 571 parents and 27 teachers voted in favour of their school being opened (opposed to 275 parents and 16 teachers against such a move (The Star, 21 May 1989). Until February 1990 the only black children attending white state schools were children of consular and diplomatic staff. However, three black American children were admitted to a white school that month, after the children's father had taken the matter to the press when the children were originally refused admission. Mr. Clase said, 'This is the first time an exception has been made and I used my discretion on the merits of the application. I did so in the interests of education and of the children (The Star, 14 February 1989).

5.2   COMMUNITIES RESPOND TO NEW SCHOOL MOVE

Many reactions were enlisted from a number and variety of persons and organizations. Most of these reactions were found in different newspapers throughout the country. This section of the chapter provides these responses.

5.2.1   NECC wary of new move (New Nation, May 25-30)

The announcement by the government of its intention to open white schools to all races received mixed reaction from the National Education Co-ordinating Committee (NECC). Speaking about opening white schools to all and creating a single education department, the NECC general secretary, Ihron Rensburg, said the NECC welcomed the announcement, but did not want to forget that "whatever proposals that emerge from the government have no legitimacy ... They come from a government that is not accountable to the people, is not accountable to South Africa ... is only accountable to a minority" (New Nations, May 25-30, 1990). He said the government was wrong in putting forward proposals and expecting the community and the NECC to react to them. He said the NECC could not function as a liaison structure, which would only be consulted by the government on education issues. Dealing with the issue of opening white schools, to all, Rensburg criticised the government, saying that the remarks made by the minister of education and culture in the house of assembly, Piet Clase, were unacceptable because these still gave the minority the right to decide on the utilisation of education resources. Rensburg was referring to government's proposals that the opening of the schools would depend on white parents in each school.

He said the potential barrier of parents' vote set by the government was unacceptable. The government said a majority of about 90 percent of parents needed to vote in favour of the opening of a school. Referring to government's statements that other issues such as culture needed to be taken into account even after white parents' approval, Rensburg said the government was trying to shift away from its definition of group: "They are moving away from the division of society into black and white to a new division into culture, religion and other forms" (New Nations, May 25-30, 1990). He said this new division also meant the protection of white minority rights. Rensburg condemned the second proposal put by the government that, where a community was willing to open the school to all races, it could take a decision to buy it and it could then admit whoever it wishes. He gave an example of a Mayfair school where parents had taken a decision to open it to all races because it was not economically viable as it had only about one-third of its capacity. The government rejected the parents' decision, saying it would not be politically viable to open the school to al races, and would therefore be closed. If parents wished, they could buy it and open it to all races.

Rensburg also referred to the Human Rights Commission's report that only 40 percent of whites were against the opening of schools to all races, but the government still put questions about opening them. He said this was clear evidence that the government still wanted to reserve the right to decide on the country's resources by a "minority of a minority". About the issue of moving towards a single education department, Rensburg said the NECC welcomed the statements made in parliament by the Minister of Education and Training, Stoffel van der Merwe, and his deputy, Piet Marais, that they recognised that the model of education constructed in parliament without the participation of the people could not be acceptable. "We endorse those statements and say that the model of education that will be quantitative and qualitative can only be constructed together with the people", (New Nations, May 25-30, 1990) he said. But, he said, the NECC felt that in order for the crisis in education to be resolved, they need to be looked at, in the short term, by an interim government and, in the medium term, by a constituent assembly. He said only them would the NECC participate in a committee which could look at the issue of forming a single education department.

5.2.2 Educationist deeply suspicious of open schools plan
       (Sunday Tribune, March 25)

Many educationist in South Africa were "deeply suspicious" that the announcements concerning the opening of white schools to all races were simply a Government ploy to keep white schools white, while outwardly appeasing calls for a single, open education system. Reacting to the announcements, the president of the Natal Teachers' Society, Mr. Gavin Kedian, said cautiously that "any move towards opening schools, however tenuous, is a step in the right direction" (Sunday Tribune, March 25, 1990). However, NTS sources said they were "deeply suspicious" as to the motives behind the government's announcement. "The two options which he suggests are open to schools are really routes enabling schools to stay white. We also have the problem of right-wing prejudice to contend with. It is highly unlikely that 90 % of parents at many schools will vote for open schools" (Sunday Tribune, March 25, 1990). The regional secretary of the National Education Union of South Africa, Mr. Duncan Hindle, said both of the conditions attached to the opening of schools were 'an absolute cop-out'. "This is a hopelessly inadequate response to the black schooling crisis".

He said essentially what the government was asking parents to do through the privatisation option was to pay more to admit blacks to their schools. "I don't believe many parents will be willing to do this". The 'school community' option was more attractive, 'but Clase put a block in it by saying that pupils from the school community would be given preference, and as long as the Group Areas Act remains on the statutes, essentially the racial nature of school will remain'. However, not all reactions to the controversial announcement were negative.

The chairman of the Parents' Association of Natal, Mr. Len Harris, said he was pleased that parents were being given the option to determine the schools' intake. He said the issue of opening schools would be discussed on a Tuesday at Panno's AGM at Glenwood High School. The headmasters of two non-racial schools in Natal, Mr. Richard Thompson from Uthogathi School near Tongaat and Mr. John Mitchell from Kings at Nottingham Road, both welcomed the announcements. Mr. Thompson said it was very important that people were given as many choices as possible, so they could make a free decision on where to send their children. Mr. Mitchell said as an intermediary step the announcements were "quite reasonable" and, in his experience, opening a school to all races did not present a problem. "The open school is a sensible and rational procedure".

5.2.3   Almost two million white parents to vote (Sunday Tribune, September 16)

About 1,8 million white parents were called on to vote in what would effectively be a referendum on whether or not to creak open the doors of learning to allow black pupils to enter all-white schools. In a flurry of activity following the government's announcement that schools can choose various models to admit black pupils, schools were rushing into meetings to debate whether or not to go to the vote, and detailed circulars explaining the models were being sent to parents. It was learnt that many Natal schools already had long lists of black pupils waiting for the green light for admission, but schools canvassed kept a tight lid on their plans. Parents of pupils at some schools in Durban, such as Glenwood High School and Maidstone Primary, had previously requested permission to admit black pupils, but it was to be seen if parents shared their views and if there were enough in favour (nine out of 10) to approve it. The acting headmaster of Glenwood, Ted Maddams, did not wish to comment on parents' feelings for fear of prejudicing the vote on a "sensitive" issue. "Even though many people involved in education have expressed disappointment in the models, they should still be seen as a beginning on the road to restructuring education in a new South Africa" (Sunday Tribune, September 16, 1990).

Sources at some schools in more conservative areas such as the Bluff, which some believed would choose to remain white, welcomed the Minister's granting parents an option. According to educationist and other sources, it was likely that most schools would opt to remain public schools, with some retaining an all-white pupil body, because parents would not be able to meet fee hikes if they opted for private school or state-aided school status. Clever wording ensured that even if a public school opted to open its doors "within the provision of the Constitution", most pupils would still be white. If the number of black pupils were to reach the 50 percent mark, the school would have to register with a department other than the white department - and take a cut in funds.

Some educationist interpreted the models as an attempt to "soften the blow" for white parents when schools inevitably open to all children, while others believed the moves were an attempt to appease white fears on open schools. Although many parents, pupils and educationist believed schools would be enriched by non- racialism, many others voiced fears that the quality of teaching would drop, classes would have pupils of vastly different ages, schools would become politicised, affluent parents would have to subsidise fees of less well-off children, the Christian ethos of schools would be threatened, or they would be swamped by different cultures. "The state should be advocating a non-racial schooling policy, recognising that in the initial stages, white fears will have to be addressed. One way would be to point at the successes of non- racial private schools", Democratic Party spokesman on education Roger Burrows said (Sunday Tribune, September 6, 1990). A wealth of information on the practicalities of opening schools already existed. The Open Schools Association, for instance, had developed detailed packages on guidelines on the transition to non-racial education. Mr. Burrows said it was essential that parents prepare for inevitable non- racial education. "Parents should take this opportunity in both hands and vote to open their schools as ordinary government schools. If they do not do it now, they will be forced to do it later." (Sunday Tribune, September 6, 1990).

5.2.4 What they voted for (Sunday Tribune, September 16)

There were four choices:

-     If a school opted for Model A, it would become a private school under an "owner", who could hire or buy buildings and equipment. Over three years the state would phase in a 45 percent subsidy of operating expenses. A departmental circular dispatched to white parents across the country said that if the parent/school community wished to maintain existing standard, it would have to contribute about R2 250 per child per year. Some educationist believed parents would have to fork out about R4 500 per high school pupils per year.

-     If a school remained a Government school (Model B), it could determine its own admission policy and criteria for admission "within the provisions of the Constitution", which meant more than 50 percent of pupils had to be white.

      Democratic Party education spokesman Roger Burrows explained: "It means that if the number of white pupils drops below that level, the school will have to register with another department" (Sunday Tribune, September 16, 1990).

-     If parents opted for Model C, the school became a state- aided ordinary school, such as present pre-primary schools, special education schools and technical colleges. Buildings would be transferred free of charge to a managing body, which would manage the school's funds, appoint or dismiss staff, and be responsible for the maintenance and extension of buildings. The state would subsidise 75 percent of the school's operating expenses, which would cover salaries of staff appointed "within the prescribed norms". Costs to parents would be about R900 per child a year, which in most cases represents a rise in fees.

-     The fourth option was to retain the status quo. The Minister of Education and Culture, Piet Clase, stressed the present system would still exist for communities satisfied with it.

The departmental circular said schools needed not to take a decision on alternative models immediately, as they could do so later, but a decision to opt for an additional model "cannot lightly be reversed".

An outvoted parent in a school which opted for an alternative model would also be accommodated. The government said provincial education departments would "do everything in their power to provide alternative provision of schooling" for pupils who wished to attend another school.

Alternative models would have to operate within prescribed parameters and would have to:

- Provide education with a Christian and "broadly national" character;

- Mother-tongue instructions;

- Give preference to white pupils, "the primary target of the department", from the school's feeder area, and

- Provide "culturally determined" education.

5.2.5 Parents' veto on non-racial schools unacceptable
(Weekly Mail, September 14-20)

The National Education Co-ordinating Committee rejected the government's announcement that approval for white schools to be opened to all races had to be a 90 percent vote in favour by parents. NECC executive member Ihron Rensburg said it was "unacceptable" for a minority of white parents to veto a decision by a community to open its school to pupils of other races. "The 90 percent vote required by the government effectively means, for instance, that 15 percent of the schools' parents can veto the opening of those schools in the face of 85 percent having voted in favour", (Weekly Mail, September 16, 1990).

The NECC was responding to the announcement by the government in which it had the go-ahead for white state schools to accept black people in 1991. The government had accepted in principle that parents should decide who should be admitted to white schools. It proposed that the integrated schools could either remain as state schools or to register as private schools, but still receive substantial subsidy from the government. Rensburg said it was unacceptable for the government to allow only white communities to take decisions on under- utilised schools that might be closed in five years.

Democratic Party spokesman on Education and Culture, Roger Burrows, said approval for opening white state schools to all races should be about 66 percent. "The DP believes strongly this figure is purely an interim measure and that the government, in moving away from social apartheid, is having to placate what it sees as white fears. Under those circumstances we would believe a figure of about $^2/_3$ would be more appropriate," (Weekly Mail, September 16, 1990).

5.2.6 Move impractical, dictatorial and racist (Daily News, September 11)

The government's three routes to opening up white schools to all races met with disdain, scepticism and disappointment from leading education authorities. The long-awaited announcement had been described by some as frustrating and impractical, by others as "another example of the Government's dictatorial style" and by others as "a last-ditch attempt to keep white schools white".

An embittered Dr. Edward Ndaba, Chief Director of the Department of Education and Training for Natal, said: "The blacks are not impressed. Whites are at liberty to determine what type of education they would like their children to have, but to date, blacks have had their education prescribed to them. What the black people in South Africa want is quite clearly a system of education that offers equality of opportunities and which is non-racial in the true sense of the word" (Daily News, September 11, 1990).

Mr. Roger Burrows, Democratic Party spokesman on education, described the announcement as "profoundly disappointing". The DP was convinced that the position adopted by Mr. Clase did not reflect the aims or desires of the majority of South Africans: "This almost total entrenchment of the racist concept of 'whites only' schools is directly contrary to everything that has been paraded as possible in the new South Africa. We call on the State President to remove Mr. Clase from this portfolio and to announce that there will be one Ministry of Education and that all South African schools will have a non-racial admissions policy. It appears that Mr. Clase has quite deliberately made it as difficult as possible for schools to become open" (Daily News, September 11, 1990). Mr. Ian Corbishley, president of the Natal Teachers' Society, said the NTS had warned that schools could not be opened on an ad hoc basis. There were too many practical difficulties. "The announcement is little more than a last-ditch attempt to keep white schools white in the new South Africa. It will force those who are in favour of a normalisation of education to pay financially for this while Government continues to fund whites-only education." (Daily News, September 11, 1990).

Mr. Poobie Naicker, president of the Teachers' Association of South Africa, said Tasa did not support the government's model. "Tasa advocates open schools for all. There must be a sincere, honest attempt to admit all South African pupils to all schools." (Daily News, September 11, 1990). Mr. Austin Green Thompson, president of the coloured Society of Natal Teachers, said the new models did nothing to get rid of apartheid. Mr. Duncan Hindle, Natal secretary of the National Education Union of South Africa (Neusa) described the moves as "clearly unacceptable" and reiterated Neusa's call for a single Ministry of Education.

5.2.7   New models of schools rejected across spectrum (Weekly Mail, September 14-20)

Announcement by the South African government, of three "new models" which allowed schools to determine their own admissions policies - and theoretically provide mechanisms by which they could become non-racial - was rejected by political and education groups across the spectrum. Strini Moodley, publicity secretary of the Azanian People's Organisation (Azapo) said the prospect of a reduction in subsidies if schools adopted one of the models which takes them out of the present government sphere of influence, "shall either influence white parents to vote in their financial interest on this matter or choose to go private, in which case, consequent financial burden shall have a debilitating effect on the poor black parents" (Weekly Mail, September 14-20, 1990).

Another aspect of government's new plans which had been criticised, was the requirement that 72 percent of parents with children at the school would have to pass the motion for a change to admissions policies, before they could be adopted, and even then, the minister would have the right to veto their decision. "The minimum percentage of 72 percent of all who have the right to vote must vote in favour of change, on condition, that at least 80 percent of the parents/legal guardians ... participated in the poll". The percentage vote in favour of change, although important, will not necessarily be a deciding factor. The government will naturally take other factors, like alternative provision of schooling, into account" (Weekly Mail, September 14-20, 1990).

Democratic Party education spokesman Roger Burrows said the parent vote requirement was an "almost total entrenchment of the racist concept of 'white only' schools (and) is directly contrary to everything that has been paraded as possible in the 'new' South Africa. It appears the Minister Clase has quite deliberately made it as difficult as possible for schools to open". According to Moodley, the voting condition, "illustrates the high racist standard against which the government obviously wants to judge and control the imminent influx of black students in white schools" (Weekly Mail, September 14-20, 1990). A further subject for concern in government's proposals was the principle the preference would be given to white pupils, in schools under the control of the DEC. "The department's primary responsibility is to server the whites. Our constitution at the moment makes provision for separate education and that is our constitution until a new one is drawn up".

Conservative Party spokesman on education and culture, Andrew Gerber, said that it appeared the government had abandoned education principles and this would result in conflict and division in every school community. "The CP will ceaselessly continue to mobilise parents to prevent the destruction of own affairs education" (Weekly Mail, September 14-20, 1990).

Representatives from most progressive education and political organisations as well as concerned parents and pupils urged the government to channel its energy into the creation of one education department and fully non-racial education, instead of dully-dallying with useless half-measures, such as those announced by Clase. In the interim however, and despite their strong reservations, the DP and the Teacher's Federal Council decided to co-operate with Clase's proposals and called upon "every parent or guardian who would have the opportunity to vote in the referendum called as schools, to drive open the doors of that school to normal admission requirements" (Weekly Mail, September 14-20, 1990).

5.2.8 <u>Models for opening white schools fall far short of what</u>
       <u>is necessary (Sunday Times, September 16)</u>

The government's new deal for schools struck educationist like
a bolt from al long-gone era. They had anticipated a far more
substantial move by authorities, and most were dismayed and
even outraged at the cautiously-worded "alternative models"
presented to a waiting public. South African education is
racked by conflict and deep mistrust, and educationist feared
the new deal, clearly aimed at appeasing white fears,
exacerbated tensions as mobilisation around non-racial
education continued and grew, rather than move education into
calmer waters.

"Coming during a time of great political change, there is no
doubt the new models are seen as divisive, patronising,
insulting to blacks, and not in the spirit of F.W. de Klerk's
challenge to us all to create an equal and equitable South
Africa", Education Foundation executive director Dr. John van
Ziyl said (Sunday Times, September 16, 1990). "If we are to
respond to that challenge we must also create a new education
system. And the design process for such a system must include
all the key players, stake-holders and communities. We have to
recognise the time is past for any single agency or player to
develop new policy options in isolation. The focus must be on
a consultative process involving all key parties." The lack of
consultation with grassroots organisations in devising the
models was indeed a crucial issue. According to a statement by
the government it had given "thorough consideration" to
comments from "statutorily recognised advisory bodies"
following its announcement on proposed models in March
1990. "One cannot tinker with an inherently unjust and
ineffectual system. This could be a very exciting phase if it is
managed properly and if there is real consultations", Dr. van
Ziyl said, (Daily News, August 10, 1990).

The head of the African National Congress education
department, John Samuel, said there were far more

stockholders in education than those the minister had consulted. The government had missed a unique opportunity to express its intentions to move away from a racist and ethnic society. "We need to see such evidence, and these models are totally at odds with any shift. It makes one wonder what the government will produce with this Educational Renewal Strategy" (Sunday Times, September 16, 1991). He said the models further entrenched racism and were fundamentally flawed by the premise of continued racial separation. The concern was that the state could begin implementing a system which would be difficult to dismantle and rebuild later, rather than helping to lay groundwork for a new system now.

The Democratic Party education spokesman, Roger Burrows, said his party welcomed the models proposed as the first sign that the state was moving away from rigid segregated education, "but six months later, after significant advances in reform in other sectors, education has not moved forward at all". Former KwaZulu Minister of Education and Culture, Dr. Oscar Dhlomo, said the government had failed to address the dire shortage of classrooms for black pupils and made it virtually impossible for white schools to admit black pupils. The situation was urgent. The Education Foundation estimated that to cater for pupils under the present inadequate conditions, there would have to be 6 827 schools (almost double the number in 1988) just in Natal/KwaZulu by the year 2000. In contrast, research by the S.A. Institute of Race Relations showed that 196 white schools closed in the past decade due to dwindling pupil numbers and that the remaining white schools had about 250 000 vacancies.

A major bugbear, and one which made it extremely difficult for even a "liberal" school to open its doors, was the high poll demanded for what the government described as a "convincing majority".   As Mr. Burrows pointed out, that meant a whopping 90 percent of parents who voted had to approve a model, which effectively allowed a few conservative parents to veto a decision. Assuming every pupil in a 1 000- pupil school had two parents, 1 600 parents would had to vote and 1 440 would had to be in favour of an open school. Applying the same criteria to a school of 300 pupils, if only 28 parents out of 600 opposed opening the school, it remained white. "Such high polls are not even obtained in major elections", one educationist observed.

However, the ministerial representative in Natal, Dr. Gerald Hoskings, said the presentation of the new models was "part of a process". "If it is proved in practice that the percentage required is too high, I am certain representations to the minister will result in that aspect's being reviewed. This is a learning experience, not only for the public, but also for the department" (Sunday Times, September 16, 1990). He said the government had consulted the Teachers' Federal Council and the four provincial education councils: "If the minister had consulted every organisation, he would have been faced with so many diametrically opposed views". Dr. Hoskings added: "The days of using coercion to enforce a defined system are limited. One feature of the new system is that it is certainly democratic and does not seek to enforce a particular model. There is no doubt that at this stage, the opinions and concerns of parents must be a major factor." (Sunday Times, September 16, 1990).

In all likelihood, the models will be thrown out when they are overtaken by major constitutional changes. Against the probable demise of the Population Registration and Group Areas Acts, the models take on an almost bizarre things. Dr. Dhlomo said that even if a school did open, against the odds, parents had to dig deeply into their pockets "while those who wish to see racial discrimination entrenched in our society are allowed this luxury free of charge with the tacit support of the state and its ministries" (Sunday Times, September 16, 1990). Ironically, the situation will probably by reversed in a post-apartheid society, with parents paying dearly for clinging to segregated schooling. The models also have to be looked at in terms of education authorities stated intentions to achieve parity in education. In 1989, R3 739 per capita was spent on white pupils, and R930 on African pupils. In KwaZulu, the per capita expenditure was R545. Parity will mean per capita expenditure will be brought up or down to about R1 383. Adjustments will also have to be made to pupil-teacher ratios, which now range from 1:17 for whites to 1:51 in KwaZulu.

5.2.9 Left wingers reject Clase plan as a farce (Daily News, September 19)

While Government-supporting newspapers gave a low-key response to the Minister of Education's cautious scheme for multi-racial schools, left-wing Afrikaans papers slammed it as a farce and unacceptable to all. The Durban-based Tempo said the announcement had sparked off might row. The government's scheme was vague, evasive, fragmentary and unacceptable to everyone. The editorial writer said bluntly it was time for South Africans to wake up and realise the writing was on the wall: schools will be opened unconditionally in the future, and the quicker people accepted this fact and co-operated in making South Africa a new country with a future, the less painful will be the transition.

The independent Vrye Weekblad said: "The so-called opening of white schools to all races is a farce. One wonders why the Conservative Party rejects it since it fortifies apartheid so well." People who would gladly open their children's schools because they believe in the cultural cross-pollination of a multi-racial system, or merely because they wanted to improve their children's Zulu in preparation for the "New South Africa", would have to pay for it. They would also have to launch a full-scale campaign to win the support of 72 percent of other parents. "Such percentages are not even expected when the constitution of the country is changed."

Beeld described the scheme as "a step forward" but queried the need for a decision by parents on a school's status to be subject to approval by the authorities. The paper said there were so many in-built reservations that, with few exceptions, there was likely to be precious little integration on a scale which would pose any threat to whites. Die Burger said the plan was a careful approach to a sensitive issue and had to make adaptations possible without any great disruption. The paper warned parents, however, that the Conservative Party would try to gain as much political advantage as possible over the issue.

5.4   THE IMPLICATIONS OF NON-RACIAL EDUCATION

The Government's plan to hand white parents the keys which open their school doors to all races was widely rejected. But it had the reality of non-racial schooling across to very black and white family. However flawed, it made John Citizen sit up and consider the implications of sending his son or daughter to school with Sipho Mkhize's children. While many prophets of doom faced this inevitability with dread, there were educationist who regarded the presence of people from different cultures in the same classroom as a positive resource for education rather than a problem.

One authority on multi-cultural education, the Vice-Rector of Edgewood College in Pinetown, Dr. Alex Coutts, believes a degree of Africanisation and Orientalisation of the present, largely Western, system must be anticipated. "In view of the fierce objections raised by black youngsters against a school system perceived to be discriminatory, tokenism and the assimilation of small numbers of black pupils into other systems is not likely to prove politically acceptable in the long term. Delay in effecting integration is likely to exacerbate tensions, with increasingly serious repercussions for the most privileged members of the population." (Mercury, September 14, 1990). In his second doctoral thesis, Dr. Coutts has outlined the experiences of Western democracies with multi-cultural education in the three decades following World War II when they had to provide appropriate schooling that accommodated the diverse needs of their growing immigrant minorities. These minorities agitated vociferously for a more substantial recognition of their cultural heritages. As a result, ethnic revitalisation movements that affirmed the importance of such cultures, became prominent in the 1960's and 1970's, with seriously disruptive affects. Steeped in a liberal philosophy that embraced a positive view of humanity, several states responded by shifting gradually towards a school dispensation that recognised the right of smaller cultural groups to assimilate into the mainstream, "western industrialised" culture while retaining the essentials of their own cultures. In turn, children from the mainstream society would be more exposed to the immigrant cultures.

While some schools threw themselves at the challenge and fundamentally changed their admission policies and their staff composition, other institutions relied on the 'ethnic additive' approach where blacks and Asians were not allowed to have much impact on the character of the school. Dr. Coutts said the policy of integrating yet nurturing cultural minorities has remained controversial and harsh criticism is still levelled at overseas countries where corrective strategies have been used to compel racial mixing. He agrees that such a policy cannot be easily applied in this country where the groups excluded from the dominant industrial culture form an indigenous majority rather than an immigrant minority. However, he is certain that the goal of exposing children to a variety of culture- based viewpoints is worth the teething pains of transition. "There is much advantage to be gained by the creation of a vehicle through which greater social solidarity can be fostered". (Mercury, September 14, 1990).

Describing the approach private schools in South Africa have had to admitting pupils of other races, Dr. Coutts said that in some cases only small numbers of blacks had been enrolled to avoid drastically altering the ethos of schools. Entrance criteria have provided a selection mechanism that has tended to ensure the compatibility of newcomers ... potential culture clashes thus tend to be minimised. It is such a mechanism which educationist believe the government is trying to install at schools which adopt its models. Entry policies were, of course, a central issue. The deprived learning histories of large sectors of our population make laissez faire open policies highly contentious amongst more privileged members who fear "a drop in standards. Open policies admittedly necessitate deep- seated adjustments to curricula and teaching methods as well as the use of bridging programmes and academic support systems.

One form of multi-cultural education would emphasise equality at entrance - setting admission criteria and providing bridging programmes for pupils in their first year. This system, based on meritocratic free-market principles, would probably favour those who are already economically advantaged. The other form of multi-cultural education would emphasise equality at exit - with academic support programmes to help struggling pupils right through their school years. Specific activities would also be designed to promote social cohesion. This system would probably favour the academically disadvantaged. Regardless of the method used to produce school-leavers of the same quality, a change in the way schools are administered was necessary. "Open management system, the creation of Student Representative Councils rather than a prefect system and the satisfactory representation of all community on parent bodies is essential if diversity of our society is to be accommodated. Also, teachers will require a comprehensive vocabulary of skills and considerable awareness if they are to avoid teaching from their own ethnic perspective ... they will have to be competent in the management of remedial courses". (Mercury, September 14, 1990).

5.4   CONCLUSION

South Africa needs a coherent and a comprehensive attack on the problems of Black education if we mean to produce citizens who will inhabit the new South Africa in peace and prosperity. What we do not need is a proliferation of numerous haphazard, ad hoc and poorly planned education projects which have no effects at all on the total system. Properly considered, this is what a demand for one Department of Education is all about.

There is a need for a precise and a clear definition of the problems in education in preparation for a new South Africa. If a concerted and a well co-ordinated effort is launched to produce a new philosophy, a new administration and new policies in a new Department of Education, then this proposed one department can be a solution.

Almost all the Black communities have called for the scrapping of discriminating education systems and they desire the establishment of one Department of Education, a non-racial, democratic system of education.

"The concern is that the state could start implementing a system which will be difficult to dismantle and rebuild later".
    - John Samual
  (Sunday Times, January 6, 1991)

THE DOORS OF WHITE SCHOOLS CREAK OPEN

6.1   INTRODUCTION

A flurry of excitement was sweeping through "white" schools which opted to open their doors to black children. Thousands of prospective pupils of colour were being interviewed at white schools for enrolment in 1991. But the late presentation of the "additional models", differing subject packages from school to school, and in rare cases the already full pupil body meant that just a fraction of black applicants would find a place at the schools in 1991. It appeared that only about 2 000 black children would enter white schools (where vacancies hovered around the 30 000 number), although the numbers could go up during the year, and rise substantially by the beginning of 1992. But this had to be seen against the apparent huge number of applications to white schools - an indication of the glaring under-provision in black education.

6.2   TRANSVAAL SCHOOLS CAUGHT OFF-GUARD

Several Transvaal schools chose to vote on government's optional school models only in 1991 after being caught off- guard by the stringent voting requirements. A Sunday Star survey revealed that Witwatersrand schools were choosing to vote on the issue in 1991 because of the limited time available to canvass parents. They were also concerned that parents of pupils writing matric or leaving school for other reasons would not bother to vote. This could be a problem in the light of the high percentage poll that was needed. A number of schools applied for more information on the models before putting the issue to a vote.

The Transvaal Education Department was not prepared to say which schools had applied and a returning officer would be appointed in order to hold a poll. First on the mark to the polls was Johannesburg Girls Preparatory School in Berea which voted on November 3, 1990. Next was Parktown Girls High which voted on November 9 with

Melville Primary voting on November 16. The prestigious Pretoria High School for Girls voted on November 20. A high voting percentage poll was needed. In order for the school to adopt one of the optional models, 90 percent of the parents in an 80 percent poll would have to agree. Polls were hampered by the end of the year exams, declining interest in the issue by parents of school-leavers and the limited time available before schools closed at the end of the year. Polls taken in 1991, if successful, pupils of other races could be admitted during the year or in 1992. The Transvaal English Medium Parents' Association (Tempa) held several meetings with schools council members and other interested parties in the province to inform them about the three models.

Tempa spokesman Glen Stuart said the organisation welcomed the models even though they were not perfect. "It gives parents the opportunity to put their money where their mouths are," (Sunday Star, October 28, 1990). Mr. Stuart said Tempa was giving schools every encouragement to vote on the issue. He admitted it was difficult to set the vote in motion with the limited time available and there were people saying it would be best to deal with the issue only in 1991. There were, however, others who were encouraging schools to "go for it". One advantage in voting in 1991 would be to increase interest of the matric parents in the school's future. Tempa - an officially recognised body which represented between 200 000 and 300 000 English-speaking parents in the Transvaal - was encouraging schools which were voting on the issue in 1990 to go about the matter professionally. One school which tried to overcome the apathy among parents of matric pupils was Northview High School in Highlands North which voted on Model B on November 12.

The school's management council held information meetings on the issue and did a lot of foot-slogging in order to elicit interest from parents. Council chairman Natie Wasserman said they had decided not to postpone voting until 1991 in order to sustain the present impetus. Also, the working members of the group could not afford a long campaign. Mr. Wasserman said the matric parents were their "weak area". The only way they would get their votes would be to treat the matrics as individuals and approach all of them.

6.3   CONSERVATIVE PARTY FIGHT SCHOOL INTEGRATION IN
       NATAL

The Conservative Party in the country was in the meantime going all-out to fight the integration of blacks into white schools - with some parents even considering placard demonstrations and school boycotts to drive their point home. The chairman of the CP in Natal, Mr. Francis Hitchcock, told the Daily News (January 19, 1991) that his party remained firmly committed to self-determination for whites and to guarding white rights and interests.

Following a national CP meeting in Pretoria, he returned to Natal determine to attempt to maintain and preserve our First World standards. "We are very much aware of the seriousness of the direction Government policy is taking. We are very worried about the situation, especially the education issues." (Daily News, January 17, 1991). A former headmaster, Mr. Hitchcock believed integration of blacks into white schools would lead to a dramatic drop in academic standards and an erosion of white culture. He said most people were unaware of the fact that when voting whether to open schools, they could also opt for the status quo and did not have to vote for change.

In Natal about 93 schools decided not to vote in 1990 and retained the status quo. "There is not much we can do except go all-out to enlighten people, warn them, and tell them that if they are unhappy with the situation, at this stage they can opt for the status quo." (Daily News, January 17, 1991). One parent said that the high school's parents' committee on which she sat were discussing what kinds of protest action they could take to voice their unhappiness with the situation. "We are trying to contact parents' committees from other schools and organise a placard protest in the city centre, objecting to forced integration. Some of the parents on our committee are even in favour of their children boycotting school if any blacks are admitted. We have to take some action soon because the situation is becoming unbearable." (Daily News, January 17, 1991).

6.4   NO ROOM IN 'SCHOOLS OF DESPAIR'

The hope that accompanied the opening of schools to all races faded as the thousands of black pupils were turned away and charges of elitism levelled at strict admissions criteria. A ray of hope that came with the opening of previously all-white government schools to all races faded away as other thousands of black pupils who sought admission to these schools were turned away. What had promised to be "schools of hope" became schools of despair, either because the "open schools" could not accommodate more pupils or because prospective pupils did not satisfy entrance requirements. Only 1 048 black, Indian and coloured pupils were accepted at 37 newly- opened white schools in the Transvaal, according to the Department of Education and Culture (DEC). "The announcement to open white schools to all races was good news and I had high hopes for a better education for my children," said Kenny Nyovane, whose daughter was turned down at a Johannesburg school. (The Weekly Mail, January 4-11, 1991).

A number of black parents were angry at the methods used by these schools to select black pupils, saying the exercise was "racist". Black pupils who sought admission had to write mathematics and English tests before they could be admitted. In some cases local residence or proximity to the school area were given as primary requirement for admission. "It is really crazy because most of us live in the townships," said Nyovane, adding, "and how do they expect our kids to be proficient in English or mathematics when they have been deprived of better education all these years? My understanding is that we send kids to school to learn, not to be expected to know things even before the are taught." (The Weekly Mail, January 4-11, 1991). Transvaal Education Department (TED) spokesman Willie van Staden said 269 black pupils had been enrolled at open high schools and 779 at primary schools.

According to TED estimates there were 480 000 white pupils attending the 940 Transvaal government schools, which made the intake of black pupils at white schools opted for model B a drop in the ocean. It was in the matter of admissions criteria that charged of elitism and hypocrisy had been raised. In an effort to assure "standards" were maintained and classrooms did not become overcrowded, many of the schools laid down strict admissions criteria which, parents and observers said, made it difficult for black children to gain a place at the school. Many of the schools were encouraging new pupils only in the lower standards, as they were concerned about the difficulties that children from different educational backgrounds could have in adjusting to a new curriculum. Another restriction was on age: most schools set age limits within two years of the average of the class, which excluded many black children who had lost years of learning because of disruptions in township schools.

The National Education Co-ordinating Committee (NECC) said it rejected the manner in which the state and the DEC, by way of the A, B and C models, were proceeding with the opening of previously white schools, and declared that all schools be opened to all people. "The models are an attempt by the state to privatise education which is in contradiction to what the NECC believes should be the approach, which is to make education accessible to all. The NECC locals, regions and organisational components are discussing which appropriate actions should be taken to cause the state and its 18 education departments to open all schools with immediate effect. The NECC further wishes to encourage our white compatriots to move speedily, together with the rest of the South African community, towards the establishment of a single, non- racial an democratic education system for all South Africans." (The Weekly Mail, January 4-11, 1991). English tests that applicants were required to write came in for strong criticism. "It is funny that our children are subjected to such tests when the same does not apply to Portuguese, Italian or Greek foreigners' kids when they apply for admission," said Skwila Makenete, a Soweto parent whose child was not admitted. "There are so many foreigners who come here and their kinds are accepted just like that without testing their knowledge of English," he said. (The Weekly Mail, January 19-26, 1991). Many parents charged that "open schools" was just a label and the government had once again failed the black community by not fulfilling promises.

DEC information officer Dr. Chris Pretorius said 33 government schools in the Transvaal had opted to open their doors to all races, one in the Orange Free State, 107 in the Cape and 64 in Natal. The DEC was, however, unable to give The Weekly Mail enrolment figures for black pupils attending previously whites-only schools for the first time. In a random survey among Johannesburg schools which had opted for the open-door policy, The Weekly Mail (January 19-26, 1991) found the enrolment figures very low.

-    Parktown Boys' High School, which had a total roll of 825 pupils, only admitted 46 students from races other than white, a mere six percent of the school.

-    At Glenvista High School, only 20 out of 800 pupils were black.

-    Parktown Girls' High School admitted 15 black pupils. The school's principal, Pamela Quin, said: "Unfortunately, we were only able to accept a handful as the standard of prospective pupils was low and we only have a limited number of available places in the classrooms." (The Weekly Mail, January 19-26, 1991).

-    Athlone Boys' High School principal Louie White said many pupils were rejected because of "low standards" but could not provide figures.

-    Bertrams Junior School principal David Patland declined to give figures to the press.

Other schools contacted during the same week said they were still interviewing parents as they had only received permission to admit blacks at the end of December 1990.

"The discrepancy between education offered in schools under the Department of Education and Training and those controlled by the House of Assembly is vast," said Tom Clarke,

Parktown Boys' principal. "It is still too early to flood schools with pupils from different educational backgrounds. These pupils should grow with the school. The open-door system is a step in the right direction because whites are going to learn to share." (The Weekly Mail, January 19-26, 1991).

6.5   MOST BLACK PUPILS STILL FACE CRISIS

Only a small number of blacks benefited from the opening of white schools in 1991 - leaving the majority of black pupils facing an ongoing education crisis. Critics expressed concern that the focus could be shifted away from the crisis facing township schools now that white schools were opening to all races. In the Transvaal 1 084 black pupils enrolled in former whites-only schools. Only one school in the Free State adopted model B (giving parents autonomy over black admissions) - and expected about 120 black pupils.

Although statistics were not yet available for Cape and Natal schools, it was estimated that about 1 000 black pupils were enrolled in Natal and 1 500 to 2 000 in the Cape. Democratic Party spokesman on education Roger Burrows said the opening of "only 10 percent" of white schools was "merely a small opening". "It is highly improbable that these schools could in any way alleviate the massive problems facing black education." (The Star, January 14, 1991). It was recognised that the opening would have "teething problems" but it was important to note that the psychological effect of opening schools was probably more important than actual numbers involved. "What needs to be wrestled with is whether the remaining whites only schools can pay for their empty spaces," he said. At the same time, the critical shortage of teachers and material in black schools needed urgent attention, which unless addressed, would mean the government being continuously accused of apartheid education.

The DP believed that all schools should be open for pupils, irrespective of race. Gillian Maskell, director of the New Era Schools Trust, said there was concern over the eye of educators being shifted off the objective of a unitary education body. "We are also concerned that people are being blinded by the word 'open'. These schools have been opened by whites and it is still very much a case of whites deciding for blacks - which implies continued white supremacy in education." (The Star, January 14, 1991). Of further concern was the fact that teachers had no extra help in how to set about multi- cultural teaching. "However, we would rather have some black children in whites schools than none at all." The opening of white schools has also been criticised by the National Education Co-ordinating Committee (NECC), which claims the state does not have a commitment to open all schools and, therefore, to a single education system. The Pan Africanist Students' Organisation said co-opting blacks into white schools was "running away from the problem" - which include the failure to build more schools.

6.6   TOO FEW PUPILS, 22 GOVERNMENT SCHOOLS SHUT

In the meantime dwindling numbers forced the Transvaal Education Department to close 22 State schools in 1990, a spokesman for the DET confirmed on the 13th of February 1991. Many of the schools were standing empty. Others were taken over by the Department of Management, Housing and Works, which would decide their fate, and some were being considered for other educational purposes. "Some of the schools are in older suburbs, now populated largely by older people. However, we estimate white pupil enrolment in the Transvaal is declining at the rate of 5 000 a year". (The Star, February 14, 1991). This department said it was not possible for the TED to open the schools to pupils of other races.

The spokesman could not give an official valuation of the school buildings and equipment, but the estimated value could run into tens of millions of rands. One school closed was Blairgowrie High, which was not yet 20 years old. Schools closed by the TED were: Lanseria Primary (Afrikaans medium), Bez Vally Junior (English), Dullstroom Primary (Afrikaans), Rooiberg Primary near Warmbaths (Afrikaans), Beestekraal Primary near Brits (Afrikaans), Blairgowrie High (English), Western High, Johannesburg (English), Ontdekkers High, Roodepoort (Afrikaans), Golfpark, Meyerton (Afrikaans), Malvern

West Primary, Johannesburg (English), Orange Grove Primary, Johannesburg (English), Greenhills Primary, Randburg (English), Hendriksdal Primary, Thabazimbi (Afrikaans), Trichardtspoort Primary, Bronkhorstspruit (Afrikaans), Hercules Primary, Pretoria (English), Tobie Winterbach Primary, Grootvlei, near Heidelberg (Afrikaans), Saambou Primary, Klerksdorp (Afrikaans), Homedene Primary, Standerton (English), Biesiesvlei Primary, Lichtenburg (Afrikaans), Joubert Park Primary, Johannesburg (English), Elandsbos, Naboomspuit (Afrikaans), and the Marong Primary at Vaalwater near Nylstroom (Afrikaans).

6.7   A.N.C. PLAN TO FLOOD WHITE SCHOOLS

In the light of certain white schools being closed down the ANC embarked on a campaign encouraging black children to apply for admission to all white schools in the province - regardless of whether parents at these schools had voted to open to all races. Although applications would be refused by schools which had not voted to adopt the 'models' for autonomous admissions policies, the organisation hoped to force the Government's hand into opening all white schools across-the-board.

The regional secretary of the ANC's southern Natal branch, Mr. Sbu Ndebele, told the Mercury (December 1, 1990) that a decision had been made at its conference that all white schools should be flooded with applications. "It is ridiculous for the Government to retain whites-only schools with declining enrolments when most black schools are terribly overcrowded." (Mercury, December 1, 1990). However, it had not yet singled out any particular white school which it felt should open to all.

The organisation's determination to act was shown during a protest staged by ANC supporters outside a white primary school in Hillbrow, Johannesburg, against the school's refusal to vote to go to the polls on the models which would allow it to open to other races. Pamphlets distributed at the scene pointed out that black children living in Hillbrow and Berea had no schools and parents had to send their children great distances to township schools or at great expense to private institutions in the city centre.

6.8   WHITE ELEPHANT SCHOOLS FACE INVASION

Empty white schools all over South Africa were being targeted by the National Education Co-ordinating Committee, which intended moving in black pupils and teachers. At least 78 white schools had been closed, with another 85 due to shut in 1991. The NECC, a non-racial activist group, has targeted for occupation empty schools in Kempton Park, Edenvale and Midrand, close to Tembisa. It planed to take over the first school, Johannesburg's Orange Grove Primary. After the NECC announced it would bus in Alexandra pupils to the school, the government responded by saying it had already allocated Orange Grove to the SA Jewish Board of Education.

This was not expected to thwart the black occupation, which the government said would be "unlawful". Outlining the nation-wide strategy, NECC Southern Transvaal regional general secretary Amon Msane said :

"Hundreds of black children and their teachers plan to move into dozens of these empty schools to highlight the black pupils' plight. At the same time we will be enrolling in white schools. Action will be taken during the coming week. This is just the beginning". (Sunday Times, June 23, 1991). It was intended that all or most of the empty white schools would be taken over.

In April 1991 Roger Burrows (DP Pinetown) said by the end of 1991, 163 white schools would have closed. He added that 33 Cape schools, 30 or more in Natal and 22 in the Transvaal were to close. This pattern of moving the entire student body plus its teachers would be followed in subsequent occupations. The first occupation would be carried out under the auspices of the NECC, Southern Transvaal, and the Alexandra Education Co-ordinating Committee. Mr. Msane would not reveal details of the take- over. The Orange Grove occupation would be the first of many.

NECC was surprised that empty schools had been handed over by the Education Department to the Department of Local Government, Housing and Works. Mr. Frank Gerber, Department of Local Government chief director, said: "Occupying the premises without permission would be an unlawful act." (Sunday Times, June 23, 1991). Twenty-eight schools had been taken over by his department from the white Ministry of Education and Culture. Of these, one school would be used by the DET, two as private schools for blacks, one would become a multi-racial private school, two would go to Education and Culture: House of Delegates, two to welfare organisations and one to a state department for training purposes. The NECC, in an open letter to Education and Training Minister Dr. Stoffer van der Merwe - with a copy to President F.W. de Klerk - challenged him to support the planned take-over of the Orange Grove school.

In a strongly-worded statement and position paper, Dr. Van der Merwe replied: "A multitude of problems related to continuing unrest, social impoverishment, unfavourable home circumstances and unemployment have combined to create a crippling milieu which fosters discontent, destabilisation and delinquency. Efforts to curb drug taking, drinking at school, gambling, revenge attacks and rape, address the same ills which are at the very heart of poor scholastic performance. The 'crisis' in education should rather be viewed as 'education in crisis'." (Sunday Times, June 23, 1991). He said part of the Orange Grove school building was being used for a pre-primary school by the Transvaal Education Department and, as far as the rest of the school was concerned, Local Government Minister Sam de Beer would be making an announcement "soon".

Among the white schools standing empty because of dwindling student numbers are Blairgowrie High on the Johannesburg/Randburg border, the Swartkops and Albatros primary schools in Port Elizabeth, Kafferrivier Primary in Bloemfontein, Pomona Primary in Kempton Park, Highflats Primary and Mitchell Girls High in Durban, and Voortrekker Primary in Pietermaritzburg. The NECC resorted to mass action following a "negative response" from Minister of Education and Training Stoffel van der Merwe, who refused to meet the Southern Transvaal regional chairman because negotiations were taking place at a higher level in the Joint Working Group (JWG) on education. But the JWG - meant to address the educational crisis in the short-term - was reportedly running aground.

The government was now moving fast to allocate the empty schools, whereas it had been dragging its feet before the campaign was announced. Welfare, Housing and Works Minister Sam de Beer announced the allocation of nine schools, mostly to private institutions. Among these were Marlandia Primary in Maraisburg to the Light House Christian Schools Ministry, Jubileum Primary in Mayfair West to he Educare Training Trust, Johan Rissik Primary in Johannesburg to the Department of Education and Culture and Malvern West Primary to the Johannesburg Tutorial College. Once the earmarked schools had been occupied, the NECC would hand them over to the Department of Education and Training. This was potentially a fresh source of conflict, as most of the empty schools, although structurally intact, had been stripped of educational facilities. Meanwhile, at a press conference the Azanian People's Organisation distanced itself from the campaign. "We should not settle for crumbs from the table of white people", said Azapo education secretariat spokesman Dr. Gomolemo Mokae. "The onus is not on blacks to decide what to do with these institutions. We should demand that the government build more schools in the townships rather, because pupils moving to white areas will lose their sense of belonging and develop other cultural tendencies." (The Weekly Mail, July 11, 1991). The Pan Africanist Congress, however, supported the campaign.

6.9   PLAN TO SEIZE WHITE SCHOOLS CRITICISED

The Johannesburg regional management schools' council condemned plans by the National Education Co-ordinating Committee (NECC) to move black pupils to empty and under- utilised white schools in the PWV area. Council chairman Steve Ramoetsane said it had resolved to oppose plans by the NECC to use children as "cannon fodder". "As a body of biological parents in the true sense of the word, and non-aligned to any political organisation, we categorically condemn the methods used by the NECC and are not going to stand and watch while our children are being used." (The Star, July 22, 1991).

Management councils are recognised by the Government in terms of the regulations of the Department of Education and Training, and members are elected by parents in black schools. Mr. Ramoetsane said the regional council, which was composed of individual councils in Soweto and Alexandra schools, had held a parents' meeting in Johannesburg, where it had been decided to oppose plans by the NECC region to take over white schools. "I still believe that such action can only allow the Government to find an excuse to delay the negotiations process." (Weekly Mail, July 22, 1991). He accused the NECC of creating unnecessary hardships for underpaid parents who were struggling to make ends meet - "sacrificing their hard-earned money for the welfare of their children". He was equally disappointed by the involvement of the South African Democratic Teachers Union in the NECC-sponsored campaign.

The NECC region announced plans to move black pupils to about 50 unused white schools in the PWV area by August 5, 1991. NECC regional general-secretary Amon Msane said the organisation had failed to persuade the Government to allow black pupils from overcrowded schools to use empty white facilities. As a result, the NECC would go ahead to occupy these schools even if it meant breaking the law. Mr. Ramoetsane said the NECC would fail again in its attempts to occupy white schools because parents were against the move. In June the NECC had to call off its plans to move Alexandra pupils to Orange Grove Primary School after the police threatened to take action. Mr. Ramoetsane said the NECC had failed to carry out its treat, not because the police had stopped them, but because the parents had not allowed their children to go to school that day. Mr. Msane said the management councils had no support base in the black community and had lost their credibility since 1976.

Meanwhile, Acting Commissioner of Police Lieutenant- General Mulder van Eyk said: "In view of the increasing frequency of illegal seizure of both Government and private property, and of publicised campaigns by various organisations to do so, the SAP is committed to protecting the rights of all people of South Africa. The SAP is therefore ready and prepared to take action in terms of the law against those who violate the property rights of individuals or institutions." (The Star, July 22, 1991).

6.10   CONCLUSIONS

When South Africans tot up the enormous damage caused to this country through apartheid, any positive move away from this hideous policy, however small, can only be counted as a blessing. Just over 1 000 black pupils enrolled at 34 formerly white provincial schools in the Transvaal and by all accounts, it was a pretty normal day. A further 800 was admitted to classes in Natal. In terms of numbers, this was probably a drop in the ocean, but it certainly represented an important milestone in the move away from apartheid education. All right-thinking South Africans has come to realise the devastation caused by apartheid, and support the process towards the total integration of all schools. In such a climate reform, the call for the PAC and its student wing, Paso, on black pupils not to enrol at white schools was regarded by many as completely out of step.

EDUCATION AND RESPECT
FOR DIVERSITY OF CULTURES

7.1 INTRODUCTION

Historically plural societies have been created by conquest, political agreement and economic necessity. Traditionally educational policies represented the outcome of battles and conflicts of long ago and were formulated and implemented as a consequence or imposition. In Europe, for instance, the growth of nationalism was associated with the use of Christian denominationalism and the use of vernaculars as media of instruction. Somewhat later it involved the suppression of dialects or regional languages in favour of a national language. Economic incentives, political power and the schools helped to mould nation/states out of communities speaking different languages and holding different beliefs. Frequently the geographical boundaries which served to separate one community from another were ignored in creating a national territory. Examples of sovereign states created out of cultural diversity include Spain, Switzerland, the United Kingdom, Belgium, Yugoslavia and so on. Indeed the list could be extended greatly to include all those nations throughout Europe in which cultural diversity is found.

Another influence made plural societies the rule rather than the exception. The migration of the Europeans in the nineteenth century before and after the abolition of slavery created plural societies out of which nations have been forged. Since 1945 the movement of people from one country to another has been a vast and world-wide scale. Numbers and rates of entry have varied but relatively few industrialized countries have failed to admit on a temporary or permanent basis immigrants from a range of countries and possessing a range for professional and technical skills. Urbanism and urbanization also characterise plural societies. Population movements within and from outside sovereign states have helped to create, in centres of political and economic power, highly complex mini-societies in which social class, occupation and political expertise as criteria of diversity complicate any analysis. Well-known models suggest how in

North America and Europe as migrants move into the old city, the more prosperous old inhabitants flee to the suburbs and the inner city decays.

European association with Southern Africa began with the Portuguese circumnavigation of the Cape at the end of the 15th century (Davenport, 1977:18). After this a number of people of different nationalities from different parts of the world came to Southern Africa hence the birth of a plural South African society. The implications for education in the plural South African society is that the work of the school, as any experienced educator can testify, is constantly conducted in the midst of a conflicting network of social, economic and political pressures exerted directly or indirectly by the South Africa's interest groups. These organized groups are by no means a new phenomenon; nor is the concern of these groups with education of recent origin.

The school is highly significant in moulding the attitudes, loyalties, and beliefs which set the limits of social fundamental ends of education will not be, and should not be left to the exclusive determination of professional educators.

The South African Society cannot, nor can any society afford to be indifferent about the underlying and controlling conceptions which determine the education of its children. Hence no group of educators, or even the profession as a whole, can define the social purposes of education or shape its policies apart from a consideration of the ideals and aspirations of the public, upon which education is dependent for support. It is possible to argue that a considerable degree of educational autonomy is possible and desirable in a democracy. But it must be an autonomy within a broad framework of purposes approved by the public; and the grant of autonomy itself, as well as the uses which are made of it, must rest on the consent of the public.

Community participation in the shaping of educational policies means, in large measure, the participation of organized South Africa's group interests. It cannot be said that groups in a society have no legitimate interest in education. For education touches, at a thousand points, the web of interests, purposes, beliefs, and practices represented by these groups. To educate is, inevitably to build character; to build character is to shape the habits, attitudes, standards and values upon which, thought, judgement and choice are predicted. Hence neutrality is impossible; to teach at all is to support, in some measure, the ideals and beliefs which certain interest groups are seeking to promote, and to undermine, to some extent, the ideals and beliefs cherished by others. Obviously, therefore, every organized group in South Africa whether Black of White has an interest in education since its fortunes and its aspirations are inescapably affected by education. To question their right in education is to question their right to exist; and to question either their right to exist or their right to participate in the decisions which affect them is to deny the large section of the society any effective voice in the determination of public affairs.

In education, which is by far the most extensive of the socials services, each year in South Africa sees the rise of fresh enthusiasm: the devising of new remedies for old problems, the identification of new problems and the discarding of tried solutions. However, the tension between conformity and diversity is at its greatest.

7.2   SOUTH AFRICA'S PLURALITY PROBLEM

Before discussing South Africa's plurality problem, let us first look at what a plural society is. Triandis, in Madgil et al (ed, 1986:77) observes that pluralism, in contrast to monism:

> ... was first used by philosophers to deal with questions: 'How many things are there in the world?' and 'How many kinds of things are there in the world?' When translated to social issues these questions become: 'How many kinds of cultures can co-exist in a given society?'

Despite the fact that pluralism is the usual situation, the concept of pluralism thus plural society is not as familiar or as well defined as some other concepts which have application to social environment.

Plainly to talk of plurality is to talk of more than one of something. In social terms then pluralism refers to the variety of basic social groups that exist in a society. Two such groupings which have been found to be of great importance in schooling and level of educational attainment are those of ethnic and racial origin and of socio-economic status. These two groupings are frequently systematically related. If a person belongs to an ethnic or racial group other than the one which clearly predominates in the society, he is more likely than not to belong to a particular socio-economic category. This is often to be explained by the fact that membership of either group is likely once more to be systematically related to certain levels of educational attainment. Groupings in society are also associated with systems of belief, norms of behaviour and general ways of conduct. Hon-Chan Chai (1971:11) says that a more recent attempt at defining a plural society distinguished between cultural pluralism and social pluralism. He says:

> Cultural pluralism usually develops from the presence in a given society of several ethnic or racial groups with different cultural traditions. Social pluralism is found where the society is structurally divided into analogous and duplicatory but culturally similar groups of institutions and the corporate groups are differentiated on a basis

other than culture. (p.11)

Watson, (1980:79) lists the following as attributes typifying a plural society:

> ... the relative absence of a value consensus; therelative presence of conflict between major corporate groups; the relative autonomy between parts of the social system; the relative political domination by one of the corporate groups over the other; tension and racial conflict resulting from perceived rather than actual differences and a belief that prejudice and discrimination are exerted by the majority group against minorities.

Furnival, in Barth (ed, 1969:16) sees the plural society as:

... a poly-ethnic society integrated in the marked place, under the control of a state system dominated by one of the (ethnic) groups, but leaving large areas of cultural diversity in the religious and domestic sectors of activity.

In this definition the nation of the integrated poly- ethnicity becomes important although it may appear to be a contradiction in terms. Finally a plural society is a society with the following observable features:

-       the presence of ethnic cultural groups observable in all their demographic social and cultural manifestations;

-       the facts and effects of ethnic identity and a sense of community with no cultural or structural concomitants, i.e. the question of self-ascribed ethnicity.

When there is consideration of cultural pluralism in South Africa which is the mosaic of norms and values existing in her multi-nationalities the tension between conformity and diversity in education is at its peak. The description and analysis of a great variety of problems the plural South African society meets in providing plural education gives a hint at an inescapable conclusion - that the task may well be impossible. The journey towards a just society seems to be as rocky as ever. The plural South African society has its dominant ethnocultural group (The White minority group) which controls power over the access other ethnocultural groups have to social rewards and economic resources. Part of this control is exercised through education and in particular through the curriculum and provision. Education is an institutionalized way of formally transmitting the culture of a society. Schools and other enculturation agencies employ the curriculum as their main strategy for ordering the selection of knowledge for which they are responsible.

Among the many aspects of the aims of education which are considered, that of the selection process itself is crucial. It entails South Africa's education planners of various kinds coming to value-based decisions about the type of society which the education system serves. Some of these decisions take account of the empirical realities of the society; others are more ideological. All decisions inevitably involve control over the type of knowledge to be transmitted, to whom, under what conditions and so on. In short South Africa's education planners control power through the way they make knowledge accessible to children. Of which social and ethnic groups the children are deemed more "worthy" of receiving more knowledge, or receiving it under more favourable circumstances, is related to the way they see and view the place and status of these groups in their society. In South Africa the way is thus open for education planners to control the life chances of children from "unworthy" ethnic groups through the education system - a form of ethnic hegemony.

A society possessing a relatively homogeneous culture, with little variation of beliefs or practice, is likely to share the universal concern for social continuity. If that society is industrialized and democratic, it may also have commitment to social change. Its schools may seek to convey standards of accomplishments, ingenuity, diligence and sincerity beyond those to be found in the homes, offices and factories in the streets outside. But where a society has more heterogeneous culture as South Africa is and there is a variety of family types, religious and moral codes, even spoken languages, what then? Is the school to make provision for all these variations? Or, should it ignore them, and concentrate on its more conservative function, and seek assimilation? This is what this book is all about, exploring this issue with special reference to South Africa. Current debates about what education in the South African society ought to be seem so far not to have been productive in directing the course the education system should take. Studies indicate that there have always been opposing schools of thought. For instance, one school of thought advocates that education for Blacks and Whites, should be completely separate (separatism). Whereas this school of thought recognizes the existence of different groups it considers racial and cultural diversities to be a threat and not an asset. Another school of thought consists of two opposing extremes - one of which acknowledges racial diversities, but wish them to be removed so that there is complete cultural fusion (assimilation/melting pot theory); whilst the other is based on the principles of integration (cultural pluralism theory).

Consciousness of ethnic identity and awareness of the White minority status have been growing rapidly in South Africa. In as much as both these have been happening, the problems have been underscored by politically vocal and even violent protest. Deeper and more widespread problems underlie these violent surface signs and they recur in different forms. In the interpretation of the theme of education for cultural, pluralism, there is a recognition that cultural, linguistic, psychological and sociological factors are all closely connected. However language and culture are very strong. Language is not only a clearly "visible" identifier of many interest groups - more reliable, often than physical characteristics. It is also a vehicle by which human beings persuade, manipulate and exercise power over each other. Language competence and power are intimately connected.

Part of the problem also, is how far the language and cultural differences between the politically dominant minority group and the politically subservient majority group are viewed as deficits. Cultural relativists argue that one culture is not superior to another, nor one language richer, though a multi-lingual individual might be considered better equipped, for life in the modern world than a person who is limited to one language and culture. On this view the problem is not merely how to educate the politically subservient majority group to know about and adapt to the world of the politically dominant minority group, but also how to educate the minority in majority ways, culture and language, not just so that they can understand the problems of the disadvantaged, but because their education is otherwise incomplete. In other words the problem in South Africa is how all ethnic groups - dominant or subordinate, indigenous or immigrant, privileged or underprivileged - should be educated for a plural society.

There are problems in this standpoint, though it should first be noted that it is a welcome corrective to the ethnocentrism for centuries. However enlightened and well- informed teachers may be, however free of racial prejudice, however many second languages are on offer, however balanced the syllabuses taught, it takes more than verbal learning to shake unthinking egocentrism and ethnocentrism. Direct experience of living and learning with other ethnic groups may be a short-cut to greater awareness of other cultures and races, but unless the dominant group is physically displaced from its home ground its complacency is unlikely to be shaken.

Even the problem of deciding what language should be spoken and taught in schools presents intractable difficulties.

Today's South African children, black or white, live in a busy and hustling world worse of it all this life is lived in separation because of the laws of the country, hence limited chances to interact with and accept one another. South Africa is a country divided against itself in which racial goodwill and trust have rapidly dissipated. It is a country in which fear, hatred and bitterness are in danger of taking over. If this is the state of the South African nation, what then should be the aims and purposes of education under these circumstances? Firstly, the purposes of education must have as their concern the kind of people being produced by the educational process now and in the future. South Africa has a need of warm and compassionate and caring people, people who believe that to be different is not to be inferior, people who have realized that one may be different and equal at the same time. (See De Lange Report p208 (e)). Does South Africa's education measure up to this demand?

The aims and purposes of education should also be concerned with the kind of society that the young people are prepared for, what Immanuel Kant called "possibly improved condition of man in the future". Does any one seriously believe that the kind of society in the year 2000 in South Africa, at which point these black and white children now in school will be young adults, will not be very different from the one in which we live now.

A society in which there is recognition both of what is common and diverse is on the one hand a society in which people have greater freedom to follow their heritages, traditions and aspirations, but at the same time a society of greater unity, a greater oneness over the fundamentals of common humanity and common South Africanism. The problem indeed lies with the genuine difficulties for well intended politicians and educators to decide what policy is best, let alone how to implement it. This is the current problem for South Africa.

7.3   POST-APARTHEID AIMS OF EDUCATION

Redden and Ryan (1956:128) maintain that many answers have been given to the question, "What are the aims of education?" Some answers have been definite and of positive value; others have been exclusive, because they are based on false interpretations of man's nature, his final end, and the functions of the educative process. The diversity of answers has begotten uncertainty, confusion and bewilderment in education. They, however, functionally define aims of education, thus:

> Broadly speaking educational aims and objectives give a long range perspective and an overall sense of direction; but very practically they also determine where things should start at any given moment ...

This definition implies that educational aims are therefore both highly theoretical and extremely practical determiners of educational policy and practice. Hansen (1960:111) elaborates:

Every question of choice among educational practices, ways of teaching, kinds of curriculum, or specific classroom activities come down
ultimately to a question of educational aims.

The aims of education are the directions in which educators seek to guide the development of those under their care. Hansen (1985:134) claims that there is no better general definition of the aim of education than as a preparation for life. By this definition is meant of education as a preparation for every part of living. Phenix (1958:552) in analysing the nature of the aims of education contends that they can be looked at as directions (directions of growth); as goals (destination to be reached).

In the light of the already mentioned and analyzed concepts in aims of education the writer now wishes to turn to the concept of <u>post-apartheid education</u> and its aims. Unesco (1972) described the biggest threat to human education as follows:

> Education, being a sub-system of society necessarily reflects the main features of that society. It would be vain to hope for a rational, human education in an unjust society. Regimes based on authority from the top and obedience from the bottom cannot develop an education for freedom. An hour can one imagine a society woven out of privileges and discrimination developing a democratic education system.

This observation points to the very clear correlation between the demand for education for democracy in South Africa and the educational perspective of the international community. Van den Heever (1987:1) therefore defines post- apartheid education as that education

> ... which prepares people for total human liberation; one which helps people to be creative, to develop a critical mind, one that prepares people for full participation in all social,
> political or cultural spheres of society.

Thembela (Education Towards Post-Apartheid) qualifies the above definition comprehensively when he states that post- apartheid education is education which

> ... has as its aim the development of the whole person through the intellectual and physical, emotional and social, moral and spiritual development of a rational, responsible, humane and compassionate individual who, having formed his own convictions and, guided by them, is equipped and prepared to live as a reasonable citizen in South Africa capable of adapting and adjusting to a changing society.

Post-apartheid education presupposes as its end-products the following kind of adults:

-      warm, compassionate, caring people, liberated from fear and hate for whom life has sense and purpose;

-      thinking, critical people, capable of independent judgement and of coping with new ideas and changes; and

-      skilled, competent, knowledgeable people capable of coping in modern political economy in Africa and elsewhere, citizens who respect the rule of law, the democratic process, who in the end accepts that "above all nations stands humanity".

This means that post-apartheid education fosters a sense of nationhood and promotes national unity. It helps the youth to acquire this sense of nationhood by removing conflict which enables them to live together in harmony and to make a positive contribution to the national life.

Basic components of post-apartheid education are therefore, as follows:

-      equal provision of and access to education of all learners;

-      provision of facilities and opportunities for the training of teachers to meet the needs of a unitary education system;

-      provision of open-ended, non-racial public education in a common system which takes into account relevant differences;

-      the organization and administration of education should furnish opportunities for co-operation among all those concerned, i.e. teachers, pupils, authorities, private sector and the community at large;

- the devolution of management of all educational resources to the appropriate lowest level of authority;

- the recognition and encouragement of the value of non-formal education as a supplement to the formal system;

- child-centred system of formal education consciously seeking to uphold common values as well as seeking to cater for children's ability, interests and aptitudes.

The real object of post-apartheid education is therefore to give children resources that will endure as long as life endures; habits that time will ameliorate, not destroy; occupations that will render sickness tolerable, solitude pleasant, age vulnerable, life more dignified and useful and death less terrible.

7.4   RESPECT FOR DIVERSITY

During the past decades there has been a renewed interest in the role of education in culturally plural societies partly because education has often been used as a weapon for uniting different groups with a sense of nationhood, but largely because many ethnic groups in the called advanced countries have begun to demand their own identity in educational terms (ironically, in many developing countries, this is a battle that has already been engaged and frequently lost by smaller ethnic groups). A major part of the debate in this sub-section focuses on education as this key social institution is responsible for producing citizens on the one hand and individuals on the other. As future citizens, children must be quipped with whatever it takes to enable them to lead lives that are personally satisfying, provided it is not inimical to the lives of other individuals. Education, to achieve these twin aims is relatively straight forward when children come from backgrounds that are broadly similar in cultural and socio- economic composition. When these are dissimilar as does occur in societies that are plural, i.e. composed of a number of distinguishable cultural groups as is the case in South Africa, the pluralist dilemma affects education. Education has cultural foundations. The institution of education is closely related to the culture of the society, and this relationship is now fully recognized and accepted by most cultural anthropologists. Culture is taken to exist as part of socio-culture system and can be identified and analyzed. The education system in South Africa should develop within the premises that people belong to and live in groups. They do not live in or belong to culture. People are born into a social group and inherit its culture. They also play their part in modifying and adopting the culture, so that it is not a static feature of a society, but is constantly changing in response to the circumstances in which the society finds itself. The importance of culture rests on what it is for. Culture may be seen as a form of problem-solving device or survival programme which enables a social group to cope with problems of living within its environment.

A related perspective, emerging among some anthropologists of education, is to see culture in terms of knowledge, meanings and conceptions, for instance Goodenough, in Hynes (ed, 1964:36) maintains:

> A society's culture consists of whatever it is one has to know or believe in order to operate in a manner acceptable to its members ... Culture, being what people have to learn as distinct from their biological heritage must consist of the end product of the end product of learning: knowledge, in the most general, if relative, sense of term.

Dobert, in Roberts & Akinsanya (eds, 1976:207) takes an almost cybernetic systems theory view:

Culture is a system for mapping information from the environment. This information is stored in shared conceptual interaction and in patterns social interaction and in patterns for getting a living.

The idea that culture involves knowledge and needs to be learned

The idea that culture involves knowledge and needs to be learned relates to the environment in which a group finds itself, and is also a form of perpetual "template". It also makes a definition that endeavours to incorporate all of these ideas useful in the context of an analysis of education. However, it is also important to draw attention to the mechanism or mode through which culture is transmitted, and also to take into account the mutability of culture in response to a social group's changing definitions of its environment and survival problems.

The main goal and significance of the analysis that has been done lies in the explicit exposition that prejudice, racism, and discrimination are consequent outcomes of South African whites' failure to realize fully the potential worth that lies in diversity. Respect for diversity is fundamental for without it all those who are different are excluded from full participation in the society. The dominant white group as well as the subordinate Black group in South Africa have to believe and see the value of diversity if there is to be self-respect and respect for others as well. All groups, Black or White have to be invited to join in the mainstream of the South African nation's life and culture.

A pluralistic society should be seen as compatible with the nation's highest ideals. To the extent that pluralism is realized, all people may retain a healthy ethnic pride, an abiding sense of their own culture and respect for, and appreciation of, the people and individuals from ethnically and culturally different heritages. The fact that this condition has not been fully realized South Africa is painfully obvious. One is often struck by the dichotomy found in some sections of the South African society where people from a dominant white cultural group have positive attitudes toward an individual from another culture but express intolerance for that culture as a whole; or the converse dichotomy in other sections where some people from the dominant white culture group manifest the opposite position and accept another ethnic people as a group but reject them as the individuals.

The thrust of this analysis, lies in the development and commitment by the South African society to the principle that to be different is not to be inferior, that one may be different and equal at the same time. The reality of the situation is that many persons have until the present viewed plural societies a s mono-cultural or uni-cultural, and this perspective has created insensitivity to the many cultures which have built plural nations and have as much still to offer. As a result the contributions of many Black subordinate groups in South Africa have been treated as "non-facts" and these achievements have either been excluded from the society's history and textbooks or twisted. Cultural differences have either been de-emphasized or over-emphasized in the name of narrow and parochial nationalism. Instead the theme of the potential that springs from diversity might have been used as a stronger bond than does spurious uniformity. As a result there is an absence in schools of an understanding of cultural pluralism and there is a dearth of material for use by teachers and students alike to build that understanding.

If there is to be respect for diversity in South Africa, the following developments must immediately be encouraged:

- There must be a development of a respect for, and an appreciation of diversity in order to stamp out fears, prejudice an discrimination which stem from inadequate understanding of the positive values of difference, of diversity and of pluralism. How does this development take root? Firstly, there must be movement in South Africa towards reduction of discrimination against diverse cultural groups and provision of equal educational opportunities in order to present all students with cultural alternatives. This can be done by creation of a school atmosphere with positive institutional norms towards diverse cultural groups.

- Secondly, there must be reduction of discrimination against ethnic groups and a provision for all pupils with equal opportunities, and also the reduction of ethnic isolation and encapsulation. This can be affected through the modification of the total school environment to make it reflective of the lives within the society.

- Thirdly, students must be helped to develop valid concepts, generalizations and theories about ethnic groups in this plural society, to clarify their attitudes towards them, and to learn how to make efforts to eliminate racial and ethnic problems within the entire society.

- Students must also be helped to develop ethnic literacy. These two issues may be attained through the modification of course objectives, teaching strategies, materials, and evaluation strategies so that they include content and information about ethnic groups in the society. These arguments will be developed later on in this study.

7.5   CONCLUSION

The essence as well as the complexity of the pluralist dilemma may now be appreciated. From the point of view of adult members of ethnic groups within a pluralist society, programmes of 'multi-cultural' education that cater for their life-styles and culture maintenance have an obvious attraction, which might even be shared by some of their children. However, the components that make up these programmes, their place in the school curriculum, and the way that curriculum is devised provide almost unlimited opportunity for the dominant education planners to exercise hegemony over the life chances of children from specific ethnic backgrounds. There is a corollary to this in the neglect of or much less emphasis placed on programmes that might improve the life chances of children from these ethnic backgrounds. Not only do these run counter to the dominant group's goal of maintaining ethnic hegemony, but in any case they are very difficult to effect, and may have little success in the final analysis as life chances are determined by political, structural, economic and historical forces within society. These cannot be greatly altered by schooling and education, although educational programmes that heighten the consciousness of children and increase their sense of power and social competence may increase their potential capacity to contribute to reforming society when they are adults.

Even to encourage the preservation and transmission of ethnic life-styles, languages, traditions and other aspects of the heritage risks placing education planners in a tricky situation. Such aspects can function to heighten ethnic identity, group cohesion, and politicise ethnic groups' aspirations to the point where they may try to establish separate institutions and live as separate ethno-cultural groups within the society in the true sense of the model of cultural pluralism proposed by Despres (1968). Idealism of this kind is as misplaced as many programmes of multi- cultural education, as control over the central resources of the state is in the hands of the Minister of Finance, and must stay there for the benefit of the majority. Of necessity, ethnic groups must strive within the system to get their share of these resources, through the rules of the game set down, unless they can change them by political processes. Is there a model that can conceptualise these issues and avoid the trap of reification, or of degenerating into more myth?

On the other hand pluralism is the development of interdependence, appreciation and the skills to interact intimately with persons from other cultures. Current legislation and practice of separation in South Africa based on legal framework, overstress individual differences and this is as dangerous as eliminating cultural differences. This book intends proposing ways of shifting from this perspective to one that provides for a marriage of the legal framework with the understanding of social psychology principles. Rather than separation as conceived in South Africa, which involves the stress on cultural structural differences, this book advocates for additive multi- culturalism where people learn to be effective and to appreciate others who are different in culture. Additive multi-culturalism is by its very nature something that needs to be instilled in the white ruling minority in South Africa rather than the subordinate Black majority of the population. As more members of the subordinate majority group learn to integrate in jobs and other spheres the ruling minority must learn to relate to the subordinate majority with a perspective of additive multi-culturalism. Within that framework and over a period of many years, there should be the development of pluralism that given self- respect to all, appreciation of cultural differences and social skills leading to interpersonal relationships with more rewards than costs. Ignorance of multi-culturalism is as much a deficiency of the South African educational system today as in ignorance of history or geography.

THE EDUCATION RENEWAL STRATEGY -
A FURTHER PLOY TO KEEP
WHITE SCHOOLS WHITE

8.1 INTRODUCTION

In May 1990 the Minister of National Education announced the development of an Education Renewal Strategy (ERS) for education in South Africa. This strategy was to be developed in conjunction with the Ministers of departments of State responsible for education and was to be carried out under the auspices of the Committee of Heads of Education Departments (CHED). A target date of one year was set for the finalisation of this strategy, which would seek short and medium term managerial solutions for some of the most pressing problems in education.

A number of factors gave rise to the ERS initiative. The first can be traced back to the development of the so- called ten-year plan announced by the Minister of National Education in 1986. Against the background of an annual increase in learner numbers in the education system of approximately 4,4 % at that time, this plan was based on an annual real increase in the education budget of 4,1 % and aimed at achieving full implementation of the subsidy formula for the college and school related education sector with equal funding levels for the various education departments.

Instead of the education budget increasing annually in real terms since 1986, the very low economic growth rate, coupled to the State's commitment to curtail public expenditure, actually led to a decrease in real terms in the education budget. This led to the Minister of National Education's announcement in May 1989 that the ten- year plan was to be shelved, at least for the time being, and that alternative solutions to the problem of funding an expanding education system would have to be found. In this regard the Cabinet subsequently, in December 1989, requested "that the Minister of National Education obtain the co-operation of his education colleagues regarding a co-ordinated approach towards rationalisation in education".

Secondly, the Committee of Education Ministers (CEM) and the Committee of Heads of Education Departments (CHED) had since their inception in 1984 regularly considered a variety of problems and difficulties encountered in education. Various extensive and sophisticated information systems developed by the Department of National Education proved invaluable in this regard. From the information systems it was possible to make a regular analysis of the condition of the education system, and from these analyses a number of distinct issues were identified which needed to be addressed.

A third factor leading to the launching of the ERS initiative was the continued criticism of the education system in terms of which the following are alleged to be the defects :

-       The present education model enjoys little support from the majority of South Africans because of its racial base, as expressed in separate education departments for the various population groups.

-       Educational programmes are not sufficiently relevant for both learners and eventual employers and do not sufficiently take into account the economic and personpower needs of the country.

-       Education is a "closed shop operation" and does not sufficiently allow for inputs from the various sectors in society which in some way or another are stakeholders in education.

-       The structural changes effected since the inception of an own/general affairs basis in education in 1984 have not solved the problem of what is perceived as a bloated educational bureaucracy.

-       Education has not proposed solutions to the problem of accommodating ever increasing numbers of pupils and students during the next few decades and how it intends to provide better and more extensive education within the same broad budgetary allocation for education.

- The existing patterns of financing education are not equitable in respect of the various population groups, and progress made towards creating equal education opportunities for all learners has been insufficient.

- In some cases fixed assets are being under-utilised whilst in other cases sever overcrowding exists.

A fourth, and more general, factor stems from the fact that South Africa encompasses both developed and developing communities.

Education systems in developing countries are characterized by a number of traits. The most important area: low but increasing participation rates, high drop- out rates, a lack of suitably qualified teachers, unequal access to educational opportunities, overcrowding of facilities and the absence of a culture of learning. In all developing countries the provision of education sooner or later creates difficulties for the governments concerned. Developing communities invariably see education as the means to a higher standard of living and consequently such countries as a rule have to contend with strong social, economic and political demands for education of a high quality. Furthermore, in such countries a developed and skilled labour force is essential for economic development, which adds to the demand for education. A meaningful extension of the base of political participation in such countries also demands and educated population.

Owing to the composition of populations in developing countries one finds, moreover, that one the average one adult assumes responsibility for two dependents, whereas in developed countries two adults normally accept responsibility for one dependent. This is one of the factors that make the establishment of a very necessary sound school and learning tradition difficult in developing countries.

The state, on the other hand, usually lacks the resources to meet these demands satisfactory. In addition to this, the period before an investment in education yields appreciable outcomes in terms of contributions to increasing the wealth of a country, is long. Furthermore, the state's inability to meet the demands for education in such countries often heightens frustration and can easily lead to social disturbances. In South Africa, reconciling the above-mentioned forces necessitates fundamental renewal of the education system to prevent the country from ending up in a never-ending spiral of poverty, frustration and unfulfilled expectations.

Against this background solutions will in the first place have to be found through which the education system will be acceptable to the majority of South Africans and will thus enjoy their understanding and support, and through which equal educational opportunities for all entrants to our education system can be achieved. Secondly, education will, to a great extent than is already the case, have to equip learners to make a meaningful contribution to economic growth in South Africa. Given the country's limited financial resources and the ever-increasing number of learners in the education system, structural changes in education will have to be introduced to make the provision of education more affordable. This has to be done without compromising existing high educational standards.

The Education Ministers therefore requested the CHED to carry out the development of the ERS by means of working groups composed of experts within the various education departments, from universities, technikons, the organised teaching profession and in some cases other departments of State and the private sector. The various working groups are listed in Appendix 1. Furthermore, in announcing the ERS the Minister of National Education requested submissions on the matters to be investigated from any interested person or body. More than 200 submissions were received from a wide spectrum of stakeholders in education. These submissions were all evaluated and channelled to the various working groups for consideration.

The CHED in turn established an Integrating Committee (ICOM) to evaluate the various briefs of the working groups, to identify additional matters requiring investigation, to evaluate the different memoranda of the working groups and to integrate these memoranda into a coherent management strategy. This Committee consisted of the chairpersons of the various groups, together with representation from the universities, technikons, private sector, the organised teaching profession and the Universities and Technikons Advisory Council. The reports by the various working groups contain detailed information which cannot be accommodated in the publication of this size.

8.2   A BOAT WITH TOO MANY HOLES

The crisis in black education which ignited the 1976 student rebellion has degenerated into nothing less than a national disaster. The critical issues in black education in 1976 - the attempts to force high school scholars to learn through the medium of Afrikaans and the inferior quality of education - were both susceptible to being reformed. But since then, black education has experienced "10 years of continued crisis" which, accumulatively, has transformed severe but manageable problems into a fully- fledged national disaster. Black children of school-going age not attending school outnumber those in school, 8 million against 7 million. And of the some 200 000 black students who sat matric in 1990, a miniscule 12 obtained an A-level pass in mathematics. Many of the 8 million youngsters outside the school system have become alienated. They are "outsiders" teetering on the verge of, if already falling into, the abyss of iconoclasm and nihilism. Some dub themselves "comrades". But their political affiliations are often shallow. Their political zealotry can easily degenerate into banditry. They are a problem to President de Klerk's white-controlled reformist regime and to the propertied classes which support it. But they are simultaneously a potential problem to a future black government.

The 8 million mentioned can be divided into three broad categories: those who have little or no formal education and who are illiterate and innumerate; those who dropped out after six or seven years at school;

and those who have had some secondary school education but who have no certificates to show achievement. The secondary school dropouts have been poignantly described by the educationist Ken Hartshorne: "For many of these unsuccessful school leavers, with little or no prospect of obtaining satisfying job or employment at all, their outlets are the streets. Rejected by the education system, they have become leaders of the street children." (The Star, June 15, 1991).

His calculations show that only 10 of every 100 school children who enrol in Grade 1 reach Std 10 (and of those only half end up with the appropriate certificate). Dr. Hartshorne's figures, made five years ago, have since been superseded. New statistics show a small improvement in retention rates. According to the Education Renewal Strategy (ERS) discussion document, the number of the black pupils who reach Std 10 is now 16 for every 100 enrolled in Grade 1. But, as the ERS document reflects, the drop out rate remains "inordinately high". Another pointer to the calamitous situation in black education are the disastrous matric results: in 1990 the pass rate was barely over 34 percent, compared to 87,2 percent in 1976.

The declining proportion of black matric candidates who pass - the overwhelming majority with secondary leaving rather than matric exemption certificates - is part of an established pattern and not just a freak result. Pass rates for 1978 and 1984 offer a broader chronological background against which to view the 1976 and 1990 results: 1978 - 76 percent; 1984 - 49 percent. These developments provide the context for the contention that disaster is not an inappropriate word with which to describe the situation in black education. It explains and motivates the call for an education policy of national reconstruction rather than a "renewal strategy". This also calls for a Bill of Education Rights to specifically address the needs of the vast number of people who, for one reason or another, are excluded from the education system. There is a realization that there is an element of irony, perhaps even tragic irony, in the situation. The "national disaster" has occurred in spite of increased expenditure on black education and concomitant improvements in some spheres.

To cite figures for the Department of Education and Training (DET), which is responsible for education of blacks living outside the tribal states: in 1976-77 the DET budget was R82 million in 1990-91 it was R3 300 million. In 1976 there were less than 155 000 pupils in secondary schools, by 1990 the number had grown to just under 570 000; in 1976 there were only 185 secondary schools, in 1990 there were more than 980. Similar trends are reflected in the "homeland" education departments which control education in the tribal territories. The tale of black education, it must be emphasised, is not without successes. They are ably summarised by Monica Bot in the Institute of Race Relations' publication "Social and Economic Update 13". To mention a few: spending on black education rose from R3,4 billion in 1987-88 to R5,2 billion in 1989-90, an increase of 53 percent against an increase of 32 percent on white education over the same period; consequently the gap between per capita expenditure on white and black pupils dropped from more than 5-to-1 to 4-to-1. Ms. Bot writes that there has been a "substantial improvement" in the proportion of black teachers with the officially required minimum qualification of Std 10 and a three-year teaching training certificate.

Between 1987 and 1989 it more than doubled from 14 to 29 percent. There are improvements of different kind. Black education in South Africa is no longer run by insensitive, arrogant whites who think they know what is good for blacks. One thinks here of Andries Treurnicht in 1976 when he was the Deputy Minister of Bantu Education. Faced with signs of revolt against the attempt to force black high school pupils to learn through the medium of Afrikaans and English on a 50-50 basis, Dr. Treurnicht declared, as Alan Brooks and Jeremy Brickhall recall in their penetrating analysis of the student revolt: "In the white area of South Africa, where the Government pays, it is certainly our right to decide on the language division." (The Star, June 15, 1991). But, it seems, black education is like a boat with too many holes to plug: the moment one leak is mended another two spout vigorously and the boat continues to sink.

Reading through the 104-page ERS discussion document, one finds another image coming to mind: running on a treadmill with prodigious energy but little or no forward movement. "From 1987 to 1990 the total education budget (for all races) increased by 57 percent," the document says. (p.39) But, it adds, taking the increasing cost of education into account, the real increase was only 6 percent. Against that the increased enrolment of pupils requires a 14 percent annual increase in the education budget merely to keep pace. Another example relates to the improved retention or lower drop-out rate. Reflecting on 1990 disastrous matric results, the ESP discussion document says: "Nearly half of the pupils who wrote the examination only managed an aggregate mark of 29 percent or less." (p.33) It then ponders on the cause and asks "whether these pupils did not proceed through the education system virtually unchecked, only to fail the final examination." (p36) If so, it concludes that the higher retention rate may be achieved by automatic promotion of pupils, hardly a sound pedagogical principle. Analysing pre-matriculation and matric pass rates - 85 percent in Std 5 and 62 percent in Std 9 as against 34 percent in matric - the ERS document suggests strongly that pupils are routinely passed before matric, irrespective of their ability to advance. The problems which lie ahead are immense: the number of children clamouring for education is increasing, particularly in the tribal homelands, where enrolment increases by 6,6 percent a year.

The cost of meeting their demands is growing proportionately. The economy, however, is stagnant. Expenditure on education already accounts for a fifth of the budget, well above that of most countries. Perhaps one can end on a hopeful note. The disaster is not merely a problem for the De Klerk administration or the DET or the "homeland" education departments. It is a major concern for the whole of South Africa, including the potential heirs to power in the extra-parliamentary opposition forces. No one gains by exploiting the disaster politically. It is truly a national challenge requiring a national solution in which all South Africans have a vested interest.

8.3   WHERE DO THE CHILDREN FIGURE?

Reading the report of the Education Renewal Strategy (ERS) committee, something felt missing. Rereading it, "seven managerial fields were explored". The missing aspect was: children. The fields explored were "systems affairs, programme affairs, client affairs (meaning the personpower needs of the country), service dispensations, fixed assets, financing of education, and information systems. But there's no feeling that we're discussing how children can be given a better deal - decent buildings, enough desk space and books, places to work and to play. It is sad that after the comprehensive De Lange investigation and report in 1981 another investigation was needed to "identify major problem areas and obtain input" But then the 1980's were largely occupied by tricameral experiment which brought "own affairs" education and, while excluding most of the people, saw new levels of education being created as well as labour protests and other upheavals. These destabilised black education so gravely that it has not yet recovered. Some schools are out of control. These will not recover until the teaching profession and the students accept that learning in classrooms must become exempt from "protest action". Such action must happen only outside pupil learning time, otherwise "the doors of learning and culture" will not open as they should. It is known that the gravest problem is that "State education for black and 'coloured' pupils has lost credibility with the people concerned". To regain credibility, improvements are not enough. There must be visible change towards shared policy control at the centre; black educators and public figures must have a share in determining both policies and priorities. If the new Department of National Education had some really senior officials other than white, this might help. Well, in 1991 the ERS integrating committee - which presumably decided what to include and what to omit from the 20 work group reports - has no women on it, no men other than white and nearly all of them are Afrikaans-speaking. Where is the "shared policy control at the centre"?

The committee, in the spirit of current policies, recommends "race should not feature in structuring the provision of education in ... future ... and justice in opportunities must be ensured". (p.47) But it also explains that exploding pupil numbers and the state of the economy make State funding problematic; one of its thrusts is cutting costs where this seems justifiable. One can accept many, though not all, recommendations in this regard:

-     Reduced statutory building norms for schools. We are told these currently cost R2 million each. Quite specific recommendations are made which should be carried out at once.

-     Use of under-used facilities "optimally for educational purposes ... as far as practically possible".

-     Rationalise overlapping university and technikon courses.

-     Use spare capacity in teacher training colleges, possibly for bridging (academic support) programmes.

-     Increase student-lecturer ratios in teacher training colleges, which can be done without impairing efficiency.

-     Do the same in education departments where the public-teacher ratio is way below the nationally accepted 1:30 norm.

These make good sense, though there is some doubt whether the State will show the political will needed to carry them out. Redistributing cash, teachers, buildings, resources more fairly will be unpopular with white voters. The idea for making parents pay a greater share of education costs are more problematical for this benefits the children of the well-to-do. If the wealthy "augment teachers' salaries" the best teachers won't be attracted to the schools of the disadvantaged. This already happens. It is known. Setting limits to compulsory attendance possibly after seven years' schooling is hardly just when whites have had compulsory schooling up to age 14 since 1913 (later extended to 16). We should not set a "set number of years" but an age limit to start with - perhaps 14. But this needs to be worked through with parent and political structures, and with the teaching profession. Those who earn money can be expected to "bear an increasing share of the cost associated with their schooling", but one can hardly apply this to youngsters of 13 ... though the ERS document says "the period should be extended as soon as circumstances permit".

There are excellent proposals about community learning centres.

These have been made before, but have not "take off". Political responsibility for education at both national and regional level is recommended, though the committee speaks of "various", not "non-racial", regional education departments. Regarding eight years' teaching experience as a form of exemption from writing Std 10 exams is a sound idea (for which there are certain legal precedents). The promotion of national unity as a prime goal is welcome, though it must be firmly put above "allowing for the accommodation of diversity (religion, language, culture)". To promote this, it's high time we trained teachers from different backgrounds together, so that they learn to appreciate "other" cultures. There is no space here to discuss other sections, for example on technology, universities, etc. The major complaint is that the document says nothing about how we must move to achieve equal educational opportunities. In all homelands, parents still have to find the money for building schools (they get half back from the government after the completion of the building, though they often have to wait a long time for this). For more than 20 years, the DET has accepted responsibility for building schools, but only 2 million of the 7 million African pupils at school are cared for by the DET.

Some 3 million are in "SGT" (self-governing territories) schools and a further 2 million in independent homelands schools (which, alas, don't figure in the ERS, except in Std 10 exam statistics). Because of this extra backlog, there's a very severe shortage of desks and rooms in homeland schools which is much worse than in DET ones. More than a year ago we saw a KwaZulu primary school in which 1 600 pupils had two toilets, and shared 26 classrooms - it has not changed since then. We need to implement a minimum entitlement per child - irrespective of area, sex, "race", language, religion or level of parental support - to his/her own desk (or sharing a double desk with ONE classmate) in a classroom with unbroken windows and enough light and heat to be able to learn in comfort - and with proper stationery and textbook supply. Is this beyond the state's capacity? One welcome the idea of including a pre-school year in the State system, though experience leads one to state that this must not be telescoped into the beginners' year, for then the pre-school content isn't handled properly. At least the critical importance of pre-primary education is accepted.

Proposals for distance education at this level through parent involvement are interesting and commendable but, with few homes having electricity (relatively speaking) and many mothers illiterate, progress would be slow.

Other uses of distance learning are more promising, as are proposals about school management councils, student loan schemes (why only at tertiary level if secondary schooling will not be fully funded by the State?) and the recognition that "progress made towards creating equal educational opportunity for all learners has been insufficient". It is this problem that needs to be addressed: HOW to get a desk for each child, and a well-motivated teacher, and decent education resources? The shocking inefficiency of much of the educational "delivery system" isn't addressed (textbooks, desks, correct pay cheques on time for all staff each month, building maintenance, and much else). To achieve a little more "justice in educational opportunities" there is also a need to provide school feeling at least for the most disadvantaged, and transport subsidies for pupils other than whites (who have them now) where needed.

These two items would cost relatively little - the committee rightly reminds that 75 percent and more of education spending goes on teachers' salaries - but they would demonstrate that there is seriousness about giving all children a fair chance to profit by their schooling, and to enjoy it. Learning should be fun for inquisitive young people. Many would disagree with some of the assumptions and reasoning in the (weighty) introduction, and with other items, but one welcomes the open-ended nature of the "discussion document". There is need to involve political and educational interest groups, including student structures, in the further discussion that's foreseen even at the cost of accepting their preconditions. While that happens let the "seven managerial fields" produce some visible improvements NOW in the "worst" schools and thus begin to restore faith in our education systems.

8.4   EDUCATION RENEWAL STRATEGY PLAN DOES NOT PASS THE TEST

The Education Renewal Strategy for the first time indicates a government commitment to seriously redress South Africa's education crisis, but falls far short of expectations for radical restructuring. Essentially the document shirks the resounding call for a single and unitary education department, proposing instead a central policy unit - much like the present Department of National Education (DNE) - and relatively autonomous regional bodies and school management councils, on the lowest tier, with power to decide on admissions. The central department will take on the functions of the present DNE: financing, conditions of service and professional registration of educators, and the norms and standards of syllabi, exams and certification. But it is unclear who will handle other critical issues. "Race" has been abandoned as the corner-stone of apartheid education, but the new decentralised model allows for classroom composition to be determined by "cultural and language diversity". "If parents want white-only education, it remains a possibility," National Education Department director-general Johan Garbers acknowledged. Multiculturalism cannot be denied, but education can play a critical role in forging a national culture in South Africa. Of course, the ERS must be seen in the context of the fact that it does not have a financial plan and cannot effect constitutional changes. The age-old issue of resources and funding - cited as a red herring by some - remains untouched. Educational changes, under this model, will have to fall within the present 19 percent allocation of the national budget. And the report acknowledges that, although government funding for education increased by 57 percent from 1987 to 1990, growing pupil numbers mean this represents a decrease of six percent in real terms.

All of its 68 recommendations pend constitutional debate, although it is likely that the government will view them favourably. But the National Education Co-ordinating Committee (NECC) - and other players active in the field at a grassroots level - have slammed the document for failing to transform the quality of education currently provided. "Nowhere does the ERS proposal refer to a plan to address the historical imbalances in the provision and distribution of textbooks, classrooms, teachers, racial budgetary allocations, white schools and private schools". (Weekly Mail, June 1991). Garbers is humble in his approach. All "stakeholders" were invited to participate in the drafting, but only 200 responses were received. Now it's an open discussion document, and they are hoping for feedback from all quarters. The Joint Working Group on Education - which comprises delegations of government and educationist led by the African National Congress and has an almost parallel brief - has been advised of the recommendations, but has not commented. Duplication appears unnecessary. The government, it appears, is once again playing both referee and player in policy-making for a "new South Africa". Some strides have been made towards addressing the country's despicable track record in providing quality education for all its citizens. And the ambit of the document is very broad. It is tragic though the learning in the 1980's had to be sacrificed via the "own affairs" model, which caused massive destabilisation and disillusionment. If only the powers-that-be had not chosen to reject the 1979 proposal of the De Lange Commission for a single education department. Now, it may still be too little, too late.

Black education may, for the first time, be compulsory for the first seven years. Three years of junior primary and four years' senior primary schooling are envisaged, with a more uniform curriculum than the present one and an emphasis on general formative education. But this is far from ideal. "Yet again, the rich will get general education and continue to dominate the economic sphere, while the poor will leave school young and enter into the vocationally orientated streams paid for by the private sector, or underfunded by the state," said the NECC in its statement. (The Weekly Mail, June 7-13, 1991). The large number of "over-age" pupils in classrooms at present appear to be left out of the equation. And clients of higher schooling will be encouraged to pay their way. This, as well as the general trend towards decentralisation - which makes management councils responsible for financing electricity, water, sanitation and sewerage at schools where the state cannot provide - indicates that the government intends absolving itself of very basic obligations. Decentralisation is the optimum strategy to "eliminate bureaucratic inertia and encourage community involvement", the ERS says, but the NECC counters that it in no way reflects "the people's demands for empowerment and democratic control".

Growth in learner numbers is regarded as central to the crisis - an overall annual average of 4,3 percent is cited at colleges and schools for the past five years. The number of senior certificates awarded to Africans has escalated from 20 to 562 in 1980 to 175 963 in 1990. To address this glut of pupils with little hope of further education as well as the "lost generation" of marginalised youth, illiterate or semi-literate adults and workers who have exhausted accessible educational opportunities, the ERS proposes a new concept called "Edukons", greater linkage between formal and informal systems, and extensive distance education. Creative use of print and audio-visual media (like the SABC) is proposed in providing distance learning for the illiterate, pre-schoolers, under- qualified teachers and those at secondary school. The side-stepping of on-the-job training for teachers is, of course, potentially dangerous. For school-going learners, a "school of the air" is envisaged in the long-term, and for early childhood American models are regarded as worth emulating to enhance school readiness. Qualification structures are proposed for literacy and vocational training - a very healthy development but one which needs to be much more refined. There are no commitment though to a general education component in skills training, which the trade union movement demands. Provision is made for the transfer of under-utilised schools to other departments for educational purposes and some technical colleges, in particular, could be used as centres for advanced education.

Universities are encouraged to increase standards for admission in certain fields "in the light of the cost of unsuccessful studies to the country and personpower needs". Along with technikons, they should also consider setting intake limits. Because the recent annual rise in study fees at these institutions has been far above the rate of inflation, creating a huge financial squeeze for students, guarantee loan funds are suggested to alleviate the crisis. The Independent Development Trust has been approached to provide such funds. Pre-primary education - for which no general policy exists - was once again left out in the cold. The ERS did recommend though, that the SA Council for Education development a national strategy and possibly use the first school year as a bridging year to be integrated in the initial seven years. A report on revised curricula will be made shortly but, said Garber, these are only likely to see the light of day in classrooms in 1994-95, "with plain sailing". There is a commitment though to "carefully evaluating all subjects as to relevancy and application to the real-life world". Of course, designing course content is an ideologically- loaded and highly subjective exercise, and the nature of what comes forth will depend on who participates in this crucial process. The implications of the ERS are far- reaching, but if it is not accredited basic legitimacy by those on the ground to whom it is handed down, it will remain a paper tiger with little real impact.

8.5 PLOT TO KEEP SCHOOLS WHITE

The Government launched a secret plan to ensure that most white schools remain mainly white without any statutory race bars. This has been disclosed by informed parliamentarians who have received an insight into the Government's strategy. The plan, which has already been put into action, is to close under-utilised white schools, effectively cramming white pupils into the remaining white schools. These remaining white schools are filling up rapidly, leaving little surplus space for children of other races.

The plan is that when "own affairs" education is finally abolished there will be few desks available at most white schools for other children. White own affairs educations Minister Piet Clase has drawn most of the political flak for the recent closure of a large number of white schools and five teacher-training colleges. It is understood he is resentful about being made to look like the "bad guy" of the Government and becoming the main scapegoat for Government policy. The Government has already responded to signals from Mr. Clase to take the pressure off him by broadening responsibility for the policy - it has been vigorously defended by other Ministers, including Stoffel van der Merwe, the Minister of Education and Training.

Since schools still give preference to children from nearby areas, the effect of the Government plan is to further limit space for children from other race groups, most of whom live in other suburbs - the legacy of the Group Areas Act which was repealed this month. Government believes this strategy will ensure that formerly whites-only schools, including those which have already become non-racial by adopting the Model B option, will tend to retain their previous characters. The plan is aimed at preventing white children becoming a minority in previously white schools and to make it difficult, in practice, for large numbers of other children to find accommodation in these schools.

It is being implemented as a prelude to the final lifting of racial barriers in schools, which has become inevitable following the repeal of the Population Registration Act as newly born children are no longer classified by race. The recently-released Education Renewal Strategy commissioned by the Government recommended non-racial education, but stated it was "equally important that adequate and satisfactory allowance be made for the accommodation of diversity (such as language religion or culture)." The State President F.W. de Klerk said that in a new constitutional dispensation community rights would be safe- guarded, including "community-orientated education".

The secret Government plan has been resolved as pupils from the Skeen Combined School in Alexandra plan to occupy the empty Orange Grove Primary School to spotlight their plight. While the Alexandra school is badly overcrowded, the school in Orange Grove, a few kilometres away, has been empty since the beginning of the year, 1991. Mr. Clase launched the Government strategy by announcing the closing of a number of under-used white schools - including nearly 30 in Natal - as well as the closure of five white teacher-training colleges. While some of these closed schools near black areas will be transferred to the Department of Education and Training, the rest will be closed. Government believes that large numbers of black pupils bused into largely white suburbs to fill such schools would result in friction. In addition Government spokesman say that annual salaries at a school are the main expense, rather than buildings. Closing white schools and laying off teachers will make more money available for black education, they say. But Democratic Party education spokesman Roger Burrows insists under- utilised white schools should be opened to all races, rather than close them and retrench hundreds of teachers.

8.6   GOVERNMENT ARITHMETIC ON TEACHERS IS PUZZLING

At least 65 000 more teachers are required if the Government is to implement its compulsory education strategy - but there is no money to train or appoint anything like this number in the foreseeable future. At the same time the Government is being slammed by its own traditionally supportive press for closing down schools and colleges of education at a time when these facilities should be used to the maximum to meet the crisis in black education.

Roger Burrows, the DP's education spokesman this week said: "The Minister of Education and Training (Stoffel van der Merwe) must be challenged regarding his nonsensical statements ... he has said he has enough teachers and more teacher training facilities are not needed. He said he cannot even employ the persons his department has trained. But he has also conceded that the teacher-pupil ratio in his department has progressed. He clearly agreed he needs more, not fewer teachers." (Sunday Star, June 16, 1991). To reach the officially approved ratio of one teacher to 30 pupils Mr. Van der Merwe's department would need 13 000.

He estimated that at present here we have two million children between the ages of six and 13 who were not in school and another 65 000 teachers, at least, would be required to teach them. He called for every college of education to be opened to all to train enough teachers to fill the posts. Dr. Van der Merwe said his department did not need extra teachers now. "Black education now and for the foreseeable future has an excess of teacher training facilities. We are training more teachers than we can employ." (Sunday Star, June 16, 1991). He also denied that any of the facilities which are being closed would be lost to education. The five colleges of education which are being closed, for example would be turned into multi- racial "Educhons". In addition to providing teacher training they would turn out graduates with technical skills.

We need people with technical skills to get the economy going, to generate the money with which teachers will be paid. He also noted that formerly white schools were being used by blacks, but that they could not always be used because of where they were located. He said bussing black children into white areas would be a prohibitively expensive exercise. "It is more economical to build schools in the community. This way they can be used for other purposes as well." (Sunday Star, June 16, 1991). Piet Clase, the own affairs minister of education and culture in the House of Assembly, has been slammed twice in the editorial columns of Die Burger, the NP Mouthpiece in the Cape. It accused him of "inexplicable and indefensible" conduct at a time when anarchy reigned in black education. Mr. Clase pleaded poverty and claimed no institutions would be lost to education.

8.7   CONCLUSION

The Education Renewal Strategy (ERS) unveiled by the government reveals only one thing - just how well and alive apartheid strategies still remain in place. While the majority of the people in the country are looking at making a giant leap forward by accepting the basic tenets of democracy and its culture of consensus, there still remain in our midst those who seek to achieve, by hook or by crook, objectives that must now be recognised as belonging to an era gone by. Attempts to surreptitiously remove important areas of struggle such as education, and place them outside of the political processes that are now unfolding - as is the case of the education strategy - must be rejected outright.

Education in our country is, first and foremost, a political problem, because it is the political practices of apartheid that inform the distortions that have been built into our education system and that have now given us the so-called "education crisis". Without first correcting the political distortions inherent in our education system, we cannot hope to save the future of our education by merely addressing its technical aspects, as the ERS tries to do. That there are today over three million children of school-going age who are not at school, a backlog that would require at least 100 000 new teachers, is a political problem.

The ERS shows the continuing aversion to reality that Nationalist Party bureaucrats still cling to, and that is of paramount concern to us. This is because it is strategies such as the ERS that give rise to suspicions about this government's commitment to fundamental change. That the government has some general commitment to change is without question, but the question that arises is whether this change is designed to empower the black majority or to buy time for the perpetuation of white privilege. The formulators of these strategies are neither naive nor foolish, since they categorically acknowledge that they are unlikely to come to fruition before the new constitution. They understand that they will not always control the political agenda, and therefore the education agenda, for any significant period of time. What they seek to do however, is to define the parameters of debate on education and ensure that white privilege is secured for generations to come. We have argued that the question of education in this country is serious and that ways forward must be found, even before the new constitution, to address the question of a national education policy of South Africa.

The working committee founded after the meeting between ANC deputy president Nelson Mandela and president F.W. de Klerk gave promise that this would materialise. However, the fact that there was no consultation in the drawing up of the report shows that "the toy telephone" remains a permanent feature of Nationalist Party thinking.

THE NATIONAL, NON-RACIAL AND DEMOCRATIC EDUCATION SYSTEM - THE ONLY SOLUTION FOR SOUTH AFRICA'S EDUCATION CRISIS

9.1   INTRODUCTION

It might make sense to talk about post-apartheid South Africa at this point - where South Africa is approaching a new era in her history. This era I prefer to call the post-apartheid era, due to the fact that South Africa's history is moving and developing in a dramatic way.

Before I mention a few pointers illustrative of this assertion, the following observation must be mentioned: South Africa evokes a morbid fascination. Multitudes of literature of condemnation wallow in moral predicaments. Ambivalent friends of Pretoria respond with ever more sophisticated justifications of the unjustifiable. Foreigners cherish the easy accessibility to an English- speaking police state, where the press is critical, intellectuals are tolerated and repression occurs out of sight. The apartheid issue allows even die-hard conservatives to look radical in a unique laboratory of social engineers. A worthy cause attracts causeless entrepreneurs. Instant experts pontificate about ready options for a creeping revolution. Some claim to seek 'moral clarity' that derives from the 'scale of the land and its antagonism'. Many more, secretly enjoy what Gordimer calls 'the last colonial extravaganza'.

Referring back to the pointers of the post-apartheid era - minority domination, no longer totally secure on a solid base, finds itself in a state of ideological and strategic fragmentation. Gone are the confident dogmatism and ideological solidarity of the Verwoerdian era and dreams. Contradictory policies rather than consistent repression characterise state behaviour. A deeply split ruling class now makes concessions forced by the anticipation of worse alternatives and searches for legitimacy alternately with upholding past practices. This fluctuation opens new avenues for forces of emancipation, through unanticipated consequences of new policies, and as a result of formerly excluded groups being drawn into the ruling sector.

The South African state is in the process of reorganisation. Its constituent groups formed new alliances that transcend the monolithic conception of black/white antagonism. It would, however, be misleading to see these developments as white capitulation and black victory. The scenario is far more complex and includes actors with a number of different interests and goals. In the significant restructuring of domination, white control is only being revised not abolished. Exclusive apartheid ideology was modified to allow political co-option of the coloured and Indian middle classes, who control substantial administrative areas of their 'own affairs'. African collaborating elites were cultivated at the regional and municipal levels. This reorganisation of central political institutions occurs at the behest of the ruling party and is aimed at strengthening Nationalist Party hegemony. Political power-sharing in the sense of diminished Afrikaner control has not taken place. Hence the struggle for post-apartheid era could yet continue for a long time. It is not known yet when the final victory will be achieved.

9.2   EDUCATION AND CULTURE

The South African government believes that education is transmission of culture. If this is the case, education should be an 'own affair'.

> ... The belief that education is an 'own affair' is likely to be ideological, at least in part, but that it is, nevertheless, historically significant, and that arguments about whether it is right to have some role to play. The argument about whether the belief is right moves through a consideration of the view that education is the transmission of culture (Marrow, 1986:245).

Arguments throughout this book have implicated that education is not merely the transmission of culture and therefore it is incorrect to see education as an 'own affair'. Education is to be distinguished from upbringing and is related to emancipation. To perceive education as an 'own affair' means that it is to be understood, and pursued, within particular social groups. This also implies that it is wrong for members of one group to interfere with the education of another group, and for one group to impose its view of education on members of another group.

The ideological belief that education is merely the transmission of culture and therefore an 'own affair' is in the interest of the dominant group in South Africa, since it provides a plausible rationale for the reproduction of the current relations of domination and exploitation. No special problem is coupled to why the oppressed of the society come to accept the ideology, this is called maintaining hegemony and hegemony is maintained by all the organs of the state - from the media, through the school (which reproduce the ideology by their organisation and content), to the intellectuals (who with great sincerity and seriousness argue that it is a 'scientific' truth that education is an 'own affair').

Schooling has economic, social and political functions. It selects and prepares people for positions in the occupational social and political hierarchies of society. Thus, schooling is one of the principle agencies for the distribution of the 'goods' of society, including access to the exercise of power. In cases where 'different' schooling is provided for 'different' people, people are prepared for facing advantages and disadvantages. However, it is unjust that a schooling system is used to advance the interest of a particular group in a society. Thus, it is wrong to think of education as an own affair when education is thought of as being equivalent to schooling. There are a great number of facets that need to be discussed in this argument.

Basically this argument is conclusive against most of the uses in South Africa's political and academic world of the idea that education is an own affair. Defenders of this idea try to escape from the conclusion by denying that South Africa should be regarded as a single 'nation' or society. South Africa has, until very recently, been saddled with the Population Registration Act, the Group Areas Act and the Separate Amenities Act, in addition to more than 35 years of propagating and ideology that South Africa is not a single 'nation' but a collection of 'nations', which should each have their own hierarchies of power.

Once an intimate link between education and culture is accepted and the former is the transmission of the latter, then two exclusive possibilities seem to present themselves in a society in which there are different cultures (and South Africa is generally accepted as such a society).

*   There should be different educational systems for each of the different cultures (in official rhetoric this is the traditional South African solution).

*   One of the cultures will dominate education (and the other cultures will be suppressed, distorted, ignored, colonised or undermined in some other way). This might be called cultural imperialism or mono- culture education.

The extent to which the opposition between these two possibilities, conceived as the only alternatives, has provided the framework for argumentation about schooling policy in South Africa. There are, however, two strong objections to both these alternatives. The first alternative leads to a kind of cultural exclusiveness which not only hinders the development of culture, since each of the cultures becomes stultified in its own forms, but also does not contribute to prepare people for the world in which they live their lives (people of South Africa do not only live in the cultural richness of South Africa, but also within the 'global village'). Furthermore, such a view underwrites schooling policies which lead to polarisation of cultural groups, mutual misunderstanding and unresolvable conflict.

The second alternative is based on disrespect for other cultures, and the unjustifiable assumption of the superiority of one culture. The idea that all people should be assimilated into a single, dominant culture fails to take the detailed behavioral fabric of people's day to day social lives into account, and how precious this fabric is for the self-concept and esteem. Once this social fabric is ruptured self identity is at risk and anomie and demoralisation are not far behind. Again, there ought to be a serious consideration of the conceptual link between education and emancipation. Through education one is able to escape from the blind adherence to the common convictions and prevailing practices of one's social group. Paradoxically, one of the central thrust of phenomenology was to encourage people to render problematic commonsense and the taken-for- granted syndromes of the world. To be able to do so is one of the characteristic achievements of being educated.

On can make these same points using the world culture. An educated person is one who has escaped from being embedded in a particular culture. This is a person who has achieved a critical understanding of how much is simply conventional in the cultural group within which he happened to have been raised. This does not imply that an educated person is one who rejects the convictions and practices of his cultural group. The idea is that a person is educated to such an extent that he is capable of critically reflecting on his life circumstances, the influences which formed his fundamental beliefs, and the customs and habits which constitute the framework of his daily life. If this is correct, then it is incorrect to perceive education and culture as being intimately linked in a way which makes it correct to think that education is the transmission of culture, thus an 'own affair'. Unfortunately, such a conflict of beliefs is the problem bedeviling the South African education scene.

In South Africa there is a conflict of beliefs in as far as educational decisions and policy making are concerned between the whites and the blacks. Perhaps the first question to ask is, whether the aims and purposes of education in South Africa are different from those of the rest of the world, or more importantly, should they be? Secondly, can and should the aims of education be the same for everyone in South Africa? Do we believe in the same values? Can there be one philosophy of education for all the people in South Africa? What do South African people hold in common? Dewey's cautionary note should always ring in any honest educationist's mind.

It is well to remind ourselves that education as such has no aims. Only persons, parents, teachers and others have aims, not an abstract process like education (1925:125).

Increasingly in South Africa, the attempt of society to shape, train, or mould its young, to bring them up, in the way they should develop according to its own ideals of life, has been taken over by the state, and more particularly, by the National Party which has been controlling the machinery of state since 1984, It is the power base in society, the establishment that now tends to make the decisions on the purposes, objectives and intentions of the education system. Some of these decisions are open, for example, in public statements of educational policy, legislation and regulations, but some are hidden and achieved rather through the persons placed in positions of power in the education system.

It must also be remembered that when the authority exercised by the establishment is not regarded as legitimate by, or acceptable to some of the clients of the education system, those clients may well have their own hidden aims and purposes which (to the extent they are able) they use the systems to achieve. One example of this points to the aims of the Bantu Education Act, as put forward in the parliamentary debates of 1953 and the outcomes as reflected in the events of Soweto 1976. In general, the universal debate on the aims and purposes of education revolves around the relative emphasis to be given, on the one hand, to what it is intended to achieve for the individual and, on the other, for the society of which he is part. These cannot be separated.

The conflict of beliefs about education produced an education system which, among other aspects, is characterised by the following :-

*   The present education system has failed to cope with the economic developmental needs of South Africa. Two main issues need to be highlighted: the need for an effective educational base for further education and training, and the need to attach much more importance to technical, vocational, careers education.

*   Grave dissatisfaction throughout the teaching profession, not only in terms of salaries and conditions of service, but also in the inadequacy of teachers' participation in educational decision making at all levels.

* A growing unease among parents and community bodies because of their limited say in the education of their children, accompanied by a growing bureaucratic arrogance expressed in a 'we know best' attitude.

* Finally, there is a rejection of the education system (with all its implications by large sections of the community, who perceived the education system as being based on ideological separation and therefore entrenching isolation and discriminatory practices, and also failing to meet the needs and aspirations of the people it was set up to serve.

South Africa is a country divided against itself, in which goodwill and trust have rapidly dissipated. Fear, hatred and bitterness are growing and may potentially take over. In this country the quality of life of millions of citizens is in constant reproach, and poverty and preventable disease have not been conquered. Grave limitations have been placed on freedom of expression, individual liberties, and the rule of law in which there is growing uncertainty and insecurity. Most importantly, however, South Africa is a country within tremendous potential, with rich material and human resources, much of them still untapped with the capacity, if given the opportunity, to cope with the human and social problems that now bedevil the land and sap its strength.

If all the mentioned factors are taken into consideration what should then be regarded as the aims and purposes of education under these circumstances? Firstly, the purposes of education must have as their primary concern the kind of people being produces by the educational process now and in the future. Above all, South Africa has a need for warm, compassionate, caring people, (see De Lange report, 208) as well as thinking people, capable of making independent decisions. South Africa also needs skilled, competent, knowledgeable people, capable of earning their own living and maintaining an independent livelihood and therefore able to contribute to society and its general welfare; capable of responding the change.

The aims and purposes of education should be concerned with the kind of society that young people are prepared for, what Kant called 'a possibly improved condition of man in the future'. In Chapter Two a question was raised: Does anyone seriously believe that the kind of society in the year 2000 (at which point those children now in school will be young adults) will not be very different from the one in which we now live. It seems as if there is a recognition of this, for example, in the 11 basic principles postulated by the HSRC committee. An illustration from the first three principles will highlight this.

*   Is it not possible to continue with a society in which discrimination continues and privilege is protected if equal opportunities, norms, and standards are to be achieved? (Principle 1).

*   A society in which there is recognition both of what is common and what is diverse would be on the one hand a society in which people had greater freedom to follow their own heritages, traditions and aspirations, but at the same time a society of greater unity, a greater oneness over the fundamentals of common humanity and common South Africanism (Principle 2). (See also 5.21, Main Report, 206).

*   A society in which freedom of choice is exercised will be very different from the closed, authoritarian society today; it will have to be open and flexible and certainly not a society in which the State tries to enforce its own stamp on every one (Principle 3).

What cannot be preserved is an education with the main purpose of preserving and maintaining the status quo. More than ever before education has become a future's activity. Tensions will inevitably arise in the search for the right balance between creativity and conservation. The De Lange report, for example, is firmly committed to an education relevant to an 'improved condition of man in the future'. It recommends 'a system of education that will remain sensitive and responsible to changes (social, economic and political) ... so that it contributes positively to the creation of the society in which equality of opportunity becomes increasingly attainable'. (Main Report, 4.17 (d) 194).

One of the main purposes of education should be to place those who have been discriminated against in the past, in a position (as quickly as is possible) where their educational background will enable them :

* to compete on an equal basis in the market place and to make their contribution to the economic welfare of South Africa

* to take their place freely in society and to contribute to its richness and diversity

* to share in the decision-making process of the country at all levels, in education as well as the wide range of other human activities - social, economic and political

* to live as citizens with their fellow citizens in a common South Africa and to share the same regard and affection for the country because it commands that regard by the quality of the human state it has made possible.

In South Africa a very particular and special responsibility rests on education, namely, a responsibility to the great majority of children of this country :

* to right the wrongs of the past
* to restore fairness and justice
* to open up the opportunities that only some South African children have had in the past
* to provide education that is relevant to their needs and responsive to their aspirations (Hartshorne 1982).

9.3 WHY DE KLERK COULD NOT RISK REFORMING EDUCATION IN 1991

In his speech President De Klerk went slightly but significantly further than many observers had expected him to do. The significant advance on what was expected was the fact that he announced that the Population Registration Act would be repealed and that temporary legislation would be produced to maintain the present voters' rolls for the final test of the constitution. The significance of this lies in the fact that in repealing the Population Registration Act he indicated that the dismantling of apartheid is completely irreversible and this quite clearly is directed at the United States Congress and perhaps other marginal sanctions that still remain in Europe. Therefore one can expect that the sanctions campaign will die completely from now on. Aspects of his speech which some people regarded as disappointing are the fact that he did not announce one education department and that he did not refer to the issue of hit squads and controversy surrounding the case involving General Lothar Neethling.

In these regards one might bear in mind that he did place considerable emphasis on the rule of law and due process in proposed provision to the South African legal system and it goes some way towards reassuring people on the issue of civil rights and liberties. As regards education, the explanation is simply that it is impossible for him to confront the white electorate with a dismantling of Group Areas Act, repeal of the Land Act, of the Population Registration Act and of the whole white educational system in one fell swoop. It is arguable that he would have risked a groundswell of opposition from within his own party support base had he done that.

What he said about education suggests that by this time in 1992 the proposed system will be for the major educational provision to be non-racial and unitary and for there to be some special protection built in for those whites of Afrikaans schools wishing to maintain their identity. One can understand the disappointment about his failure to make any concessions to the demand for an interim government and constitutional assembly. However the general tone of his speech suggested that he is open to creative co-operation between all major parties.

Although the State President did not announce any immediate changes to the education system, it is clear that the Government now sees this as a major priority. And his reference to "fragmented State administration" - a euphemism for 19 education departments - raises the hope of a new unity in the country's classrooms. Since he spoke several Cabinet ministers have also told Press briefings that the expenditure gap between white and black children must be eliminated and pupil/teacher ratios equalised. Funds from cuts in other departments are likely to be channelled into these needs.

The awareness that every child is entitled to the same standard of education has been slow in dawning. Years of official neglect, rubber-stamped by Verwoerdian legislation, have made radicals of young black people, caused mindless destruction of scarce resources and led to appalling academic results. Widespread adult illiteracy and lack of skills continue to cost the economy dearly. "Separate but equal" is a discredited concept; so is the unrealistic "pass one, pass all" call of agitators. These are the lessons that Mr. F.W. de Klerk and Mr. Nelson Mandela must heed when they discuss education.

9.4   OPEN SCHOOLS: A DROP IN AN OCEAN OF DEMOCRACY

The opening of white state schools is seen by many as a damp squib which makes no significant impact on the enormity of the education crisis and does not begin to address the fundamental demand for a single, unitary, non- racial and democratic education system. It may also be seen as a momentous event where for the first time in the history of the nation racial segregation in state schools is beginning to crumble and the erosion of apartheid education is becoming a reality in the suburbs.   The opening of these schools is clearly not quantitatively significant in terms of the numbers of children who have been admitted - a mere 5 360 black pupils have been admitted to white schools, which is probably in the region of 0,8 percent of the white and 0,08 percent of the African schooling population. The departure to greener pastures of such a small number can offer no relief to a critically overburdened education system. The political significance of the policy (the Clase models) which made this minimal opening possible has been contested because firstly, the models are fundamentally undemocratic in that they exclude most parents from decisions about where their children may go to school and allow a small minority to make decisions for the majority - a further disenfranchising of the disenfranchised. Secondly, the significance of the Clase models may be dismissed because the policy is fundamentally wedded to an apartheid-style commitment to race and to Christian National Education. This is perhaps the clearest indication that De Klerk has given of what he might mean by "distinctive community- based education".

All open state schools are permitted to admit a maximum of 49 percent of children classified as other than white. If this figure is exceeded, they are obliged to register with the racially "appropriate" education authority for the majority of the pupils in the school. One previously white school registered with the Transvaal Education Department exceeded the 49 percent quota, causing some consternation in Transvaal Education Department circles. Teachers who have worked for the TED for years might suddenly find themselves working for the Department of Education and Training. This concern with registration based on race classification is absurdly anachronistic. Another consequence of the 49 percent policy is that schools with dwindling white populations, some of which may have as few as 100 pupils, may only admit 49 black children. As schools have on the whole shown some reluctance to rapidly change their racial composition, the pattern is that few schools are exceeding a 25 percent black enrolment. Thus a small school that proudly announces its opening may in fact only have "space" for 25 black children while the school buildings could accommodate at least another 400. Another anomaly is the fee-paying implications of trying to school together children for whom different educational laws apply. For white children, education is compulsory and free. Schools do request school funds and these are voluntarily paid by the majority of parents, but there is always a minority who do not pay and because education is compulsory these children cannot be sent home. For black children education is not compulsory, and no open white school is obliged to take any black child for whom the school funds have not been paid. Many open schools are acutely aware of the injustice of this but would argue that they are the victims of confusion in macro-politics over which they have no control.

The management committees of the open state schools individually determine the admission policy of the school and the restrictive criteria that have been adopted have contributed to the widespread dissatisfaction with open schools. All of them have had to select pupils because in all cases the demand has far outstripped the places that were available. The mechanisms of selection varied but a pattern is emerging. Some schools operated on a first come, first served basis. The race was won by those who had access to the information and the means to apply. Others knew the exact individuals they were going to admit before they even voted to become an open school. Most schools have used one or more of the following selection mechanisms for black applicants: parents must live in the area; parents must own property in the area; pupils will only be admitted into Grade One; only pupils who have been to an English-speaking pre-primary school will be admitted to Grade One and pupils must be no older than the average age of the standard to which they are being admitted. Again, these conditions apply to black children only, and for most black parents these conditions are insurmountable obstacles put in place by people who have no understanding of the conditions under which they live.

Most schools have required black applicants to complete selection tests which have emphasised English Language proficiency and have explored other areas of scholastic achievement such as maths. These tests have tended either to select black children previously schooled in traditional private schools that have satisfied these criteria; or the school has decided how many black children it can admit and has taken the best of the applicants to achieve this number. One school working on the "meet our standards" model initially accepted only three or four black pupils before it reconsidered and then accepted five black children per class. Many black parents have gone to great lengths to try to have their children admitted to the open white schools despite the conditions outlined above and the enormous inconvenience of commuting from one Group Area to another. I know several families who battle 60 km or more across the traffic every morning to get their children to the open school they consider themselves to be fortunate to attend. This indicates strong rejection of the conditions under which children are being schooled in the DET and a determination to escape this. It also indicates the high regard in which the educational provision for whites is held. But the move towards non-racialism in schools previously reserved for whites cannot solve the education crisis. Non-segregated schooling is a preoccupation of a minority; the numbers of children who will even in a post- apartheid education system ever attend a racially mixed school will be relatively small. De-segregating schools will make a negligible quantitative contribution to alleviating the crisis and our efforts and hopes must be invested in the transformation of the entire system.

While it is understood that the opening of white schools is in itself not a solution to the current crisis, the failure of the state to respond more decisively to the racial restrictions on access to school is unacceptable. It is unacceptable that children living with their families in Joubert park and Hillbrow have no access to a local school while Joubert Park Laerskool is empty. It is unacceptable that 1 200 students at East Bank High in Alexandra have classes together in a hall while Orange Grove Primary stands empty. Such wastage of resources serves nobody's interests. In fact, the unanticipated strength of support for opening schools among white parents may have been largely due to the compelling logic of using resources effectively. When Clase announced the models so late in 1990, and when he stipulated what seemed to be such prohibitively high percentage poll requirements (80 percent participation and 72 percent affirmative), it was not expected that as many as 10 percent of all white schools would have achieved open status by the beginning of the 1991 school year, as is quite remarkably the case. Anyone who has had anything to do with the Clase voting procedures will know that the opening of the school could not happen unless there was a group of parents and teachers expending enormous efforts to complete the prescribed steps in the given time. Special meetings had to be held and official requirements completed in a highly constrained time frame. Imaginative campaigns were run, parents were given stickers saying "I have voted" only when they had done so, schools had competitions between classes and the winning class was the one with the highest percentage poll.

Teachers and parents spent week-nights and weekends collecting parents, driving them to the school to cast their special votes and taking them home. Schools did not open as a result of casual effort. Despite the reservations that might be expressed about the nature of open schools, that one out of every 10 white schools managed to open in the space of a few months is an indication of something positive. Open schools may be the vehicle that will take the reality of political change into the family rooms in the suburbs. The white open schools have dominated the attention of the media, but the realisation of a unitary educational system will mean the "opening" of all schools. While much interest has been expressed in how black pupils will adjust to open schools, the more central issue is what are the processes by which all of the previously, and currently, racially exclusive schools will adjust to a non-racial and unitary education system. And we haven't even begun to talk democratic and non-sexist yet!

9.5   FUTURE PROSPECTS AND PROBLEMS

In one form or another, the quest for equality has been the dominant activity of the black man throughout his history in South Africa since the arrival of the white man. He has always been seeking full participation in all aspects of South African life. The goal has not been achieved, because the minority racial group in South Africa has managed to deny the black man full citizenship through subtle and direct means.

This has been true especially in the area of education, which the black man has through the years perceived as the gateway to a better life, even in a race-conscious society. The denial of equal educational opportunity has led to feelings of frustration and hopelessness, it has also led to challenges to authorities, and the rise of a general militancy demanding better and equal education for South Africa's black population.

No attempt is made here to review the sweep of history that has led to the sense of frustration and hopelessness of many black people and is reflected in the current militant attitude of some blacks. The search for education has always been a struggle won by comparatively few. A few examples of this status quo are given next.

* The South African government has not as yet fully committed itself to uphold fundamental human rights in a free, open and just society. The problems underlying education in South Africa are not merely educational, but have political undertones, predominantly because of the inequality and exclusivity of the ideology of apartheid.

* There is no open education system which allows any child free access to any public education institution. South Africa insists on racially exclusive schools and departments.

* South Africa does not have a single ministry of education characterised by a policy of cultural diversity, which takes cognizance of the different languages which are prevalent, differences in culture and historical heritages and differences between First World and Third World orientations.

* The principle of equality of opportunity in education is still lacking and limited efforts are made to eradicate the historic backlogs and disadvantages in black education.

* Democratic participation of local parent communities in education is still lacking.

On the other hand, feelings from the victims of the status quo just described amount to the following.

* Prejudice, racism and discrimination in education are

consequent results of South Africa's failure to realise the potential worth that lies in the diversity of her population groups.

* Equality of educational opportunities comes from self- respect and respect for others where all groups are invited to join in the mainstream of the nation's life and culture.

* South Africa's white minority does not perceive that to be different is not to be inferior, and that one may be different and equal at the same time.

* Fears of diversity in South Africa have led to perceived fears, prejudice and discrimination in education and other spheres of life, which stem from inadequate understanding of the positive values of difference, of diversity and of pluralism.

In terms of education in South Africa, it must surely be clear to us now that matters have moved beyond the stage at which better buildings and facilities, higher levels of financing, more efficient instruction can offer a solution to the education crisis of 1986 (important as these are to providing a base for equality). If one is listening to what is going on 'out there', then one should be in touch with terms such as liberation education, worker education, community education, alternative education, post-apartheid education and, in the words of the National Education Crisis Committee, people's education for people's power - a far cry from the 'pupil power' of 1976. It is all too easy to interpret these messages as slogans, although they do have the emotive appeal of the slogan they embody, they are more than that.

It is essential to realise and accept that most of these new messages, certainly in the voices of younger people, are rooted in the principles of socialism (this is the new emphasis of 1991 as opposed to 1976). Their scepticism about the benefits of capitalism, their perceptions of exploitation by those holding economic power, their disbelief in the inevitability of the rewards of greater economic growth 'filtering down' to those economically as well as politically disenfranchised, are now all too well documented. In the light of frequent collaboration between the state and capitalist interest in the past and compromises in the present, this is fully understandable. The rise of the trade union movement, with its realisation of the crucial importance, has also led to a greater awareness of the economic, as well as the political factors involved in societal change. Economic as well as political reform is now on the agenda.

Clearly many conservative people (political leaders, academics down to the 'man in the street') perceive an introduction of socialist principles in the debate on the future of South Africa as threatening and difficult to cope with. And yet it is an inevitable debate - one that every country has had to face and continues to face. In South Africa it is very much a debate which is long overdue: it is both inevitable and necessary, and has moved from the realm of academic discourse into the school, factories, homes and political process of South Africa. I do not believe this debate should be seen to be threatening to anyone, except to those who are concerned with the protection of privilege and power, or who see the debate in bold terms of communism or capitalism, as though either of these provide the only answer. The all-in-or- nothing solution offers little hope to South Africa.

In entering this debate and seeking solutions, everyone has to have a starting point. My starting point is that the achievement of a democratic society in South Africa is the primary requirement - whatever else South Africa might be, it is not democratic. This has implications for the economic as well as the political organisation of our society. In principle, socialism is not incompatible with a democratic order. Similarly, I believe that the principles of 'free enterprise' are not divorced from democracy, but in practice this excludes unbridled, exploitative capitalism, cartels and monopolies, whether private or state controlled. In biblical terms, the poor, the weak and the oppressed have to be protected and delivered from those with power. Subsequently, in the economic as in the political order, we must seek a just and democratic path to the future of South Africa.

As a political order democracy often has many imperfections, but is the only alternative in which man has been able to care about people as individuals, has tried to provide equal opportunities for them in education and in other spheres of life, treats individuals as equal before the law, protects them from the arrogance of office and the abuse of power, and at its best, allows for the full development of human potential and the free flow of the human spirit. An education system which reflected and cherished these values would be different from that which currently operates in South Africa. In the words of the 1986 NECC conference it would be 'unitary, free compulsory, non-racial and democratic', and, in those of the earlier Johannesburg meeting, 'programmes to promote people's education must encourage critical and creative thinking and working methods, and promote the values of democracy, non-racialism, collective work and active participation.'

In the short term, as there is a move through the transition stage towards a new South Africa, various forms of 'alternative' education will be practised. On the one hand there will be increasing numbers of projects and programmes, conducted outside the formal state system by non-government agencies and funded by the private sector, both South African and international, and by foreign governments. On the other, there will be programmes within the black school, and in direct conflict with authority, 'conceived and executed within the framework for the struggle for national liberation', which will be designed to conscientise pupils, to offer alternative economic and political models, to interpret the 'processes of exploitation and oppression and to prepare them for the liberation struggle'. The possibilities of conflict between this approach and the perceptions of the state in the immediate future are very real; so, too, are tensions between the two approaches to alternative education. Private sector programmes will have to be sensitive to this issue if they are to have credibility and acceptance in the black community; they will have to be seen, not as reinforcing the present model of education, but as contributing to a unitary, non-racial, democratic future for education.

It is to this future to which I now wish to turn my attention - to post-apartheid education, not only for black youngster, but for the whole South African youth. When looking at this future, some of my convictions about education that influence and inform my view of that future will be mentioned.

* Education does not exist in a vacuum, but in a social, economic and political context. Education reflects political and economic realities, and fundamental change in education is dependent on changes in society, politics and economic life.

* Education in its present form does not offer equal opportunities to all South Africans, and cannot do so as long as it is racially segregated: equal and separate will simply not work. As damaging and destructive as apartheid education has been for black South Africans, it has also failed privileged white South Africans in the long term.

* Only a common education system can serve the needs and aspirations of all South Africans. This does not mean the co-option or absorption of every one into the existing white-type educational model, but rather the creation of a new cross-culture mainstream South African education system. Whereas education has been a divisive force in the past, it should serve the purpose of national unity. Education based on a commitment to a common purpose could be a powerful agent for societal change.

* Commitment to a common purpose should not mean the imposition of a dull bureaucratic uniformity. Education can only live and breathe if there is room for diversity (not inferiority), flexibility, different aspirations, local initiatives, but not differentiation on grounds of race, colour or definitions of 'culture' which are mere euphemisms for them.

What is important in the education in the end is what goes on in the classroom (or whatever learning situation), that is, policies, structures, administration, syllabuses are relevant only to the extent that they help to provide the most effective and creative environment for the teacher and learner, and the way they interact with each other.

Two further comments should be made at this point. Firstly, we must expand the statement on apartheid education and white children. Not only has apartheid education separated white from black children, but it has also divided white children into separate camps. It has been authoritarian in nature, strongly influenced by Christian National principles, with an underlying philosophy of the 'moulding of good citizens to fit into ordered society', to be obedient to the state and the values of the existing order. Further it has been marked by strong and often arrogant bureaucratic control, with little freedom for parents, teachers or pupils to exercise much 'say' or influence. Its overall effect has been that generations of white children have been conditioned to privilege, to accepting separation as a natural order and to feel undue respect for authority and the status quo. They have not been given a fair chance to learn to understand, work and live with their fellow black South Africans, to find out that they have much in common. Instead, they have had to fall back on stereotypes of their fellow citizens.

Secondly, it is doubtful whether a change in government and political structures alone (even if they were democratic in nature) would bring about the 'democratisation' of education. As Franz Auerbach (1987:14) pointed out, authoritarianism in the schools 'reflects ancient and deep-seated authoritarian child- rearing patterns in the homes of all sectors of South African society'. In the schools themselves learning styles will have to change from passive, rote learning, single textbook, examination-oriented approaches to creative learning and problem solving through the active participation and involvement of pupils in the learning process, to hands-on experience in the laboratory and workshop, self-study in the library, questioning, discussion and co-operative working together in groups. There is a need for a hard look to be taken at the classroom (the inter-action of teacher, pupil and the subject-matter of learning) and the why, what and how of the learning experiences of pupils who will have to live in a new and different South Africa. 'Neither do men put new wine into old bottles!'

We will just take a brief look at the question to which the De Lange Committee was unable to address itself (except indirectly) because in its own membership it reflected deep divisions over the issue of South Africa. Through a process of agreement on what needed to be done in the provision of education. What is needed now, in the search for the basics of education beyond apartheid, is to turn to the questions of what education is for and what its purposes should be in a new South Africa?

There are two major challenges in the world in which we are living :

*   learning to live together in peace through the conquest of inhumanity, prejudice and self-interest

*   learning to cope with our everyday economic needs through the conquest of food shortages, poverty and unemployment.

Both will be best met if education enables individuals to make the most of the abilities and qualities with which they are endowed, if it encourages them to keep on learning throughout their lives, and if it prepares them to 'live themselves out' in society and to contribute to its well being.

Education, therefore, in its purposes must have a primary concern for the kind of people which emerge from the formal schooling process. At this stage of its history South Africa has particular needs in this order :

*   warm, compassionate, caring people, liberated from fear and hate, for whom life has sense and purpose

*   thinking, critical people, capable of independent judgement and of coping with new ideas and change

*   skilled, competent, knowledgeable people capable of coping in a modern political economic in Africa and elsewhere; citizens who respect the rule of law and arrogance of power; who do not believe in my country right or wrong, but always want the best for it, including the right of criticism and protest, and who

in the end accept that above all nations stand humanity.

The purpose of education must also be concerned with the kind of society in which people have to live and work, in which education systems and processes have to function effectively, and for which education should prepare young people. The creative aspect of education must have more emphasis that the 'conservation' aspect. Education, more than ever, is a 'futures' activity and must make its contributions towards change in society, rather than being used at present as a policy instrument to maintain the status quo. The aims and purposes of education should be concerned first and foremost with people, with their relations with others in society, and with the liberation of the human spirit in the individual, the family, work, worship and leisure.

These are among the fundamental issues in education which underlie all the discussions and decisions about policy, structures, finance, teacher education, curricula and syllabuses - all the matters that need to be addressed and effected in building a post-apartheid education system. These are not issues just for politicians and educationist - they concern all of us, but most of all the young people who, together with their children, will live in the post-apartheid society. Teachers, in particular, will have to be able to cope with new situations, different contexts and structures, different content and processes in education. At best this will not be easy. Unless the future is discussed and debated, the mind and spirit prepared, reconciliation and unity sought with colleagues of all colours and persuasions, history may well leave all South Africans behind. For South Africa there is only one way to face the future in education, as in other spheres of life, and that is together: unless South Africans do so, the future will be bleak for all of them. Whites must be educated to see this challenge not as threatening to them personally or professionally, but as an opportunity to contribute to a better condition of man in the future.

Whites should not abdicate from life and believe 'what is the use of talking' or 'what can they do'. They should not stick their heads in the sand and, above all, they should not despair. There have been times in the history of mankind when it has been the duty and pride of man to have done the best things in the worst times and even hoped for them in the most calamitous. Starting with 16 June 1976 in Soweto, which led to an almost complete rejection and breakdown of the old segmented systems, events of the past few years have shown conclusively that the 'users' of these systems - pupils, parents, teachers and the community - are not prepared to accept a continuation of separateness, with all the inferiorities and limitations arising from this. Whatever the divisions in the black community, there is a general consensus that the education system is inferior since it is separate and encapsulated within an 'apartheid' ideology that isolates it from the facilities and resources, both human and material, that should be available to all South Africans, whatever their colour. There may well be questions as to whether a common education system will work, and how it should work, but one thing should be clear by now - that separate systems have not worked in the past and hold no hope in the future.

At last, the South African Government has committed itself irreversibly (so it says) to a new South Africa where all the inhabitants of this country will be treated equally. In educational terms this means that the schools for Black children must also be made to provide an environment and an atmosphere where teachers can teach and educate children in such a way that these children can gain real understanding and insight into the subject matter. Black children must begin to enjoy learning. In this way they will also develop the physical, mental and moral skills and wholesome attitudes. Their home and school environment must be conducive to learning. This environment must promote the development of creativity, originality and reasoning prowess that will help them in decision-making and problem-solving. If this happens to all the children of this country, no pupils would riot or destroy his own school.

South Africa needs a coherent and a comprehensive attack on the problem of Black education if we mean to produce citizens who will inhabit the new South Africa in peace and prosperity. What we do not need is a proliferation of numerous haphazard, ad hoc and poorly planned educational projects which have no effects at all on the total system. Properly considered, this is what a demand for one

Department of Education is all about. What I am saying is that there is a need for a precise and a clear definition of the problems in education in preparation for a new South Africa. If a concerted and a well co-ordinated effort is launched to produce a new philosophy; a new administration and new policies in a new Department of Education, then this proposed one department can be a solution.

9.6   WHY A UNITARY EDUCATION SYSTEM?

* No other approach will gain the acceptance of the great majority of people in South Africa. Unless this acceptance is won, fundamental reform in education will be almost impossible, because the authority behind the reform will be suspect and will be resisted. The political dangers inherent in such a situation are considerable.

* No other approach will remove the past taints of discrimination and inferiority, and allow a fair and just allocation of resources of men and money to the education of all the people in South Africa. Furthermore, South Africa shall not be able to afford to do justice to all its peoples' educational needs unless she stops duplicating expensive, rare facilities, especially at the level of higher education. Instead the system should be such that it shares what whites already have and anticipates what still needs to be created.

* Socially South Africa has become a dangerously divided country with much underlying bitterness, in which the hurts, fears and misunderstanding go deep. For years, policies and practices in education (as in other areas of national life), have emphasised these differences and divisions. Now the people of South Africa increasingly have to learn to work together and concentrate on emphasising the common factors in our society. A unitary education system will make a major contribution to a universal sense of belonging and commitment to South Africa.

Clearly there are many difficulties ahead in achieving this kind of perception of education as a unifying force. Education does not operate in a vacuum but always in a particular social, economic, political and constitutional context. There are, therefore, those who would argue that it is meaningless to seek reform in education without radical and fundamental change in society and its political and economic systems. Considerable truth is found in this argument and it is imperative that this truth be recognised. Nonetheless the process of education itself, certainly at its best, is creative and can prepare people for change, can anticipate and facilitate change and can work as a change instrument within society. A common education system may well be ahead of its time, but could be a powerful strategy of change.

It has to be accepted, however, that in the white community , where perceptions are generally of a different kind, many people would see a 'common system' of education as endangering their 'culture'. At its best culture is used to express matters of real concern such as religious belief, values, philosophies of life and hard-won heritages. In a negative context, however, it can be manipulated as a cover for hard, exclusive attitudes, for racial prejudice and fears, and as protection of positions of privilege and of the benefits of the status quo.

The wide spectrum of meaning given to this word was well- illustrated at the 'Volkskongres' on Education held in Bloemfontein in March 1986. In historical terms this must be seen as a strong, well-organised rearguard action aimed at resisting any fundamental reform in education. Whatever the relative strength of this minority group - and this still has to be proved in political terms - it is representative of a body of people who feel threatened by such concepts as a common education system and equality. In a potential conflict situation of this nature, where the perceptions and demands of a powerful white groups are poles apart from those of black communities, one wonders what kind of common education system is possible.

In the first place it is important to note that the purpose of such a system would be to facilitate the implementation of equality of opportunity in education for everyone in South Africa and to monitor its progress. This does not imply uniformity, that schools should all be the same, that the same kind of education will meet the needs of everyone. It is fundamental to education as a process that cognizance should be taken of individual differences - differences in learning needs, talents, aspirations, interest, expectations and background. These are relevant and acceptable grounds for educational differentiation; race, colour or creed are not. A common education system does not imply the imposition of a dull uniformity on all the schools of the country, cramping either the professional independence of teachers or the local initiative of parents and communities. In fact, the present systems are characteristically 'closed' and suffering from an overdose of too much government, too much bureaucracy and too much pressure from the top. Fundamental to the spirit of the unitary education system is the strong plea made for openness, flexibility, mobility. As many decisions as possible should be left to those closest to the situation for which the decision is intended. The greatest possible freedom of choice should be exercised by the parents. The greatest possible measure of decentralisation consistent with the objectives of equal opportunity and equal standards should ideally be achieved.

What then are the essentials of a unitary education system? For a unitary education system to succeed it is imperative that representatives of all the people of South Africa and of all the major concerned with education should be consulted, participate and be involved in the decisions relating to policy on the national level. Agreements should be reached on how the school systems are to be managed and administered at regional and local levels. Due to these reasons the De Lange report recommended as first priority, that a broadly representative, non-racial South African Council for Education should be set up, replacing all the existing separate education advisory councils and having greater statutory authority. However, such a body would have little meaning or authority unless it were consulting with a single Minister of Education and working in close co- operation with one Department of Education. What is envisaged for such a department is not a massive bureaucracy, since it would not be responsible for the actual running of any schools. This would be the responsibility of smaller, lower-level education authorities.

The central, national authority would be responsible for broad, educational policy, for decisions on the allocation of financial and other resources, for the setting and maintenance of material (e.g. buildings and equipment), educational and examination standards, basic national curriculum requirements, certification requirements and conditions of service for all teachers. Most importantly it would monitor the national programme aimed at bringing about equality of opportunity and standards in education throughout the system.

Responsibility for the administration of schools would rest with regional education authorities, which ideally should be management units much smaller than the existing provinces, working in consultation with regional education councils of the kind envisaged for the national level. Many problems would be solved at this level and perhaps the most that can be hoped for in the short term, given human fears and white conservatism, will be a pattern of co-ordination of separate ethnic school groupings. Importantly, flexibility would have to be maintained. Geographical areas that are ready to go beyond this limited step should be allowed and indeed encouraged to do so.

A unitary education system is most likely to succeed under present constraint if at the local level, the level of the school governing body, for example, parents, teachers and communities are given the largest measure of freedom of choice consistent with a national programme of equalising standards. At this level the diversity of needs, perceptions and aspirations of different sections of South African society can best be satisfied. Clearly many white people want their children to go to schools little different from those existing at present, and black parents will want their children to go to improved schools but there must also be room and official support for parallel-medium schools, open non-racial schools, if this is what parents and community leaders want. The options must be available. Therefore, the author believes that a common education system can work for the four following reasons.

* If it is structures along the suggested lines and there is no dragooning from above to force people to accept either 'open' schools or segregated schools, this system should work well.

  Private schools should be allowed to make their own decisions and be freed from the need for permits. If the University of Pretoria wishes to preserve its character is should be allowed to do so; equally if the University of the Witwatersrand wishes to go 'open' its council should have the right to make that decision. South African people have to learn to agree to differ.

* Such a system will work if it has the sincere and unreserved support of government, this being more than a matter of the finance. Senior educationist who believe in what they are doing and are not shackled by past experience in separate systems should be the administrators of this system. If the government moves away rapidly from entrenched 'apartheid' in other areas of our national life, such a system is even more likely to succeed.

* It would help considerably if influential people were to take a clear and unequivocal stance on the need for a new educational dispensation, not only to satisfy manpower needs and maintain economic growth, but also to meet the human needs and aspirations of all South Africans.

* Ultimately it will work if ordinary people are encouraged to accept change, if unjustified (or even real) fears are allayed by positive, enlightened political leadership and whites are prepared to give to others what they want for themselves.

Diversity can enrich South African national life: divisions, separation and 'exclusivity' can destroy it. In education they will lead to continued discrimination and therefore rejection and the total breakdown of the system. Whites must seek a future together with their fellow South Africans or they will have a bleak future to look forward to.

The 'bottom line' is not whether or not a unitary education system will work, but the fact that there is no alternative - it must be made to work. It will not be easy and will require South Africans of all persuasions to change their minds, their considerable resources of know- how and matter, their energies and human understanding to seeking a viable solution.

9.7   ALL CONSTITUENCIES MUST BE CONSULTED

Three prime features of the present education system must inform decisions about a future dispensation: the dissatisfaction that currently exists, the limit on resources and the legitimacy of any new structures.

While there has been an impressive growth in student numbers over the past two decades, there are still millions of children without school places. On the qualitative level, the schooling system satisfies neither those families whose children drop out before attaining even the minimum skills needed to cope with our complex society, nor the captains of commerce and industry and economic planners who complain that the shortage of skills is critical in inhibiting economic growth.

The second brute fact with which we must content in reconstructing education is the limit on resources. South Africa does not have the money to expand to all our people the kind of schooling at present enjoyed by the privileged minority. Priorities will have to be set and hard choices made.

Questions concerning who makes these decisions and the processes through which they are made bring us to the third corner-stone of the new education system: the issue of legitimacy. Respect for the present system is at a low ebb. On one hand teachers have lost authority over their students, and on the other they have little faith in the impartiality of the administrative and political authorities. There is corruption, in both senses of the word, throughout the bureaucracy. Systems move at a snail's pace; officials help themselves to millions in taxpayers' money, while schools are desperately short of books, desks and even doors and windows. Frustrated school leavers wander the streets without jobs.

What is needed to restore direction and a sense of purpose to schooling, and to establish a more productive relationship between education and the economy? A representative government, an honest and efficient bureaucracy and carefully formulated policies are prerequisites for a better system, but will not in themselves guarantee success. It is not difficult to envisage a scenario in which a popular government commissions the best experts to write a set of policies which balance the interests of all constituencies, but where the implementation of these plans is met with as much hostility as the engendered by the present system. If all constituencies are not involved in feeding their concerns into the debates around setting priorities and into the bargaining through which compromises are hammered out, they are likely to feel as alienated by the "new" single department of education as they are from apartheid education.

9.8 ACTION TO BE TAKEN DURING THE PERIOD OF TRANSITION

There is no magic way of bringing the present education crisis to an end. The year 1990 has shown us just how fragile and vulnerable the schooling system is, how much the learning environment has deteriorated, how commonplace it has become for schools to be disrupted, how deep the malaise among African youth. There is no one priority that will place the schooling system on the road to recovery. It is not a matter of "either/or" but of "both/and", and a judicious mix of top-down and bottom-up action, if the long haul to transform the schooling system is to get started. It must be clear to everyone that this transformation will be constrained until fundamental political, societal and structural changes in the South African polity have taken place. But this does not mean that nothing can be done during the transition period.

-     In the first place it is clear that the transformation can begin to take place only in an atmosphere of trust in, and acceptance of the bona fides of, those initiating the changes that are necessary. It is therefore difficult to imagine anything substantial happening before the Department of Education and Training is removed from the scene. It has lost all credibility, and as an interim measure all its functions should be transferred to the Department of National Education, subject, however, to two steps being taken: the appointment of senior African educationist, from both within and without the system, to the decision-making levels of that department; and the setting up of representative regional education councils to superintend the work of the existing DET regions.

-     Secondly, there is no reason that the re-distribution of education resources should not be speeded up considerably. This has to be done in two ways: rapid progress towards equality of per capita funding so that all schools and children at the same level of schooling will be treated the same; and at the same time a review of priorities within the schooling system itself, with compulsory primary schooling up to Std Four for all South African children becoming priority number one. It is crucial that within the next five years this be done, so that a stop is put to the growth in the number of illiterate youngsters, and a sound foundation is laid for preventing another "lost generation" coming into being.

-     The third step that is necessary is to re-organise the secondary schooling system by the introduction of a "middle school" that would take in Standards Five to Seven. By the middle of to the late Nineties it should then be possible to introduce compulsory schooling for all throughout this phase. The introduction of a completely new school structure into the existing system would have strong symbolic value and would signal a fundamental change of purpose and direction. The inertia of existing systems is always powerful, and the creation of a new kind of school at the beginning of the secondary level would help to break through this inertia and make a fresh start.

- This school, more than any other, because it will be new could have a broad "nation-building" character. In it we could start to develop the new "common culture" of South Africa. In it all children could follow a broadly common curriculum, concerned with the basics of language, mathematics and science. In it pupils could begin to learn about their country and its people, the realities of the economic and political life of South Africa, what it would mean to live in a democracy, and how education and work relate to each other. At the end of Std Seven it would become necessary to introduce an economic, efficient and acceptable public examination. It should not be of the old pass/fail nature: every pupil should receive a certificate stating what he/she has achieved and at what level of competence. To a large extent it should be based on the completion of assignments, continuous assessment and the mastery of basic skills.

- The next important priority would be to create a number of options that pupils could follow after Std Seven, so that they are not all forced into the old "high school" mould. Because of the other priorities the ability of the state to fund formal schooling from Standards Eight to Ten will be limited. Within the state system parents will have to pay school fees at this level. As it will be crucial that entry to this level should be based on merit and not on ability to pay most of the state funding should be directed to assisting those who are not able to pay the fees. But other options, particularly of a technical and commercial nature, in which further education should be linked to the work situation, will have to be provided on a large scale by the business sector. In addition, because of the threats of large scale unemployment, until the economy turns around, the state, assisted by the business sector, will have to consider both a national youth training scheme and some kind of "job corps" enterprise.

Non-formal, non-school components will have to begin to play a much greater role in secondary education: nether the state nor the school, acting alone, can bring about the transformation of the schooling system. For many 15 to 16 year olds all over the world the school is neither the best nor the most attractive environment for further learning experiences. In general terms, it is a combination of work and further education and training that holds the best promise for many young people.

- Finally, little of this will have the effect hoped for unless the learning environment in the schools is restored. This cannot be done by fiat from above, important as leadership decisions and structural changes are going to be. It is the people that have interests and concerns in each individual school - parents, teachers, community leaders, local business people, the churches, and the pupils themselves - who will have to come together and make a common, shared commitment. In a sense they will have to enter into a new kind of "social compact" to get their own school "back on track" towards the future society.

If schooling is to be transformed so that it can make an effective contribution to the building of the "new South Africa", then each individual school, together with all its stakeholders, will have to enter into a new "liberation struggle" to restore the "learning culture" without which education is doomed to further disintegration.

9.9   WHAT THE THIRD WORLD CAN TEACH US

Somewhere on the horizon looms the promise of a new educational system in South Africa - a system in which, with care, black matriculation results will not longer be an annual recurrent nightmare. To achieve this, the government will have to spend a great deal more on black school education, but will it be effective? Will higher expenditure actually lead to improve health, safety and prosperity in South Africa? Or are we doomed to repeat the same mistakes that were made in many other Third World countries? Three decades ago when uhuru began to spread over Africa, new governments started pouring billions of rands into education. Euphoric predications were made that if massive amounts of money were put into education, general health would improve, population growth would "automatically" decline, and productivity levels would soar. Only the first part of the prediction came true: massive amounts of money were put into education, but the social ills which these were supposed to cure showed a peculiar immunity to the prescribed remedy.

As we in South Africa at last stand poised for major financial injections into black education, a hard look at the results of similar enterprises in other Third World countries may help to keep our feet on the ground. After years of enormous inputs into education in Africa, the development statistics are dismal. General health remains poor. For example: compared to South Africa's infant mortality rate of 72 per 1 000 births in 1985, similar rates in most other African states continued to be high - 115 per 1 000 in Uganda; 130 in Somalia; 164 in Malawi, 169 in Sierra Leone. Instead of education causing a decline in the birth rate, population growth has escalated. Compared to an average of 4,6 births per woman in South Africa (1985), the comparative figure in Uganda was 6,9; in Malawi 7,6; in Kenya 7,8; in Rwanda 8. Most disappointing of all, productivity levels in most African countries have dropped. Compared to a gross domestic product (GDP) in the United States of R39 750 per person in 1988, that of South Africa was a mere R3 500 per person. The GDP in other African states was considerably worse - in Kenya it was R643 per person; in Tanzania R605; in Malawi R349; in Zaire R213.

Why has high expenditure on education failed to raise the quality of life of Africans? No doubt political instability and defective infrastructures were major causes. But many causes are educational. To devise some kind of handle on the problem much research has been conducted in recent years in the Third World. Many of these projects were aimed at weighing the long-term effectiveness of various school reform measures in order to establish school expenditure priorities in specific countries. To circumvent the tricky problem of teachers' passing large numbers of low-achieving pupils merely to save face, standardised tests were used to identify which factors raised pupil achievement in the short term and thereby quality of life in the long term. We should take not of these findings before we latch on to fancy-sounding practices and plug them into our schools as holus-bolus measures to help us out of the educational quagmire. Two types of "reform" measures deserve close examination: those which did not improve pupils' performance in the classroom, and those which did.

Measures in Third World countries which had no effect on pupils achievement were :

*   Science laboratories in high schools:
       Seven controlled experiments in seven different Third World countries showed that science pupils who had access to laboratories did not perform better in science examinations than pupils from schools without laboratories.

*   Fewer pupils per class:
       Eleven studies in Kenya, Tanzania, India, Argentina and other developing countries found that pupils in large classes (about 40 pupils per class) performed just as well as pupils in smaller classes (10 to 20 pupils per class); in five studies pupils working in larger classes actually performed better.

*   Pupils' social class:
       Almost 30 investigations confirmed that pupils' social class affects achievement much less in the Third World than it does in developed countries.

*   Number of class shifts:
       Two experiments (one in Egypt and one in Chile) found that double sessions (the same teacher takes two classes/teaching loads per day) had no detrimental effect on pupils' performance; these pupils did not obtain lower marks in standardised tests than pupils of teaching only one shift per day.

*   Teachers' qualifications:

Projects in Kenya, Iran, Chile and Tanzania showed that upgrading teachers' schooling (for example, helping the 9 000 black teachers in KwaZulu/Natal currently without a matric to obtain matric) was not cost-effective; it did not raise pupil achievement.

*   Teachers' salaries:
        Nine Third World studies proved that pupils of higher- paid teachers do not perform better than pupils of lower-paid teachers. One investigation in Tanzania showed that higher achieving pupils actually were taught by lower-paid teachers.

These findings sound good because they suggest a variety of cost-saving processes which could make the introduction of an equal-opportunity school system more affordable. If such processes were implemented - across the board, regardless of race - they might prevent a drastic drop in academic standards on the inevitable day when all public schools will be declared open to all races.

Cost-cutting ventures, however, would only solve half the problem. The really difficult part is: while preventing a drop in academic standards, we should simultaneously try to raise academic standards where these are at lower levels.

Here, too, recent research provides meaningful guidelines. Noteworthy measures in Third World contexts which raised achievement were :

*   Quality of teachers:
        Research conducted in 22 countries like India, Ghana, Botswana and Uganda consistently showed that the number of years of initial teacher training which teachers received was by far the strongest of all factors that raised pupil achievement. Teacher qualities that led to high achieving pupils were: verbal proficiency, high quality expectations, proficiency in English, and middle class background. Length of teachers' experience had no effect on achievement.

* Textbooks:
  Sixteen experiments in South American, Far Eastern, and African countries proved that availability of textbooks had a powerful influence on pupil performance, particularly on pupils coming from rural areas, lower income families, or illiterate parents.

* Nutrition and school feeding programmes:
  Studies in Guatemala, Egypt, Chile, Thailand and Uganda indicated that school feeding programmes enhance pupil achievement. The effect of poor health was dramatic: undernourished children scored an average of 20 percent less in tests than other children.

* Length of instructional period (school days per year):
  In Tanzania, Brazil, Colombia, India and eight other developing countries it was shown that length of instructional period was significantly related to achievement. Schools in KwaZulu offering Saturday classes also obtain better matriculation results. It is interesting to note that Japan has 243 school days a year compared to 200 school days a year in white South African schools.

* Libraries:
  Fifteen specialist studies revealed that the impact of school and public libraries on pupil performance is much stronger in the Third World than it is in industrialised countries.

* Other factors:
  At least three other cost-effective factors have been proved to raise real pass rates in the Third World: the provision of desks (crucial for the improvement of handwriting and reading skills), boarding schools, and radio programmes.

Recognition of research findings like these - as opposed to quick-fix rhetoric by people living in the realm of fantasy - could be our key to recovery when it comes to priority selection in the upgrading of school education in South Africa.

9.10   PROSPECTS OF CHANGE IN SOUTH AFRICAN SOCIETY

The South African society can be described and analyzed in terms of functionalist or Marxist perspectives. Functionalists tend to be consensus-thinkers, viewing society as a entity whose solidarity is ensured by the integrated co-operation of its constituent parts. Marxists tend rather to think in terms of conflict. In their view, Western capitalist society is comprised of classes of people struggling for material gain. Functionalists and Marxists thus have radically different perspectives on change and tend to gravitate to opposed poles of the political spectrum. Indeed, writing of the sociological setting of South Africa, Christie (1986:19-23) characterises consensus-thinkers on society in terms of two groupings: conservatives and moderates. Conservatives, she points out, do not generally favour social changes, while moderates tend to support reformist changes that are neither drastic nor disruptive. Both groups have a consensus view of society and both want to retain the basic structure of the present society. They are thus essentially functionalist. Opposed to their views, Christie points out, are the conflict thinkers who argue that schools are places in which racial and class differences are perpetuated. In South Africa, they assert, schools tend to keep the different Population Registration groups separate and help to keep the society unequally divided between managers and owners on the one hand, and workers on the other. These conflict thinkers, she declares, believe that society cannot be changed by improvements in education alone. Changes in education must be accompanied by broader societal changes.

Writing of the prospect for change in South Africa, Schlemmer (1983:269) tends to confirm Christie's classification of viewpoints. He considers the radical or critical school of thought in sociology to hold to a view of change as fundamentally a consequence of conflict or pressure. It incorporates the marxist perspective. The structural-functional school of thought, on the other hand, believes change to be facilitated by internal adjustments and adaptations in the institutional systems of society. Schlemmer points out that there is very little agreement between the schools. Polarised views are common. He argues that a synthesis is possible. In assessing the prospects for change in South Africa, consensus and conflict views should both be borne in mind.

Schlemmer's synthesised theoretical approach appears to be sound. He does not attempt to explain change in South Africa as a process neatly coincident with a single theoretical perspective. A study of Contending ideologies in South Africa (Leatt et al, 1986) shows the complex matrix of ideological perspectives that prevail in South Africa at the present time. Some of the ideologies are essentially conservative, others are conflictual. Change is likely to come about as a result of an interaction of many actors who are bearers of a variety of perspectives. The complexity is clearly acknowledged by Schlemmer. A synthesised approach is congruent with the eclectic sociological approach.

Many paradigms of change are current. Schutte (1988:2-3) relies heavily on the work of Smelser and Marx in order to explain their influential theories of change, as they apply to South African society. Smelser's equilibrium model is part of the functionalist tradition. Society is seen as a number of functionally related sub-systems that endure over time, but are amenable to modification or adjustment. Schutte explains:

> Change in a particular sub-system results in a chain reaction of adjustments to restore the equilibrium in that sub-system and eventually in the large system. It is a continuous, largely self-correcting process aimed at maintaining the equilibrium of the system (ibid).

Karl Marx, by contrast to Smelser, is introduced as "a leading exponent of the conflict approach". Marx's revolutionary approach is described by Schutte. Society becomes polarised, with a developing communal consciousness in each pole leading to a breaking-point followed by revolution. Schutte discerns in the work of both Smelser and Marx, a process of conditioning that develops through progressive stages, implying a gradual heightening of the stimuli for change. Schutte (1988:9) concludes that violence is likely if the society develops a low tolerance threshold to change, leading to a violent reaction contrary to the direction of change. He points out that the "accelerated process of change" in South Africa renders it vulnerable to social insecurity and conflict, yet concedes that further drastic changes are needed. Negative stereotypes must be challenged. The problem, to Schutte's mind, is basically one of tolerance for change:

> In order to put the necessary initiatives for peaceful change into operation in the time at the country's disposal, purposeful and persistent efforts must be made to heighten the tolerance threshold for change in all relevant spheres (1988:9).

Whereas Schutte lays emphasis on the cognitive climate for reform, Marais (1988:11) points to a more open and conciliatory form of negotiation by the protagonists) as a solution. Marais points to the incredibly complex task of accommodating diverse ethnic groups in one country and gives glimpses of the world-wide loss of life that has been traceable to ethnic conflict since World War II. Africa has been deeply affected, with the loss of an estimated three million lives since 1960. Marais puts forward a model showing current and past reform endeavours and the spiral of violence that has accompanied them. He refers to the model as the reform-violence helix (1988:18- 24). In essence it shows that, because reform was not seen as a sharing of responsibility, it enjoyed little legitimacy and the spiral of violence erupted further at each stage of reform. The model reveals rising frustration and violence accompanied by more suppression and reform. The key, according to Marais, lies in substantial participation by all protagonists in the process of reform (1988:29).

Is it possible, therefore, that the development of an open, non-racial system of education might create a more pliable cognitive disposition for reform, affording a greater degree of participation in institutions than previously? Maylam (1988:97) tends to be sceptical of the liberal hope that the reform of racist attitudes will present a solution. He points to the radical argument that whites will not have a change of heart while their interests are served by apartheid. Reform is seen by radicals to be an attempt to conceal fundamental economic inequalities "beneath a mask of multi-racialism". Maylam is himself pessimistic of the chances of success via reform. There has been no softening of attitudes, while notions of reform fall far short of what is required. Nor, he argues, is the revolutionary scenario a likely outcome either. Maylam's prognosis is gloomy:

> Thus it looks as though the impasse will continue in the short-term. As long as it continues the quality of life for all South Africans will continue to deteriorate (1988:99).

Other writers are pessimistic about education as a vehicle for changing society. Swift (1977:16) believes radical or innovatory functions of education to be difficult to reconcile with its traditional role in the transmission of culture. Schools, he points out, are subject to powerful social pressures. In a highly stratified society, for example, a school would not be readily able to promote egalitarian values.

> Only when egalitarianism is accepted as part of the dominant value system of a society is it likely either to influence the organisation of education or to be part of moral and social training given by the school (1977:16).

Writing specifically of the situation in South Africa, Theo Hanf (1980:233-4) also reflects pessimism. He pointed out in 1980, at the height of reformist optimism, the extent to which enforced inequality had been entrenched between segments of the South African population. These "segments" he averred, had no free choices to make about their education.

He concludes :

> If the present educational system is counterproductive for those who designed it, it is also counterproductive to any form of peaceful and democratic conflict regulation (1980:334).

He asks :

> Could a different kind of education contribute to a peaceful
> and democratic change? Again, this is not very likely. Of
> course, an education designed to reduce prejudice instead of
> actually promoting it would be very attractive; its prospects,
> however, are very bleak. Under certain conditions education
> can contribute to reducing prejudice, and to promoting better
> understanding between different groups in a society. The main
> condition for a successful educational contribution to that end
> is, however, an overall policy and strong public support for it.
> Precisely this condition is not fulfilled in South Africa today.
> Schools may positively influence attitudes and opinions, but
> whether these can be translated into behaviour depends largely
> on factors outside schooling? (ibid).

Despite the grim pictures painted by the authors quoted, some hope
remains. Schutte has advocated the creation of an improved cognitive
climate for reform, Marais has written of a genuine process of
negotiation, while Hanf concedes that schools might positively
influence attitudes. It is a slender hope. With origins reaching back
forty years to the experiences of Deane Yates and Steyn Krige after
World War II some multi-racial schools have built on slender threads
of hope such as these.

Yates writes :

> Most of the strategies for ending the apartheid system involve
> confrontation or violence. An alternative which is at least as
> viable is to work constructively, but urgently, to confront
> apartheid with a society which is its opposite (July 1988).

They offer a programme based on social reconciliation. But does it
imply justice? Justice is, of course, a concept at the root of much
contention in political debate. As Andrew Gamble (1984:220) has
pointed out, liberalism and socialism are fundamental components of
the Western ideology. Concepts of justice have been specific to each.

Liberals have declared their detestation of public legal inequalities, while accepting social inequalities and privileges. The socialist response to liberalism proclaimed formal legal equality to be insufficient. Socialists demanded practical equality in the social sphere:

> For socialists real freedom and real quality, true universalism, required the overcoming of social as well as political and legal inequalities (Gamble, 1984:220).

9.11 THE INTEGRATED POLYETHNIC SOCIETY - A PLURALIST COMPROMISE

The more logical description of pluralist societies such as Australia - one already adopted officially in the United States - is multiethnic or polyethnic. The latter is preferable on albeit pedantic grounds of being better because it matches two Greek words, polus - much, many, and ethnos - nation. It is a term becoming increasingly accepted in recent anthropological literature on ethnicity (e.g. Despres, 1975). The term can also be used as the basis of a normative ideology or theory about pluralism.

Descriptively the term 'polyethnic' says no more of a society than that it is made up of a number of ethnic groups. We accept Schermerhorn's definition of an ethnic group (1970:12) as :

> A collectivity within a larger society having real or putative common ancestry, memories of a shared historical past, and a cultural focus on one or more symbolic elements defined as the epitome of their peoplehood. Examples of such symbolic elements are: kinship patterns, physical contiguity (as in localism or sectionalism), religious affiliation, language or other dialectical forms, tribal affiliation, nationality, phenotypical features, or any combination of these. A necessary accompaniment is some consciousness of kind among members of the group.

The combination of these two concepts - polyethnic society and ethnic group - enables us to take into account those features of the society which the cultural perspective either ignores or provides only a tenuous theoretical justification for considering. They are :

-       The presence of ethnic groups observable in all their demographic social and cultural manifestations;

-       The facts and effects of ethnic identity and sense of community with no cultural or structural concomitants, i.e. the question of self-ascribed ethnicity;

-       The facts and effects of labelling by others of those who are racially different, with or without cultural or structural concomitants, i.e. the question of socially ascribed ethnicity;

-       The fact and effects of the use of cultural symbols and traditions as a means of politicizing ethnic aspirations.

The possibility that these different forms of group life and bases for personal identification will be used to demand political separatism must also be taken into account in any model that claims to be comprehensive. Here, the notion of integrated polyethnicity becomes important although it may appear to be a contradiction in terms. This can be overcome by thinking of a society that is integrated at one level but polyethnic at another, which was the way an early theorist conceptualised the plural society. Furnivall, in Barth, (1969:16) says:

(A plural society) is a poly-ethnic society integrated in the market place, under the control of a state system dominated by one of the (ethnic) groups, but leaving large areas of cultural diversity in the religious and domestic sectors of activity.

The inevitability of some degree of political integration was a feature of cultural pluralism which was stressed by the founder of the concept, Horace Kallen, but many proponents of multi-culturalism have chosen to ignore it. A very similar ideology of pluralistic integration has been proposed by John Higham (1975:242-43); this is probably the most objective assessment of what should realistically be aimed at in Western democracies. In particular, it attempts to reconcile the needs of ethnic groups while recognizing that there is a dominant culture which must be preserved:

> In contrast to the integrationist model, it will not eliminate ethnic boundaries. But neither will it maintain them intact. It will uphold the validity of a common culture, to which all individuals have access, while sustaining the efforts of minorities to preserve and enhance their own integrity. In principle this dual commitment can be met by distinguishing between boundaries and nucleus. No ethnic group under these terms may have the support of the general community in strengthening its boundaries. All boundaries are understood to be permeable. Ethnic nuclei, on the other hand, are respected as enduring centres of social action. If self- preservation requires, they may claim exemption from certain universal rules, as the Amish now do from the school laws in some states. Both integration and ethnic cohesion are recognized as worthy goals, which different individuals will accept in different degrees. (Higman, 1975:242)

In the more idealistic, normative sense, a polyethnic society characterized by pluralistic integration, that endeavours to avoid extremes of ethnic hegemony by one ethnic group over another is all that should be aimed at for the future. The education system, curriculum development and teacher education would find much more to guide them from such a point of view: it does open the way to the consideration of questions relating to the distribution of power and access to resources experienced by ethnic minorities in society, as well as provide opportunities for them to preserve worthwhile aspects of their cultural and linguistic heritage. Regrettably, however, these very features, while worthwhile educationally, could be interpreted by some as posing a threat or challenge to the dominance of educational and other knowledge managers who are concerned to maintain their vested interests and control over the distribution of power. In fact, the degree of opposition to the model proposed above could well be directly proportional to the level of threat it poses to the current ideology of multi- culturalism. Similar resistance might apply to a supporting publication (Bullivant, 1981), which bring the argument into the practical level of school and classroom by proposing a core survival curriculum to reconcile the needs of the survival imperative of society with the individualistic claims of pluralism.

All these features must be accommodated somehow, for the survival imperative affects all and brooks no compromise. Its major corollary is the fact that equality between human beings individually and nation-states as a whole is a natural or biological impossibility. The search for the utopia in which all shall be equal is a dream, impossible to achieve. Individuals and social groups will obey a fundamental law of survival and will strive to maximize their personal or collective advantages in the struggle to cope with, and attach meanings to, the environments in which they find themselves. At the same time, they will endeavour to search for some order and regularity in the dilemmas that surround them. Such is the human condition, from which, by similar reasoning, Robert Ardrey has been led to propose the idea of the just society (1970:3): "one in which sufficient order protects members, whatever their diverse endowments, and sufficient disorder provides every individual with full opportunity to develop his genetic endowment, whatever that may be". The search for order without disorder - the quest for utopia rather than reality - is at the heart of the forms of pluralist education discussed above. In the search, knowledge about the nature of pluralist societies has been distorted, reality replaced by ideology, truth claims by rhetoric and myth.

The task for educationist is to achieve a balanced form of pluralist education which recognizes the challenge of the survival imperative. Nathan Glazer has suggested how it might be done (1977:24) :

We should still engage in the work of the creation of a single, distinct, and unique nation, and this requires that our main attention be centred on the common culture. Cultural pluralism describes a supplement to the emerging common interests and common ideals that bind all groups in the society; it does not, and should not, describe the whole.

Despite all the seductions of the multi-cultural ideology such a task is essential for our very survival. The alternative for Western democracies could well be the kind of 'desert' Barbara Falk postulates as a possible outcome for Australia, in which we could have 'no secure personal identity ... no social structure embodying our common values, and no symbolism in which to express a shared reality'.

9.12   CONCLUSION

Amid the optimism of renewed world links following the Government's commitment to remove the last vestiges of apartheid, there remains the anomaly of racially-based education and the proliferation of 19 departments. If South Africa is to take the proverbial high road to economic success and social stability, everyone needs the self-empowerment that can only be obtained through a good education. The Government's introduction of the Model B system has opened up some schools to all races but it poses the question of how this will be paid for: a school child in a white or Indian school presumably receives the same funding as his or her classmates; a pupil in an overcrowded township school still receives almost three- quarters less expenditure per capita.

It is a minefield of inequalities that has resulted, particularly since Soweto '76, in thousands of ill-educated and unemployable young people, whose resentment must threaten every effort to build a new and peaceful South Africa. The solution lies in the creation of a single ministry. Within this provinces or regions should be given autonomy to tailor education to their unique needs. Education currently takes up 19 percent of the Budget and percent of the Budget and though this is likely to be increased in years to come, every education rand must be carefully spent in the best possible way. The bitter legacies of apartheid will be truly removed only when every child enters school on an equal footing.

LIST OF ABBREVIATIONS

SA	=	South Africa(n)
HSRC	=	Human Sciences Research Council
NEC	=	National Education Council
CUP	=	Committee of University Principals
UAC	=	University Advisory Committee
SAIRR	=	South African Institute of Race Relations
GNP	=	Gross National Product
ICE	=	Interim Council for Education
SABC	=	South African Broadcasting Co-operation
DET	=	Department of Education and Training
NECC	=	National Education Co-ordinating Committee
SER	=	Strategy and Programme for Educational Renewal
ANC	=	African National Congress
PRESEC	=	Private Sector Education Council
SADTU	=	South African Democratic Teachers' Union
PTSA	=	Parent-Teacher-Student Association
SRC	=	Students' Representative Council
NP	=	National Party
PTF	=	Progressive Teachers' Federation
DP	=	Democratic Party
NEUSA	=	National Education Union of South Africa
TASA	=	Teachers' Education Union of South Africa
NTS	=	Natal Teachers' Society
CP	=	Conservative Party
NED	=	Natal Education Department
AZAPO	=	Azanian People's Organization
TFC	=	Teachers' Federal Council
DEC	=	Department of Education and Culture
EPU	=	Education Policy Unit
TEMPA	=	Transvaal English Medium Parents' Association
TED	=	Transvaal Education Department
TTA	=	Transvaal Teacher Association
JWG	=	Joint Working Group

PWV	=	Pretoria-Witwatersrand-Vereeniging
IDT	=	Independent Development Trust
COSATU	=	Congress of South African Trade Union
SACP	=	South African Communist Party
SACC	=	South African Council of Churches
AECC	=	Alexandra Education Co-ordinating Committee
NEB	=	Natal Education Board
TPR	=	Teacher-Pupil Ratio
CHED	=	Committee of Heads of Education Department
ERS	=	Education Renewal Strategy
SGT	=	Self-Governing Territories

BIBLIOGRAPHY

Arnstine, D. (1967): Philosophy of Education and Schooling, New York, Harper and Row.

Aronowitz, S. and Giroux, H. (1985): Education under siege: The conservative, liberal and radical debate over schooling, Massachusetts, Bergin and Garvey Publishers.

Barth, F. (1969): Ethnic groups and boundaries, Boston, Little Brown.

Barton, L. and Walker, S. (eds. 1983): Race, class and education, London, Croom Helm.

Beeby, C.E. (1969): The qualitative aspects of educational planning, Paris, UNESCO.

Beeld, 29 June 1989.

Bloomer, M. and Shaw, K.E. (eds, 1979): The challenge of educational change, Oxford Pergamon Press.

Booysen, P. de V. (1990): The challenges of numbers, an opening address delivered at the meeting of the C.V.P. at the University of Port Elizabeth, January 1990.

Brembeck, C. and Hill, W. (1973): Cultural challenges to education, London, Lexington Press.

Briefing paper prepared for the National Education Co-Ordinating Committee Education Policy Unit, University of the Witwatersrand, January 1990.

Brightman, E.S. (1951): An introduction to philosophy, London, Pietman and Sons.

Broadfoot, P.; Brock, C. and Tulaciewicz, W. (eds, 1981): Politics and educational change, London Croom Helm.

Bullivant, B. (1981): The pluralist dilemma in education, London, Allen and Unwin.

Business Day, 12 January 1989.

Business Day, 13 January 1989.

Business Day, 19 January 1989.

Business Day, 27 February 1989.

Business Day, 16 March 1989.

Business Day, 13 June 1989.

Business Day, 23 June 1989.

Business Day, 22 August 1989.

Business Day, 6 February 1990.

Business Day, 20 February 1990.

Business Day, 5 March 1990.

Cape Times, 18 December 1989.

Chai, H. (1971): Planning education for a plural society, Unesco, Paris, IIEP.

Christie, P. (1986): The right to learn, Braamfontein, Ravan Press.

City Press, 29 January 1989.

City Press, 5 February 1989.

City Press, 23 April 1989.

City Press, 28 January 1990.

City Press, 14 July 1991.

Coombs, P.H. (1973): New paths to learning for children and youth, Paris, ICED.

Corke, M.A. (1978): A school system for our society: South Africa's crisis in education, Johannesburg, University of the Witwatersrand.

Cosser, Social and Economic update 7.

Cosser, Social and Economic update 8 March - July 1989, SAIRR.

Coutts, A. (1989): An exploratory study of the South African new era schools trust, an unpublished D.Phil. thesis, University of Natal, Durban.

Craft, M. (ed, 1984): Education and cultural pluralism, London, The Falmer Press.

Coombs, P.H. (1968): The world educational crisis, New York, Oxford University Press.

Curle, A. (1973): Education for liberation, London, Tavistock.

Daily Dispatch, 21 January 1989.

Dale, R. (1989): The state and education policy, Philadelphia, Open University Press.

Dave, R.H. (1975): Reflections on life-long education and the school, Hamburg, Uie, Monograph III, Unesco.

DET, RP61/1989. Information supplied by the registrars of the various universities.

Department of Education and Training: Focus on education, February 1991, Vol. 6, No. 2.

Desperes, L.A. (1988): "Anthropological theory, cultural pluralism and the study of complex societies", Current Anthropology, 9(1), pp3-36.

Dewey, J. 91963): Democracy and education, New York, MacMillan.

Eastern Province Herald, 11 December 1989.

Eiselen, W.W.M. (1959): Harmonious multi-community development: A racial policy, Pretoria, Benrose, Frier and Munroe.

Entwistle, H. (1978): Class, culture and education, London Methuen.

Fafunwa, A.B. (1976): New perspectives in African education, Lagos, MacMillan.

Faure, E. et al (1972): Learning to be: the world of education today and tomorrow, Paris, Unesco.

Financial Mail, 18 August 1989.

Financial Mail, 2 March 1990.

Giroux, H.A. (1989): Schooling for democracy: critical pedagogy in the modern age, London, Routledge.

Glazer, N. (1977): Public education and American pluralism, in Coleman, J.S. et al: Parent, teachers and children: prospects for choice in American education, San Francisco, Institute of Contemporary Studies.

Grundy, K. (1971): Guerrilla struggle in Africa: an analysis and preview, New York, Grossman Publishers.

Hanf, T. (1980): Education and consociational conflict regulation in plural societies, in South Africa: dilemmas of evolutionary change, editors, Van Zyl Slabbert, F. and Copeland, J. Grahamstown, Rhodes University.

Hansard 2q Cols 34-35, 14 February 1989.

Hansard (A) 4q Col 159, 28 February 1989.

Hansard (A) 7q Cols 613-614, 22 March 1988.

Hansard (A) 5 (interpellation debate) Cols 259-265, 7 March 1989.

Hansard (A) 15q Cols 920-921, 11 March 1989.

Hansard (A) 9q Cols 727-728, 27 March 1990.

Hansard (A) 15q Cols 1173-1175, 7 May 1990.

Hansard (A) 15q Cols 930-931, 2 May 1989.

Hansard (A) 18 Cols 8904-8906, 15 May 1989.

Hansard (A) 19 Cols 1157-1160, 18 May 1989.

Hansard (A) 18q Cols 1159-1164, 18 May 1989.

Hansard (A) 4q Cols 210-211, 27 February 1990.

Hansard (A) 6q Cols 387-390, 12 March 1990.

Hartshorne, K. (no date): The unfinished business: Education for South Africa's Black people, Unpublished paper, South Africa.

Higham, J. (1975): Send these to me: Jews and other immigrants in urban America, New York, Athenaeum.

Holdstock, L. (1987): Education for a new nation, Johannesburg, University of the Witwatersrand.

Homes, B. (ed, 1980): Diversity and unity in education: a comparative analysis, London, Allen and Unwin.

House of Representatives, RP47/1989.

Hughes, A.G. (1960): Education: some fundamental problems, London, Longmans.

Hymes, D. (ed, 1964): Language in cultural society, New York, Harper and Raw.

Information supplied by the administrative registrar, Vista University, 10 January 1990.

Information provided by the committee of university principals, 1 November 1989 and 13 August 1990.

Kendall, F.E. (1983): Diversity in the classroom: a multicultural approach to the education of young children, New York, Teachers College Press.

King, E.J. (1958): Other schools and ours, New York, Holt, Rinehart and Winston.

Kirp, D.L. (1982): Just schools, Berkeley, University of California Press.

Leatt, J.; Kniefel, T. and Nurnburger, K. (1986): Contending ideologies in South Africa, Cape Town, David Philip.

MacKay, S. Quarterly Countdown 13.

MacKay Quarterly Countdown 12, South African Institute of Race Relations (SAIRR), 30 May 1989.

MacKay, S. Quarterly Countdown 13, (SAIRR), 25 August 1989.

Malherbe, E.G. (1977): Education in South Africa, Vol. 2, Cape Town, Juta.

Marais, H.C. (1988): The dynamics of change in South Africa, in South Africa: the challenge of reform, Pinetown, Owen Burgess.

Marcum, J. (1982): Education, race and social change in South Africa, California, University of California Press.

Media statement by Mr. P.J. Clase, Minister of Education and Culture (Administration: House of Assembly), 23 March 1990.

Modgil, S. et al (eds, 1986): Multicultural education: the interminable debate, London, The Falmer Press.

Morrow, W. (1986): "Education as an own affair", South African Journal of Education, 6(4), pp245-247.

Mphahlele, E. (1983): The residue of history, Energos, (Magazine of Mobil Oil).

Mylam, P. (1988): Thoughts on the historical origins and future collapse of the apartheid system, in Mentor, Vol. 69, No. 3. Autumn 1988.

New Nation, May 25-30, 1990.

New Nation, January 25-31, 1991.

New Nation, February 1-7, 1991.

New Nation, February 8-14, 1991.

New Nation, February 15-21, 1991.

New Nation, March 8-15, 1991.

New Nation, June 12-18, 1991.

North, R. (1987): Schools of tomorrow, Bide Ford, Greenbooks.

O'Keeffe, B. (ed, 1988): Schools for tomorrow: building walls or building bridges, London, The Falmer Press.

Peters, R.S. (1966): Ethics and education, New York, Random House.

Phenix, P.H. (1958): Philosophy of education, New York, Hanry Holt.

Phillips, H.M. (1975): Basic education - a world change, London, John Wiley and Sons.

Pluckrose, H. and Wilby, P. (eds, 1980): Education 2000, London, Temple Smith.

Provision for Education in RSA. (1981): Report of the main committee of the HSRC investigation into education, Pretoria, HSRC.

Redden, J.D. and Ryan, S. (1956): A catholic philosophy of education, New York, The Bruce Publishing Co.

Rist, R.C. (ed, 1979): Desegregated schools, New York, Academic Press.

Roberts, J.I. (ed, 1976): Educational patterns and cultural configuration, New York, David MacKay.

Schermerhorn, R.A. (1970): Comparative ethnic relations: a framework for theory and research, New York, Random House.

Schlemmer, L. (1983): Social indicators for change in Change in South Africa, Editors: Van Vuuren, D.J. et al. Durban, Butterworths.

Schutte, W.D. (1988): Change, an alternative approach, in South Africa: the challenge of reform, Pinetown, Owen Burgess.

Silver, H. (ed, 1973): Equal opportunity in education, London, Methuen.

Singh, R.R. (1972): Final report of a working group on research and development in teacher education, Baguio City, Philippines, 11-20 January 1972, Asian Institute for teacher educators, University of Philippines.

Sonn, F. ( ): Equal opportunity in education in South Africa.

Sowetan, 15 March 1989.

Sowetan, 5 May 1989.

Sowetan, 16 May 1989.

Sowetan, 24 May 1989.

Sowetan, 18 December 1989.

Sowetan, 1 February 1990.

Sunday Star, October 28, 1990.

Sunday Times, September 6, 1990.

Sunday Times, October 20, 1990.

Sunday Times, January 13, 1991.

Sunday Times, June 9, 1991.

Sunday Times, June 23, 1991.

Sunday Tribune, March 25, 1990.

Sunday Tribune, April 1, 1990.

Sunday Tribune, September 16, 1990.

Sunday Tribune, November 11, 1990.

Sunday Tribune, December 2, 1990.

Sunday Tribune, February 10, 1991.

Sunday Tribune, February 21, 1991.

Sunday Tribune, February 24, 1991.

Sunday Tribune, March 3, 1991.

Sunday Tribune, May 12, 1991.

Swift, D. et al (1977): <u>Schooling and society</u>, editors: Brown, C. et al, Milton Keynes, Open University Press.

The Citizen, 2 March 1989.

The Citizen, 22 May 1989.

The Citizen, 21 October 1989.

The Citizen, 12 January 1990.

The Citizen, 26 March 1990.

The Daily News, June 21, 1990.

The Daily News, August 6, 1990.

The Daily News, September 11, 1990.

The Daily News, September 12, 1990.

The Daily News, September 15, 1990.

The Daily News, September 19, 1990.

The Daily News, January 17, 1991.

The Daily News, January 25, 1991.

The Daily News, February 8, 1991.

The Daily News, February 13, 1991.

The Daily News, February 14, 1991.

The Daily News, February 22, 1991.

The Daily News, February 26, 1991.

The Daily News, February 27, 1991.

The Daily News, February 28, 1991.

The Daily News, October 23, 1991.

The Natal Mercury, June 12, 1990.

The Natal Mercury, September 11, 1990.

The Natal Mercury, September 12, 1990.

The Natal Mercury, September 13, 1990.

The Natal Mercury, September 1, 1990.

The Natal Mercury, January 19, 1991.

The Natal Mercury, January 23, 1991.

The Natal Mercury, February 17, 1991.

The Natal Mercury, February 22, 1991.

The Natal Mercury, February 26, 1991.

The Natal Mercury, February 27, 1991.

The Natal Mercury, February 28, 1991.

The Natal Mercury, March 3, 1991.

The Natal Mercury, March 5, 1991.

The Natal Witness, 11 July 1989.

The Star, 26 January 1989.

The Star, 17 May 1989.

The Star, 21 May 1989.

The Star, 17 August 1989.

The Star, 27 September 1989.

The Star, 4 December 1989.

The Star, 27 January 1990.

The Star, 14 February 1990.

The Star, 9 November 1990.

The Star, 8 January 1991.

The Star, 14 January 1991.

The Star, 31 January 1991.

The Star, 2 February 1991.

The Star, 13 February 1991.

The Star, 26 February 1991.

The Star, 27 February 1991.

The Star, 28 February 1991.

The Star, 8 June 1991.

The Star, 12 June 1991.

The Star, 15 June 1991.

The Star, 22 July 1991.

The Star, 24 July 1991.

The Star, 25 July 1991.

The Star, 31 July 1991.

The Sunday Star, 9 June 1991.

The Sunday Star, 16 June 1991.

The Sunday Star, 23 June 1991.

The Weekly Mail, 31 March 1989.

The Weekly Mail, 15 December 1989.

The Weekly Mail, 8-14 January 1990.

The Weekly Mail, 14-20 September 1990.

The Weekly Mail, 22-28 September 1990.

The Weekly Mail, 30 November - 6 December 1990.

The Weekly Mail, 7-13 December 1990.

The Weekly Mail, 15-21 February 1991.

The Weekly Mail, 1-8 March 1991.

The Weekly Mail, 7-13 June 1991.

The Weekly Mail, 5-11 July 1991.

The Weekly Mail, June 28-July 4, 1991.

The Weekly Mail, July 26-August 1, 1991.

Thembela, A.J. (no date): Education towards post-apartheid, an unpublished paper.

Thembela, A.J. (1986): "Educational obstacles to black advancement", in Smollan, R. (ed) Black advancement in the South African economy, Johannesburg, MacMillan.

Thembela, A.J. (1987): "The state of education for blacks in South Africa", in Sethi, P. (ed) South African quagmire: in search of peaceful path to democratic pluralism, Massachusetts, Ballinger Publishing Company.

Thembela, A.J. (1989): Black education in South Africa: issues, problems and perspectives, in Per Linguam, Vol. 5, No.1, 1989.

Thembela, A.J. (1990): Current education structures and black educational needs, an address delivered at a symposium - Michaelhouse, Balgowan, 23 July 1990.

Thembela, A.J. (1990): One department of education, an unpublished paper, 21 August 1990.

Troyna, B. and Carrington, B. (1990): Education, racism and reform, London, Routledge.

Unesco, (1972): Learning to be: the world of education today and tomorrow, Paris, Unesco.

Unesco, (1975): Meeting of experts on the content of education in the context of life-long education, final report, Paris, 20-25 October (Annex II).

Van den Heever, R. (1987): Alternative education: vision of a democratic alternative, Cape Town, UTASA Publication.

Vos, A.J. and Brits, V.M. (1987): <u>Comparative and international education for student teaching</u>, Durban, Butterworths.

Wai, D. (1978): Sources of conflict and secessionist politics in Africa, in <u>Ethics and racial studies</u>, 1978 July, 3, 286-305.

Warnock, M. (1988): <u>A common policy for education</u>, Oxford, Oxford University Press.

Watson, J.K.P. (1980): "Education and cultural pluralism in South East Asia with reference to Peninsula and Malaysia" <u>Comparative education</u>, Vol. 33, pp139-58.

Welsh, D. (1978): The nature of racial conflict in South Africa, <u>Social dynamics</u>, 4, 1978 (1 June) 36.

Willie, C.V. (1984): <u>School desegregation plans that work</u>, London, Greenwood Press.

Wringe, C. (1984): <u>Democracy, schooling and political education</u>, London, Allen and Unwin.

INDEX